INTERNATIONAL HUMAN RIGHTS

Universalism Versus Relativism

ALISON DUNDES RENTELN

QUID PRO BOOKS
New Orleans, Louisiana

Previously published in 1990 by Sage Publications, Inc., Newbury Park, California and London, UK, as volume six of Frontiers of Anthropology; and copyright © 1990 by Sage Publications, Inc.

Published in 2013 by Quid Pro Books. Part of the *Classics of the Social Sciences* Series, and a *Digitally Remastered Book.*™

ISBN 978-1-61027-160-8 (pbk.)
ISBN 978-1-61027-159-2 (eBook)

QUID PRO, LLC
5860 Citrus Blvd., Suite D-101
New Orleans, Louisiana 70123
www.quidprobooks.com

qp

Publisher's Cataloging-in-Publication

Renteln, Alison Dundes.
    International human rights: universalism versus relativism / by Alison Dundes Renteln.
        p. cm. — (Classics of the social sciences)
    Includes bibliographical references and index.
    ISBN 978-1-61027-160-8 (pbk.)

1. Human rights—Cross-cultural studies. 2. Human rights—Sociology. I. Title. II. Series.
JC 571.R47 2013

323'.07—dc20
2013624491
CIP

The United Nations System Chart, reproduced as Appendix B, is copyright © 2011 by the United Nations and is used with the permission of the UN Department of Public Information. Special thanks to Akiko Ito, Kashif Qadir, Maxine Smith, and Janet Teperino.

The author's photograph on back cover is © by Brian Morri, and is used with permission.

CONTENTS

[Page numbers in brackets below reference the pagination of the original 1990 edition, which are found herein embedded into the text by the use of brackets. Page numbers to the far right of the ellipses reference the pagination of the current printing, found at the bottom of the page.]

FOREWORD • 2013

Although 1948 was a crucial year in the development of human rights, because of the adoption of the Universal Declaration of Human Rights, sadly it was also the year of missed opportunities. In 1947, the Commission on Human Rights had invited comments on the draft Universal Declaration. The American Anthropologists Association replied with a statement, drafted by Melville Herskovits, in which it warned that the Universal Declaration was likely to become an ethnocentric document. According to the AAA, it was impossible to maintain that the Declaration would apply to all human beings, while at the same time only incorporating values which are prevalent in the West. In order to be truly "universal" the AAA held that the Declaration should "embrace and recognize the validity of many different ways of life."

According to Mark Goodale, the drafting committee of the Commission on Human Rights, which mainly consisted of lawyers, did not consider the AAA's statement, let alone take the lessons to be learned from it. Consequently, the opportunity to incorporate anthropological insights into the drafting process with the aim to bring in important cultural and social lenses to the field of human rights was lost. In 1948 the anthropologists left the scene; in doing so they gave a free reign to the lawyers, who virtually monopolized the field.

This monopolization has had two major consequences, which made human rights more vulnerable as an academic discipline. First, because of the dominant involvement of lawyers, the area of human rights turned into a normative rather than an empirical field. Consequently, human rights ran the risk of becoming what Raimundo Panikkar described as "Trojan horses," *i.e.* vehicles for the promotion of Western values and modernity. Second, human rights mainly became a legal discipline, which lacked the benefits of multidisciplinary scholarship.

Fortunately, in 1990, after an absence of more than 40 years, the first anthropologist returned to the field of human rights. In her book, *International Human Rights: Universalism Versus Relativism*, Alison Renteln redefines the concept of cultural relativism and adopts it as her starting point. She deals with the question, whether or not there can be any such thing as universal human rights. In her view, the central question is whether cultures other than those in the West have a concept of human rights, and if they do, whether or not it resembles that of the Universal Declaration of Human Rights or any other human-rights instruments.

As she notes on page 1, "Universalists merely presume the validity of human rights, which abnegates the need for justification." Instead of assuming that human rights are universal, she argues that the question needs to be answered empirically. If empirical research can lead to the discovery of values shared by all cultures, then the process of building human-rights standards which have genuine support across the globe can begin. In order to avoid the charge of cultural imperialism, cross-cultural support for international human-rights standards needs to be sought.

Renteln makes clear that there is no guarantee that cross-cultural universals will be found to support the international human-rights standards which are most important to either Westerners or non-Westerners. For example, there may be no worldwide support for women's rights. Renteln's study suggests a method for identifying universals that would carry moral weight in the international arena, yet cannot guarantee social change. Even if a cross-cultural universal is shown to exist—as was the case with universal condemnation of apartheid—that did not in itself bring about reforms in South Africa.

The book caused quite a splash when it was first published, because its author asked many important questions which had not been raised before. She challenged some of the normativist assumptions which characterized the field. Through this book and a number of publications in leading journals which followed it, Renteln succeeded in bringing back academic rigor and methodological sophistication to the field. Over time anthropologists like Sally Engle Merry, Marie Dembour, Richard Wilson, and Mark Goodale, and other social scientists, also entered the field, where they started to develop and explore new and more effective approaches towards human rights.

All those involved in human rights research and practice owe a debt of gratitude to Alison Renteln for writing this pioneering book. This is particularly true for the researchers involved in the so-called "Receptor Approach to Human Rights" Project conducted jointly by the Netherlands School of Human Rights Research, the International Law Institute of the Chinese Academy of Social Sciences, and the Centre for Human Rights of Shandong University School of Law.

Renteln has taught the members of our team that to solve a human rights problem one has to properly understand it. Thus, she demonstrates that child labor is not only an economic issue, as everyone will probably expect, but also has a cultural dimension related to filial piety. She also makes the point that even if Southern and Eastern societies do not express moral concerns in a framework of human rights, they may nonetheless address them in some other conceptual framework which serves as an equivalent. She therefore insists that we should look not simply for rights cast in the Western mold, but for the structural equivalents for human rights in other societies. Renteln also makes clear that moral systems which are duty based can accommodate human rights. If, for example, the members of a given society have a duty to take care of the elderly, then the elderly could be said to have a right to proper care.

Fortunately, this wonderful book, through its re-issue, will remain a very important reference text for decades to come, to be enjoyed by the next generations of students of human rights.

TOM ZWART

Professor of Human Rights, Utrecht University
Director, "Receptor Approach to Human Rights" Project

PREFACE • 2013

The debate about the relationship between cultural relativism and universal human rights remains as relevant in the twenty-first century as it was decades ago when this book first appeared. Whether the question is conflicts over Islamic religious garb in Europe, methods of punishment like stoning in Nigeria, or "coercive interrogation" in the United States, the cultural context is critical for the interpretation of the issue. How cultural relativism ought to influence the interpretation of human rights continues to be debated, and sometimes there is no obvious answer to the question of how a particular right ought to be construed. Relativism is still a source of disagreement in many circles, among activists, philosophers, policymakers, and jurists.

The argument I advanced in this monograph sparked debate partly because of the methodological approach. The book was considered novel for suggesting that scholars undertake cross-cultural empirical research to identify cross-cultural universals to bolster human rights standards. I proposed that by identifying shared principles it would be possible to provide a stronger foundation for particular rights. While not everyone agreed with this approach, prominent scholars such as An-Abdullahi An-Na'im, Sally Merry, and Tom Zwart have advanced in their own work the cross-cultural interpretation of human rights norms.

I would like to express my gratitude to Alan Childress of Quid Pro Books for his interest in my scholarship. By reissuing this monograph in the Classics of the Social Sciences series, he makes my ideas available to new generations of scholars, advocates, and students who are interested in international human rights. The aim of this project was to build the legitimacy of international human rights standards and to encourage others to develop innovative approaches to the analysis and enforcement of human rights. A culturally sensitive and nuanced approach to international human rights offers the greatest hope of establishing the legitimacy of these vitally important standards, and this global jurisprudence is of crucial importance for solving world problems. Insofar as we can identify shared values that provide foundations for particular human rights, we avoid claims that human rights advocates are ethnocentric and foisting alien values on other societies. It is my hope that this book will inspire others in their quest to promote international human rights for all peoples around the world.

ALISON DUNDES RENTELN
Los Angeles, California
2013

For Paul and David

Acknowledgments

{*page 7 in original*}

For many years I wondered how one could simultaneously respect the integrity of other cultures and retain a firm commitment to one's own moral code. In the early 1980s my father, Alan Dundes, brought to my attention a thought-provoking article by Raimundo Panikkar entitled "Is the Notion of Human Rights a Western Concept?" (1982). I am grateful to both of them for encouraging me to pursue the tension between relativism and universalism.

Many individuals have contributed to the genesis of this work. I wish to thank Frank C. Newman for sparking my interest in many areas of international human rights and Philip Alston for helping me focus on some of the more controversial theoretical issues. Laura Nader was generous in sharing her inspiring work on cross-cultural notions of justice. Conversations with Elvin Hatch and Robert LeVine were especially memorable and important to the development of this book. I am extremely grateful to Martin Shapiro for a close reading of the manuscript. I owe a great deal to H. Russell Bernard for his invaluable criticisms and editorial suggestions. I also thank the following individuals for their help: Stanley Anderson, Katherine Auspitz, Gayle Binion, Donald Brown, Seyom Brown, David L. Cingranelli, Stanley Hoffman, Herbert Kelman, Alouette Kluge, Everett Mendelsohn, Sheldon Messinger, Sara Monoson, Sally Falk Moore, Michael Rogin, Davida Weinberg, and David Wong.

The opportunity to work with Laurie Wiseberg and Jennifer Schirmer on two Human Rights Internet bibliographies on anthropology and human rights, one for UNESCO and the other for *Cultural Survival*, was a valuable one. I am also grateful to Russell Sizemore for providing me with sections of the prepublication copy of the Harvard-Berkeley Comparative Religious Ethics Bibliographical project.

I greatly appreciate the efforts of the entire staff in the Interlibrary Loan Department at the University of California, Santa Barbara: Kitty Uthe, Susan Mahaffey, Lou Smitheram, and Diane Stowell. Reference librarians Gary Peete and Carol Gibbens were particularly kind as well.

The Soroptimists Founder Region, the Mark De Wolfe Howe Fund of Harvard University, and Dean W.J. Hill at Boalt Hall, University of California, Berkeley, provided generous financial assistance during the course of this work. {*page 8 follows*}

I would like to acknowledge Dr. Jennifer Montague of the Warburg Institute at the University of London who helped me choose the photograph used for the cover of this book and Dr. Christian Theuerkauff of the Staatliche Museen in Berlin who granted permission to use it. Some of the material in this book appeared previously in a different form in "The Concept of Human Rights," *Anthropos,* 83: 343-364 (1988), by permission; "A Cross Cultural Approach to Validating International Human Rights: The Case of Retribution Tied to Proportionality," in D. L. Cingranelli (Ed.), *Human Rights: Theory and Measurement* (pp. 7–40), 1988, Macmillan and St. Martin's Press, with permission; and reproduced by permission of the American Anthropological Association from *American Anthropologist*, 90: 1, March 1988, not for further reproduction.

I am especially grateful to my husband, Paul Renteln, whose interest in my research and willingness to discuss ideas were an important source of inspiration.

A. D. R.

Los Angeles, California
1990

INTERNATIONAL HUMAN RIGHTS

Universalism Versus Relativism

Introduction

{page 9 in original}

IN THIS study I address the question of whether or not there can be any such thing as universal human rights. Their existence is asserted by human rights advocates and denied by cultural relativists. Universalists merely presume the validity of human rights, which abnegates the need for justification. Relativists reject the possibility that there can be universal moral standards because no justification can avoid being culturally based and thus limited in scope. This work attempts to reconcile the conflict between cultural/ethical relativism and universal human rights by showing that they are not diametrically opposed. Since I take the view that universal human rights are possible, the heart of the issue is where to locate their source of justification.

The content of the concept of human rights depends on the basis of moral authority from which it derives legitimacy. There tend to be four bases for human rights to which theorists refer: (1) divine authority, (2) natural law, (3) intuition (that is, certain actions are obviously wrong because they violate inalienable rights), and (4) ratification of international instruments. None of the four provides a wholly satisfying justification for the existence and defense of particular human rights. Divine authority cannot lend much assistance as there are many variations of religious ethics, none of which is subject to proof. Moreover, the tenets of one theology may conflict with those of another. Intuition is problematic for exactly the same reasons.

The most misleading source has been natural law because there is an assumption that natural rights, which have become associated with human rights, are self-evident. The rights are held by all individuals simply by virtue of their status as human beings. Of course, the underlying assumptions are a common view of human nature and an agreed-upon ranking of priorities with respect to basic human needs. It is by no means clear that there is universal assent to the ordering of human needs as is evidenced, for example, by the relative support of the two Covenants on human rights (see Chapter 1). This poses no problem for proponents of natural law since they share a worldview centered around civil and political rights. Turning to natural law nowadays for moral authority may not be advisable because it may not be inclusive enough: "The real issue [however] is whether a natural rights theory can adequately comprehend a right like the right to work" (Donnelly, 1982b, p. 398). If natural law is interpreted to justify {10} all human rights, inflated beyond recognition (Pocklington, 1982, pp. 77-86), then it may lose all credibility.

Resorting to ratification as a basis of authority is also not free from problems. First, those who ratify are the elites whose views may not correspond to those of the rest of the citizenry in a given state. Second, ratification may simply serve political and not humanitarian interests. Third, the claim that by ratification a nation-state demonstrates its commitment to and belief in a particular concept of human rights depends on a legalistic understanding of ratification (see, e.g., Sieghart, 1985, pp. xii, 40). It may be necessary to operate under the assumption that ratification of human-rights instruments conveys agreement with the concept as outlined and confers legitimacy upon it (see Alston in Anonymous, 1987a). Still, it is not true that ratification proves that there is a universal concept of human rights.

There is, indeed, reason to be concerned about the extent to which the concept of human rights is embraced worldwide. There is considerable difference of opinion as to what "true" human rights are. Some commentators assert that the concept is a Western one, while others insist that it is truly universal (for more on this debate, see Alston, 1983b; Bedau, 1982; Berger, 1977; Berman, 1979; Donnelly, 1982b, 1985; Ferguson, 1979; Henkin, 1979b; Kleinig, 1981; Manglapus, 1978; Masahiko, 1985; Murphy, 1981; Nickel, 1982; Novak, 1986; Panikkar, 1982; Pappu, 1982; Pollis & Schwab, 1979b; Raphael, 1966; Schifter, 1988a; Sinha, 1981, 1982; Tomuschat, 1981; and Tyagi, 1981). There tends to be a division into two camps: those who advocate civil and political rights and those who champion economic, social, and cultural rights. When one considers how voluminous the literature on human rights is and how much divergence there is on the question of human rights, it is startling that relatively little has been written on the subject of its conceptual basis (but see the insightful analyses of Alston, 1984; Bilder, 1969; Ramcharan, 1983; and Sinha, 1978b, 1981, 1982).

It is possible to find analyses of the concept of human rights from various national, ideological, and religious perspectives. But many of these studies are unreliable because their authors are determined to show that their cultures have human rights and thus they may be apologists for their own traditions. Others dismiss outright the possibility that there may be any notion of human rights in certain societies (see, e.g., Howard & Donnelly, 1986). There is certainly no comparative treatment of the concept of human rights across cultures (except for a few two-country comparisons: Berman, 1979; Kadarkay, 1982) and that is precisely what is needed. Some writers focus on a single right which they assert is the only valid right, e.g., Hart and the right to liberty (1979), Nickel and the right to freedom from torture (1982), {11} and Stackhouse and the right to participate (1984). Much of the literature reflects an ethnocentric bias which I have discussed elsewhere (Renteln, 1985). Based on the conflicting statements by scholars, it seems difficult to decide one way or the other if the concept of human rights is universal. Instead of assuming that the concept is universal, it would be better to investigate the question empirically.

A CROSS-CULTURAL APPROACH FOR
VALIDATING HUMAN RIGHTS

Since I do not believe that any existing approaches can effectively validate international human rights, I propose a new method for doing so. Only through cross-cultural empirical research can one discover values shared by all cultures. This book contains a case study which demonstrates the kind of approach which could confer legitimacy on specific human-rights standards.

The central question is whether other cultures have a concept of human rights, and if they do, whether or not it resembles that of the Universal Declaration of Human Rights or any other human-rights instruments. It is not clear if other societies' moral systems center on rights. Much of the debate has tended to revolve around such linguistic questions. Many peoples do not, of course, speak English and have no tradition of Enlightenment ideas, which means that looking for the literal existence of human rights will not be fruitful. Even if non-Western societies do not express moral concerns in a framework of human rights, they may nonetheless address them in some other conceptual framework. It becomes necessary to reformulate the basic question: are there any homeomorphic equivalents for human rights in other cultures? I maintain that we should look not simply for rights cast in the Western mold but for the structural equivalents for human rights in other societies. Other scholars have also advocated the approach of identifying notions comparable to human rights in other cultural systems (Panikkar, 1982; Chiba, 1987).

THE CONTEXT OF HUMAN-RIGHTS DEBATES

It is important to have some insight into the nature of the debates concerning international human rights. For those unacquainted with international {12} and regional human-rights machinery, Chapter 1 provides a succinct overview with references to more in-depth treatments in the literature. This overview of United Nations (UN) organs and instruments suggests that the failure to resolve value conflicts, both acknowledged and underlying ones, ensured future confrontations. Although there was a pretense made of recognizing the significance of cultural diversity, little effort was made to deal with culture conflicts in the international realm. The drafters of the UN documents laid the groundwork for subsequent disputes.

THE CONCEPT OF HUMAN RIGHTS AND
THE PRESUMPTION OF UNIVERSALITY

Chapter 2 reveals the fallacy common to many writings on human rights, namely the presumption of universality. What typifies this way of thinking is the belief that human rights exist independent of culture, ideology, and value systems. This absolutistic perspective is found particularly among philosophers and legal theorists. Even when scholars acknowledge that human-rights norms appear to be Western, they nevertheless assert their universality. This is a peculiar form of ethnocentrism insofar as Western ideas are presumed to be ubiquitous. My approach differs sharply from this. I contend that human rights cannot be derived philosophically, but can only be established by empirical demonstration.

Chapter 2 begins by exploring the traditional notions of human rights. After clarifying the idea of a right, I discuss some of the conceptual problems associated with human rights. In particular, I challenge the claim made by some human-rights scholars that moral systems which are duty-based cannot accommodate human rights. If, for example, the members of a given society have a duty to take care of the elderly, then the elderly could be said to have a right to proper care. The point is that just because the rubric of some peoples is not that of rights does not mean that human rights cannot be universal.

But even if all social systems contain rights, this guarantees neither that they share the same rights, nor that they ascribe comparable importance to them. Nevertheless, virtually all human-rights advocates presume that human rights are universally valid. A consideration of various international human-rights instruments reveals that some of them do not embody universal values. The practices of child labor and female circumcision give some indication of how divergent moral perspectives can be. Examples of this kind {13} show that it is futile and perhaps even counterproductive merely to assert the existence of universal human rights in the face of cultural diversity.

Whether non-Western societies have human rights remains to be seen. The literature is not helpful here since many writers simply assert the presence or absence of human rights in their traditions, but provide little documentation to support their claims. Moreover, as many have been educated in Europe or the United States, these scholars tend to cite Enlightenment sources. Eventually, there may be more data on Third World views on international human rights and international law generally (Snyder, 1987; Marasinghe & Conklin, 1984).

RELATIVISM REVISITED

Chapter 3 attempts to elucidate the theory of relativism. Unfortunately, the early cultural relativists formulated the theory in such a way that it appeared to be logically inconsistent. By arguing that relativism necessarily implied tolerance, they transformed it into a prescriptive theory and thereby made it logically self-contradictory. The correct version of the theory, I contend, is cultural relativism as a descriptive theory. Because relativism is not a value theory, it does not entail tolerance or any other value. Rather, it is a theory about moral judgments. The insight that relativism has to offer is that every culture follows its own moral precepts, which it perceives to be the best. Thus, enculturation rather than tolerance proves to be the essential contribution of the theory (for an explanation of enculturation, see Herskovits, 1964, p. 326; Shimahara, 1970). As I will show, one consequence of this reinterpretation is that moral criticism is possible for the relativist.

The fact that all societies take their standards to be most desirable does not mean that they may not share some in common. So, by rendering the theory more coherent and by giving it a more generous and, I believe, fair interpretation, I show that some human rights may be compatible with relativism. Relativism is consistent with the existence of cross-cultural universals.

There is no guarantee, of course, that cross-cultural universals will be found to support the international human-rights standards most important to either Westerners or non-Westerners. For example, there may be no worldwide support for women's rights. Cultural practices regarded as repressive by Western feminists cannot, therefore, be said to violate "universal" {14} standards. Thus, even though relativists can embrace universal human rights, it is not clear which particular human rights those will turn out to be. But my position is that universals are, in any case, preferable to absolutes. Even if there may not be a universal commitment to a certain value, a consensus could emerge with respect to that value. Absolutes, by definition, are not subject to change, whereas universals can evolve over time.

A CASE STUDY: RETRIBUTION TIED TO PROPORTIONALITY

Chapter 4 presents an example of a cross-cultural empirical investigation of a moral principle, *viz.* retribution tied to proportionality. Evidence is adduced to prove the ubiquitous nature of the principle. For example, major religious texts and many ethnographies furnish irrefutable proof of its significance throughout the world. I also draw on the literature of several social processes, for example, the feud, vendetta, and vengeance killings, whose presence I take to be evidence for adherence to the principle of retribution tied to proportionality. The reason why the principle of retribution tied to proportionality is so widespread is that it serves as a limit on violence. Therefore, if there is a worldwide commitment to this principle, this may indicate a global willingness to embrace particular human rights such as those against genocide and torture.

This finding is important because it means that it is justified to criticize repressive governments when they punish innocent citizens who have committed no wrong. State suppression of civil liberties, activities of death squads, and other forms of violence perpetrated on dissidents all violate the principle of retribution. Punishment is only justifiable when it follows some act that contravenes norms accepted by the people. Thus, government officials who inflict inappropriate penalties violate a universal standard and, by definition, their own indigenous normative standard as well. Some will argue that governments that engage in a consistent pattern of human-rights abuses do not support any universal standard. But this argument is spurious. The fact that elites ignore important rules for reasons of political expediency does not prove that the people in that society reject the rules. So, although the practice of states may leave much to be desired, as far as respect for human-rights standards is concerned, this does not undercut the universality of the standards.

This study suggests a method for identifying universals that would carry moral weight in the international arena. It cannot, however, guarantee social {15} change. Even if a cross-cultural universal is shown to exist— say universal condemnation of apartheid—that will not in itself bring about reforms in South Africa. But if empirical research can lead to the discovery of values shared by all cultures, then we can begin the process of building human-rights standards which have genuine support across the globe.

To avoid the charge of cultural imperialism, we must seek cross-cultural support for international human-rights standards. Demonstration of the existence of a universally embraced moral principle would provide a much-needed foundation for certain human rights. If this theoretical approach can lead to the justification of particular ethical values that serve to ensure the humane treatment of all, this study will have been a worthwhile enterprise.

grievances were entitled to bring claims before the League Council. According to Tolley, "For the first time some nation states became regularly accountable (to) an international body for mistreatment of individuals subject to their rule" (1982, p. 2). The principle behind the mandates system has survived in the trusteeship system of the UN, although not many "non-self-governing territories" remain (Humphrey, 1973, p. 80).

Despite the early manifestations of concern with human rights, the Covenant of the League of Nations failed to include any general reference to them whatsoever (Fareed, 1977, pp. 21-25). President Woodrow Wilson had attempted to have a provision for religious liberty incorporated in the convenant, but his proposal was rejected (Szabo, 1982, p. 21). The only apparent human-rights guarantees existing under the League of Nations pertained to the protection of minorities and indigenous populations in mandated territories. But the term "human rights" was not used in connection with either the minorities system or with the mandates system, neither of which attracted much public attention in any case. The fact that these rights were implicitly recognized at all indicates a commitment to what are called collective rights, as opposed to individual rights. According to some commentators, this commitment supposedly contributed to the failure of the League (Szabo, 1982, p. 21). In any event, the League was mostly ineffectual. Even the most heinous crimes against humanity, such as those perpetrated by Hitler, Mussolini, and Stalin, failed to elicit serious response from it.

The modern incarnation of the minorities system is the UN Subcommission on the Prevention of Discrimination and Protection of Minorities. Unfortunately, competing state interests have prevented this body from effectively {20} protecting minority rights (see below) just as was the case for its predecessor, the League.

One institution that has not only survived but has also flourished is the ILO. Its purpose was and is to ensure safe, humane, and fair labor standards, and it is invariably cited as the most successful human-rights institution, exemplary in its standard-setting as well as in its enforcement techniques (Jenks, 1970; Landy, 1980; Swepston, 1984; Valticos, 1982).

EARLY DRAFTING MOVEMENTS

Although nothing appeared in the Covenant of the League of Nations concerning human rights, a number of proposals for standards were put forward outside the context of formal UN institutions. A private body, the Institute of International Law, composed of leading international law scholars from across the globe, met at Briarcliff, New York, in 1929 to develop an "International Bill of Rights." In their first draft they set out what they regarded as state duties to respect individual rights (Fareed, 1977, p. 26). They included six specific articles: the rights to life, liberty, property, religious and linguistic freedom, and a nationality. Although their effort did not produce any tangible results, some claim they greatly influenced the movement which culminated in the human-rights provisions in the Charter of the UN (Drost, 1951, p. 19).

Another memorable articulation of human-rights ideals was President Franklin D. Roosevelt's annual message to Congress on January 26, 1941, in which he advocated the "four freedoms": freedom of speech, freedom of worship, freedom from want, and freedom from fear. Roosevelt and Winston Churchill included these notions in the Atlantic Charter, which was drawn up August 14, 1941, adding the need for self-determination, economic progress, and social security (Szabo, 1982, p. 22). The "pre-history" of the UN ended January 1, 1942, with the signing by twenty-six nations of the Declaration of the UN. The United States, Great Britain, and the Soviet Union formally endorsed the UN Declaration at the Moscow Conference of October 1943. The Moscow Declaration helped pave the way toward the development of the UN organization by formally recognizing the need for such a world body (Fareed, 1977, p. 28).

A conference of the four major powers (China, Great Britain, the Soviet Union, and the United States) at Dumbarton Oaks in the fall of 1944 was the birthplace of a preliminary draft of the constitution of the new international {21} organization. Some value conflicts emerged, e.g., China favored the inclusion of provisions for nondiscrimination and equal rights, whereas the United States and Great Britain were opposed to these because of their domestic policies at the time, specifically racial segregation and exclusionary immigration (Tolley, 1987, pp. 3-4).

THE UN CHARTER

The proposals which were developed at Dumbarton Oaks were the basis of the work undertaken at the Conference on International Organization in April 1945 (Fareed, 1977, pp. 28-30) attended by many nations and nongovernmental organizations (NGOs).[2] It was at this conference that a draft of the Charter was finally adopted. The UN Charter was the first international agreement in which the countries of the world made a commitment to promote human rights at the international level (Fareed, 1977, p. 30; Sohn, 1977). In contrast to the League of Nations Covenant, the Charter made explicit reference to human rights in its Preamble and in several different articles (1, 13, 55, 62(2), 68). Other Charter articles have proved to be instrumental to those seeking to advance the cause of human rights (11, 14, 73) (Fareed, 1977, pp. 31-33).

Considering the competing influences, though, it is perhaps not surprising that the language pertaining to human rights that was incorporated in the Charter is vague. The Charter only refers to fundamental human rights (including the idea of equality before the law) in the most general terms.[3] Considerable debate has ensued concerning the ambiguous phraseology employed by the drafters. At the San Francisco conference there had been those who proposed attaching a Declaration on Human Rights to the Charter to define more precisely the nature of the rights to be protected. The explanation given for the decision not to do so was that the drafters wanted to ensure that the scope of rights protected by the UN be expansive. In other words, an exact definition of human rights was omitted to allow the concept to evolve with the development of humankind (Fareed, 1977, p. 59, n. 39; Ganji, 1962, pp. 120-124; Lauterpacht, 1950). Evidently, there was also fear that trying to complete an "International Bill of Rights" at the San Francisco conference might result in a hastily drafted, ill-conceived project (Fareed, 1977, p. 53).

As a consequence of the imprecise language employed in the Charter, there has been substantial disagreement over the extent to which it imposes {22} legal obligations upon its signatories. Many critics hold that the vagaries of the UN Charter do not permit one to conclude that states have incurred legal obligations merely by virtue of having ratified the instrument. The content of the human-rights duties held by states is nebulous, making it impossible to determine the nature of their obligations. That is, the language used is not strong enough to support obligations (Driscoll, 1979, p. 43; Green, 1958, p. 658).

The opposing view holds that the principle of good faith in treaty interpretation requires states to observe human rights. As the UN has steadily grown, this idea has gained wider acceptance. Human-rights advocates wishing to validate international human-rights standards often point to the 1971 *Namibia* case in which the ICJ held in favor of the view that, to some extent, the Charter is legally as well as morally binding.

Even if the standards had been clearly formulated, there remained the serious issue of what modes of enforcement member states were prepared to accept. Possibly the most controversial provision in the Charter was Article 2(7), which was put forward by the four major powers:

> Nothing contained in the present Charter shall authorize the United Nations to intervene in matters which are essentially within the domestic jurisdiction of any state or shall require the members to submit such matters to settlement under the present Charter, but this principle shall not prejudice the application of enforcement measures under Chapter VII.

Intervention is justified only under Chapter VII when the Security Council finds a "threat to the peace, breach of the peace, or act of aggression" (Article 39). The Security Council must interpret gross human-rights violations as being serious enough to constitute a threat of war (Tolley, 1987, pp. 6-7).

Article 2(7) raises serious conceptual difficulties. It is not clear whether a matter is, in fact, within a state's domestic jurisdiction. Even if the issue were one traditionally viewed as "domestic," the impetus behind the movement to establish international human rights necessarily required a shift in thinking. What was formerly domestic becomes international in character. Thus, the interpretation of an issue will reflect political judgments. Those favoring international human rights tend to deemphasize 2(7), while those wary of international obligations will have the opposite inclination.

The important point is that the drafters intended some degree of intervention, despite the inclusion of 2(7) in the Charter. Otherwise, there would have been no reason to incorporate references to human rights throughout {23} the instrument. The drafters simply had to balance the competing demands for international standards with the national fear of surrendering sovereignty. With the development of UN institutions one witnesses a new perspective on national sovereignty. The treaties and institutions that emerged indicated that the traditional position was declining and foreshadowed the creation of stronger human-rights bodies, more expansive in their coverage and approach.

UNITED NATIONS MACHINERY

The Charter specified institutions empowered to promote human rights (for a comprehensive discussion, see Fareed, 1977, pp. 33-52; Farer, 1987, pp. 550-586; Schwelb & Alston, 1982, pp. 231-301). In the UN, the main responsibility for advancing the cause of human rights belongs to the General Assembly. Under its aegis, the Economic and Social Council (ECOSOC—Article 60) is authorized to pursue human-rights activities. According to Article 60 of the UN Charter, the General Assembly may decide questions directly itself in plenary sessions or rely on a report from one of the Assembly's seven main committees (Schwelb & Alston, 1982, p. 232). Ordinarily, human-rights issues are referred to the Third Committee, which is concerned with social, humanitarian, and cultural matters.

Other UN institutions wield power as far as the enforcement of human rights is concerned. Article 34 specifies that the Security Council investigate disputes which might give rise to international conflict. On occasion, the Trusteeship Council (Articles 76(c) and 87) and the ICJ have decided human-rights questions. The Secretariat is designated as a key human-rights actor in the Charter as well (Articles 97-99) (Schwelb & Alston, 1982, p. 231). Under Article 13(Ia) of the Charter, the General Assembly is responsible for the codification of international law. It therefore established the International Law Commission (ILC) in 1947 (Fareed, 1977; Sinclair, 1987, pp. 41-43). Commission members have drafted conventions and articles on a variety of international law topics, including matters of human rights. Over time, many other UN organizations have been created which address human-rights issues, e.g., the United Nations Educational, Scientific and Cultural Organization (UNESCO) (Alston, 1980; Marks, 1984; Saba, 1982; see Appendix A [and, since 2011, Appendix B] for schematic listings of the UN human-rights organizations and their interconnections). {24}

THE COMMISSION ON HUMAN RIGHTS

One of the most lasting contributions of the UN Charter was the establishment of a Commission on Human Rights, which was provided for in Article 62. In fact, it is the only Commission specifically referred to in the Chapter. Pursuant to Article 68, ECOSOC first set up a subsidiary organ, the so-called Nuclear Commission on Human Rights, which initially included nine members serving in their personal capacity. At its second session, in June 1946, ECOSOC established the eighteen-member full Commission. The principal concerns of the Commission were an international bill of rights; international conventions on specific topics; the protection of minorities; and the prevention of discrimination on the grounds of race, sex, language, or religion. (For references which focus on the operation of the Commission, see Fareed, 1977; Hoare, 1967; Humphrey, 1969; Nolde, 1946; Shestack, 1982; Smoger, 1979; Tolley, 1983, 1984, 1987; Turlington, 1945; van Boven, 1968; for a personal account of the development of the Commission and other human rights activities, see Humphrey, 1984.)

The delegates at the San Francisco conference unanimously approved the Human Rights Commission, but emphasized national sovereignty at the expense of individual rights. This view coupled with the compromises inherent in the Charter itself left the mandate of the Commission unresolved. So, between June 1945 and January 1947, when the full Commission first met, legal experts and UN representatives debated issues such as its membership and powers (Tolley, 1987, pp. 6-8).

Early on there were conflicts between ECOSOC and the Commission with regard to the role which the Commission would play. There was the question of the extent to which Article 2(7) of the UN Charter might limit the Commission in its human-rights activities. ECOSOC was also unwilling to accept the Commission's recommendation that members serve in their individual capacity. The reasoning was that the Commission should be composed of independent experts since the General Assembly and ECOSOC were comprised of government delegates. The assumption was that government representatives would be overly concerned with national sovereignty, making them disinclined to pursue human-rights violations zealously. While the United States originally advocated independent experts, the Soviet Union held that "instructed representatives would be more qualified to develop practical solutions" (Humphrey, 1984, p. 17).

ECOSOC decided to allow states to select representatives subject to consultation with the Secretary General and confirmation by ECOSOC (Tolley, *Development of Human-Rights Standards* 1987, p. 10). {25} In the years since its founding, though, there has been "no case of the Secretary-General objecting to the qualification of a representative, or of the Council refusing to confirm him" (Schwelb & Alston, 1982, p. 244). Some maintain that the decision to have governmental representatives in lieu of independent experts was a sound one: "There would be no point in preparing texts which would not be accepted by governments" (Humphrey, 1984, p. 18). Insofar as the Commission was functioning as a quasi-legislative body, it was, arguably, appropriate that it should depend on governmental approbation. When the Commission shifted its attention from standard-setting to enforcement, however, the need for independence seemed to be greater. If members of the Commission did not feel free to raise questions that would embarrass governments, then it would accomplish little.

As it turned out, subtle considerations of membership were rendered virtually moot by a Commission resolution admitting that it had "no power to take any action in regard to any complaints concerning human rights" (Commission on Human Rights, Report of the First Session, UN Doc. E/259 [1947] para. 22). This "self-denying rule" was confirmed by ECOSOC in resolution 75(V), effectively limiting the Commission to general studies and recommendations concerning alleged human-rights violations. For twenty years the Commission was in essence restricted to the role of librarian, merely cataloguing the thousands of complaints it received. It was not until 1966-67 that serious effort was made to reverse this long-standing policy of inaction. Upon the recommendation of the General Assembly, ECOSOC authorized the Commission to investigate and make recommendations to the Council concerning manifest and repeated violations of human rights (ECOSOC Res. 1235[XLII 22 UN ECOSOC [1967]). The decision as to the admissibility of certain cases was delegated by ECOSOC to the Subcommission on the Prevention of Discrimination and Protection of Minorities in 1971 (ECOSOC Res. 1503 [XLVIII] 25 UN ECOSOC [1970]; El-Kayal, 1975, pp. 107-108; Shelton, 1984; Tardu, 1980). This sequence of events marked the beginning of a dramatic shift toward a stronger commitment to the promotion of international human rights and a stronger role for the Subcommission as well.

SUBCOMMISSIONS

In 1946 and 1947, ECOSOC authorized the Commission on Human Rights to create subcommissions. Three such subcommissions were established, {26} but only one has survived. At the same time that ECOSOC set up the Nuclear Commission of Human Rights, it appointed a nuclear subcommission on the status of women. This subcommission met in the spring of 1946 and concluded that it did not wish to be "dependent on the pace of another commission" (Humphrey, 1984, p. 19). The Council acceded to the request to transform the subcommission into a Commission on the Status of Women (for discussion of this Commission, see Bruce, 1971; Farer, 1987, pp. 566-567; Galey, 1979; Guggenheim, 1977; Schwelb & Alston, 1982, pp. 254-260). Evidently, there were those who objected to this development, regarding it as discriminatory for the UN to have a separate body dealing with the rights of women (Humphrey, 1984, p. 19).

For a brief period there was also a Subcommission on Freedom of Information and of the Press. Despite the fact that it was comprised primarily of journalists, the Commission was unable to achieve a consensus on the role of the press:

...the members were soon in deep ideological conflict, and the often stormy debates quickly revealed the fundamental differences in approach that would characterize all future discussion of freedom of information at the United Nations. The issue was and remains whether the press should be an instrument of freedom or one of power (Humphrey, 1984, p. 35).

The sharply divergent approaches to this issue are reflected in the 1980s debates in UNESCO concerning the New International Information Order (Nordenstreng, 1984). In some respects it is remarkable that a definition of freedom of information should have been included (Article 19) in the Universal Declaration of Human Rights (see below), in spite of the ideological conflict. The subcommission was abolished in 1951.

As it turned out, the Subcommission on the Prevention of Discrimination and Protection of Minorities proved to be the most influential. (For detailed analysis of this subcommission, see Claude, 1951; Gardeniers, Hannum & Kruger, 1982; Haver, 1982; Humphrey, 1968, 1975; and Salzberg, 1973.) Extremely important in the field of international human rights, it has become the Commission's only permanent expert group (Tolley, 1987, pp. 163-186).

Originally the plan was to establish two separate subcommissions, one on the prevention of discrimination and the other for the protection of minorities. The Commission decided instead to combine them into a single subcommission. Some regard this as having been a mistake because: "the two functions are quite different, and giving the same body responsibility {27} for both not only helped confuse the issues but made it easier for the United Nations to shirk the politically embarrassing job of protecting minorities." (Humphrey, 1984, p. 20).

Few countries are willing to grant autonomy to minority groups. The strong tendency toward assimilation mitigates against the recognition of minority rights. This proclivity is reinforced by the composition of the subcommission. Although it is officially comprised of independent experts, in reality its members are beholden to their respective governments. Despite efforts by the subcommission to fulfill both parts of its mandate, the bulk of its efforts has been directed toward the prevention of discrimination rather than the protection of minorities.

As with the Commission, it was not clear what activities the Subcommission would be authorized to undertake. The Commission narrowly circumscribed the powers of the Subcommission, just as its own powers had been by ECOSOC. Nevertheless, over time the Subcommission has enlarged its own powers beyond what the Commission had previously approved. As it has turned out, the Subcommission has become a de facto Subcommission on Human Rights despite its more narrow title (Tolley, 1987, p. 168). The Subcommission has created working groups whose function it is to investigate specific types of human-rights abuses, such as slavery, the subjugation of indigenous populations, torture, child labor, and others. It has not only tried to set international standards but it has also attempted to influence world public opinion. Research has been a key priority for the Subcommission, and its most controversial activities have, in fact, been its efforts to investigate human-rights violations through fact finding. Alarmed by the Subcommission's "radical" nature, the Commission tried to abolish it in 1951 but was prevented from doing so by the General Assembly, which cited an overriding commitment to the principle of nondiscrimination.

THE UNIVERSAL DECLARATION OF HUMAN RIGHTS

The first and most important task which the Commission on Human Rights faced was drafting an "International Bill of Rights" (Anonymous, 1948-49). At its second session, in 1947, the expectation was that this would include a declaration, a convention on human rights, and methods of implementation (Humphrey, 1984, p. 26). The Universal Declaration of Human Rights is often referred to as the "central document for the cause of human rights," which explains why the date of its adoption, December 10, 1948, has been {28} designated "Human Rights Day" by the United Nations (Szabo, 1982, p. 23; see G. A. Res. 423[V] of December 4, 1950; for the text, see Appendix C). With its adoption, it became possible to interpret the formerly obscure human-rights provisions of the UN Charter and thus to substantiate claims of human-rights violations.

The Division of Human Rights received numerous proposals for the Declaration from individuals as well as organizations. When the Commission began its work, it had eighteen drafts to consider (Szabo, 1982, p. 21). It is noteworthy that *all* the drafts came from the democratic West and that all but two were in English (Humphrey, 1984, pp. 31-32).

It was agreed at the first session that the Commission itself could not draft the International Bill of Rights. Consequently, the project was assigned to a drafting committee comprised of Eleanor Roosevelt, first chair of the Commission; Vice-Chair P. C. Chang, representing China; and the rapporteur Charles Malik, representing Lebanon. Interestingly, despite apparent national differences, Chang held a doctorate from Columbia University, while Malik had attended Harvard University (Tolley, 1987, p. 11). As director of the Secretariat's Division of Human Rights, John Humphrey from Canada was asked to draft the Secretariat Outline, a preliminary draft of the UDHR (for his personal account, see Humphrey, 1984, pp. 29-32). He evidently relied on the draft declaration that had been sponsored at the San Francisco conference (Humphrey, 1984, p. 32). Although most of the articles pertained to civil and political rights, the mainstay of the West, Humphrey was determined to include economic rights: "Human rights without economic and social rights have little meaning for most people, particularly on empty bellies" (Humphrey, 1984, p. 2). He takes credit for the fact that economic rights ended up in the final text (1984, p. 32).

Because the Soviet Union raised objections to the composition of the drafting committee, Eleanor Roosevelt was persuaded to expand the committee to eight members, including Australia, Chile, France, the Soviet

Union, and the United Kingdom. Even though she actually lacked the authority to enlarge the committee, the Council approved her decision (Humphrey, 1984, pp. 29-30). In early June 1947 the expanded drafting committee met to review the Secretariat's detailed Outline for a Declaration including forty-eight articles which had been prepared by Humphrey. The committee reconvened in May 1948 to assess replies from governments and then voted to adopt the Declaration by June 18. The recorded vote was twelve in favor, none opposed, and four abstentions by Eastern European members (Tolley, 1987, p. 20). ECOSOC made no substantive change, and final passage was secured in the General Assembly's Third Committee at 1:00 a.m. on {29} December 8. Final approval carne in the General Assembly on December 10, 1948. (For more detailed accounts of the drafting of the UDHR, see Anonymous, 1947-48; Cassin, 1951; Kanger, 1984; Robinson, 1958; Schwelb, 1964; and Verdoodt, 1964.)

LEGAL EFFECT OF THE UDHR

Despite apparent acceptance of the UDHR, the question of its legal effect still remained. Since its passage, scholars have debated whether or not the sweeping provisions constitute customary international law (Kunz, 1949, p. 316; Lillich & Newman, 1979, pp. 53-121; Schwelb, 1959). Although it appears to have greater significance than a simple UN resolution, some scholars contend that it is not legally binding.

Eleanor Roosevelt took the tack of arguing that the UDHR would not entail legal obligations. This strengthened her campaign for United States support. If it lacked legal force, then there would be no risk in endorsing it. It is true that the General Assembly resolutions do not bind members, certainly not those who oppose the resolution (Tolley, 1987, p. 23; Driscoll, 1979, pp. 4-5).

Many simply assumed that a convention would follow the adoption of the UDHR, which would transform the Declaration provisions into enforceable norms through the ordinary ratification process. Nevertheless, some countries anticipated legal consequences and therefore abstained from the final vote on the Declaration, e.g., the Soviet Union and South Africa (Tolley, 1987, p. 24).

The dominant view now is that the UDHR constitutes the authoritative interpretation of the human-rights provisions of the UN Charter. As such, it is legally binding on member nations. Another widespread position is that the norms of the UDHR have become binding as part of customary international law, legal principles of the so-called civilized nations. This makes the standards applicable to all nations, whether or not they have expressed consent.

VALUE CONFLICTS

The swift passage of the UDHR through official channels was due in large part to the agreement of a majority of the eighteen-member Commission. {30} The fact that there were no dissenting votes should not be taken to mean that complete value consensus had been achieved. As Tolley aptly puts it: "Swift passage of the Declaration without a dissenting vote neither resulted from nor established a consensus on fundamental substantive questions" (1987, p. 20).

The UDHR contains primarily civil and political rights (those favored by Western nations) as well as a few economic, social, and cultural rights (those championed by the Third World and the Soviet bloc). Evidently, it was because the Declaration was said to be without legal effect that Western drafters were convinced to include economic, social, and cultural rights, as they would be nonjusticiable in character (Tolley, 1987, pp. 21-22). Because there were clearly divergent cultural conceptions of human rights which remained unreconciled at the time of the drafting of the UDHR, the stage was set for inevitable conflict concerning the validity of particular international human-rights standards.

There was a considerable number of value conflicts surrounding the UDHR. A few examples of the cultural clashes will suffice to make the point. Arab states unsuccessfully challenged the right to change religion, a norm which was contrary to the tenets in the Koran (Tolley, 1987, p. 22). The Soviets were opposed to the preponderance of Western civil liberties. Those acquainted with the debates are forced to conclude: "Deliberations by the Commission and its drafting committee revealed profound ideological differences over what constituted universal rights" (Tolley, 1987, p. 21). Despite the common assertion that the UDHR is "universal," since its adoption, there has been widespread recognition of cultural conflict with regard to the norms embodied in it (see Chapter 2).

EXPLANATION FOR THE WESTERN BIAS

In the literature on human rights many have argued that the concept of human rights is a Western one. If one examines the circumstances under which the UDHR was drafted, the reasons for the emphasis on Western values will become apparent. The most obvious explanation is that the membership of the drafting committee, the Commission on Human Rights, and the UN as a whole were predominantly Western. It was not until the 1950s that anticolonialism prevailed, leading to the formation of new African {31} and Asian states. The membership of the UN was most assuredly a critical factor in shaping the UDHR.

The movement to create a new international apparatus for the promotion of human rights was led largely by Americans. The U.S. Department of State orchestrated the early drafts of a proposed constitution (Tolley, 1987, p. 3). The crucial meetings took place in the United States. American NGOs were extremely influential during the formative stages of the Commission and the UDHR (Humphrey, 1979, p. 21). The efforts of more than forty private organizations brought in as consultants by the United States ensured that the Charter would contain some references to human rights (Farer, 1987, p. 554).

Even the goal itself was described as drafting an "International Bill of Rights," language which undeniably reflects an American flavor. Many writers refer to those who drafted the original human-rights documents as "founders" (Farer, 1987, p. 554; McWhinney, 1984b, p. 4). Eleanor Roosevelt was said to favor a two-stage drafting process for a declaration and convention modeled after the United States' Declaration of Independence and Bill of Rights (Tolley, 1987, p. 21). Considering the mindset of those most actively involved in the drafting of the original human-right's instruments, it should not be surprising that many of the notions resemble Western European and American political ideas:

> *Everyone* has the right to:
> • life, liberty and security of person (Article 3)
> • recognition everywhere as a person before the law (Article 6)
> • freedom of movement...to leave any country, including his own (Article 13)
> • a nationality (Article 15)
> • freedom of thought, conscience and religion (Article 18)
> • freedom of peaceful assembly and association (Article 20)
> • take part in the government of his country (Article 21)
>
> *No one* shall be:
> • held in slavery (Article 4)
> • subjected to torture (Article 5)
> • subjected to arbitrary arrest, detention or exile (Article 9)
>
> (Tolley, 1987, pp. 22-23; see also McWhinney, 1984b, p. 210).

In spite of many indications that the UDHR is Western in orientation, this remains a sensitive point. There are those who deny that the Western influence at the drafting stages resulted in any bias: {32}

> I submit to you that what the thinkers of the Enlightenment did, and what the drafters of the Universal Declaration also strove to do, was to present a set of ideals—of universal ideals on the limits of governmental authority, of goals to be attained, above all, to guarantee the individual respect for his dignity and a life of freedom from fear....
>
> Is it not a truly detestable form of racism to suggest that these should be the goals of Western civilization only and of no bearing or relevance to the rest of the world? (Schifter, 988, pp. 2-3).

Those who defend the universality of values embedded in the UDHR often cite the number of national constitutions enacted after the adoption of the UDHR which incorporated some of its provisions (for evidence of the alleged impact of the UDHR on national constitutions, municipal legislation, and court decisions, see Fareed, 1977, pp. 128-130).

The point which must be underscored is that there was in the 1940s and there remains today some question about the degree to which the "Universal" Declaration of Human Rights truly reflects "universal" values. Doubts were not laid to rest on December 10, 1948, with the consequence that the credibility of this potentially revolutionary document has been enveloped in controversy. States are probably more likely to comply with standards based on values to which they are committed. Therefore, if a document contains principally Western values, this would seem to ignore the practical problems of implementation for non-Western countries. What remains to be determined is the extent to which the UDHR is, in fact, based on values shared by all systems.

THE COVENANTS

The Commission worked on the rest of the International Bill of Rights between May 1949 and April 1954. The Covenants the Commission drafted represented an attempt to create human-rights standards which would be legally binding on signatories, since the UDHR was originally intended only as a statement of principles. Compared to the rapidity with which the Declaration was drafted and approved, the Covenants took an exceedingly long time. The General Assembly did not grant its approval for twelve years. The historical debates indicate that one of the major conflicts was the decision whether to have one or two covenants. Although some preferred to have one on civil and political rights and another on economic, social, and {33} cultural rights, others regarded this division as being highly artificial. For those subscribing to the latter view, the two sets of rights were perceived as interdependent (Szabo, 1982, p. 29).

At first the UN decided to have all the rights incorporated in a single convention. This was the position officially taken at the fifth session of the General Assembly. A year later, however, in response to Western pressure, the Assembly reversed itself, concluding that it was, after all, preferable to draft two separate conventions which would be completed concurrently and then open for signature by states on the same date (Szabo, 1982, p. 29). Some have attacked the decision to devise two discrete instruments (Szabo, 1982, p. 30). Their essential point is that the types of rights are not conceptually distinct. For example, the right to join a union could be characterized as being either political or economic. The real reason for the twin Covenants was that Western states could avoid economic rights for the most part. The claim was that more states in general would be inclined to ratify a covenant if it contained only rights which they supported. An examination of patterns of ratification, though, do not appear to bear this out. The United States, for instance, has failed to ratify many human-rights treaties, despite its professed commitment to the rights embodied in them. It ratified the Genocide Convention only in 1988 (for discussion of U.S. policy on the Genocide Convention, see Kaufman & Whiteman, 1988).

In 1966 the Convenants were finally presented in the General Assembly. The International Covenant on Civil and Political Rights (ICCPR) received 106 votes in favor with none against (for analysis of the ICCPR, see Hevener & Mosher, 1978); the International Covenant on Economic, Social, and Cultural Rights (ICESCR) received 105 votes with none against (Farer, 1987, p. 560). But despite the fact that nations voted for the Covenants, this did not mean that they would ratify them promptly. Ten years later, both Covenants finally had received the required thirty-five ratifications needed to enter into force. The delay has been attributed to the ideological diversity in the UN (Tolley, 1987, p. 24).

DIFFERENCES BETWEEN THE DECLARATION AND THE COVENANTS

Since the mainstream view now is that the declaration is customary international law and therefore binding on member states, the advantage of the Covenants is their reporting and enforcement procedures (Das, 1982, pp. 330-334; Driscoll, 1979, p. 46). {34} Whereas the UDHR contained a combination of political and economic rights, each Covenant was devoted to one kind only. Because Western opposition to economic rights was so entrenched, it seemed advisable to have two separate documents: "Realistically it appeared that if Western governments would obstruct a comprehensive covenant, two agreements would be preferable to none" (Tolley, 1987, p. 25).

Although some characterize the covenants as more detailed versions of rights in the UDHR, there are substantive differences. The final draft of the ICCPR contained fifty-one articles, twenty-two of which closely resembled provisions of the Declaration (Tolley, 1987, p. 27). Both Covenants include rights not recognized by the Declaration. For example, the Political Covenant prohibits imprisonment because of inability to fulfill a contractual obligation. Other rights in the UDHR are either modified by the Covenants or left out altogether.

Some examples of the refinements might be of interest. The ICCPR limited the free exercise of religion and removed the right guaranteed in the UDHR to change one's religion. Likewise, the Covenant qualified freedom of association according to the interests of national security or public safety. One provision incorporated into the ICCPR which may have contributed to the reluctance of the United States to ratify the Covenant concerns free speech. Specifically, several states insisted on a prohibition of speech advocating racial hatred and war. Even France joined China and the Soviet Union among others in favor of the provision. Although the United States managed to block the restrictive proposal for a few years, despite its having been recommended by the Subcommission, by 1953 supporters of the exceptions were in the majority (Tolley, 1987, p. 28).

Western nations tried to prevent the incorporation of the right to self-determination but proved unsuccessful in this enterprise. This right became Article 1 of both Covenants because of extensive support among the nations which had fought colonialism. Western states had advanced the argument that vague collective rights do not belong with the guarantees of individual freedom. They also failed to secure language ensuring just compensation for nationalized property (Tolley, 1987, p. 27).

Perhaps because of the bitter disputes surrounding the Covenants, ratification by member states has proceeded slowly. As of 1986, only eighty-five members had ratified the ICESCR and eighty-one the ICCPR. Since the total membership of the UN was approximately 150, this left about half the members unaccounted for. In light of the Western origins of the Covenants, it might be expected that more Western nations would ratify. {35} This expectation is borne out: roughly two-thirds of all European and Latin American states ratified, versus about one-third of all African and Asian nations. Although President Jimmy Carter signed both Covenants in 1977, official ratification in the United States appeared to remain unlikely (Tolley, 1987, p. 140). [The U.S. eventually ratified the ICCPR, in 1992.]

Optional Protocol

As mentioned previously, one advantage derived from the ICCPR over the UDHR is the possibility of enforcement. The ICCPR has several complaints procedures, not all of which are equally effective. The interstate complaints procedure, for example, suffers from the reluctance of member states to risk diplomatic crises by raising controversial human-rights issues. More useful perhaps is the Optional Protocol to the ICCPR. Under Article 1, ratifying states authorize the Human Rights Committee[4] "to receive and consider communications from individuals subject to its jurisdiction who claim to be the victims of a violation by that State Party of any of the rights set forth in the Covenant."

As states tend not to lodge complaints against other states, it is advantageous to permit individuals to present their own claims in international human-rights forums. It is part of the changed thinking in international circles that the individual has become a subject and not merely an object of international law.

By 1986 only 18 states had agreed to the interstate complaints procedures of the ICCPR and only 38 governments had ratified the Optional Protocol (Tolley, 1987, p. 140). No states, however, have brought complaints (Tolley, 1987, p. 269, n. 27). Since the Covenant and Optional Protocol are relatively modern creations and have only recently entered into force, it is not yet possible to assess their efficacy (Driscoll, 1979, p. 47). One can, however, anticipate at least one problem with the implementation of the Covenant and Optional Protocol: only states that are parties to the Covenant are subject to the enforcement mechanisms.

REGIONAL APPROACHES

Enforcement of human-rights standards also occurs at the regional level. The earliest and most established human-rights institutions at the regional {36} level are found in Western Europe. If the ideas from the Enlightenment provided the foundation for international standards, then it should come as no surprise that the first human-rights organizations emerged in Europe. Acceptance of the basic notions of human rights throughout Europe must have facilitated the founding of these bodies.

The three major organs of the European human-rights system are the European Commission of Human Rights, the European Court of Human Rights, and the Council of Ministers (for in-depth studies of the European institutions, see Beddard, 1980; Boyle, 1984; Fawcett, 1969; Jacobs, 1975; Robertson, 1977; and Vasak, 1982). They derive their authority from the European Convention for the Protection of Human Rights and Fundamental Freedoms, which was drafted by the Council of Europe and entered into force in 1953 (well before the International Covenants). The Convention allows states (Article 24) as well as individuals and NGOs (Article 25) to bring a complaint against a state. Applications are initially reviewed by the Commission, which rules upon admissibility and facts. If the complaint is valid, the Commission can attempt a friendly settlement. If that fails, the case is referred either to the court or the Council of Ministers, whose decisions are binding (Boyle, 1984; O'Boyle, 1980; Vasak, 1982).

Another important regional human-rights organization is that set up by the Organization of American States (LeBlanc, 1973; Buergenthal, 1984). The Inter-American Commission on Human Rights was established in 1959. Two regional documents serve as guidelines: the American Declaration on the Rights and Duties of Man (1948) and the American Convention on Human Rights (1969), which has not yet entered into force. The Commission has interpreted its powers broadly to enable it to investigate problems in member states (Gros Espiell, 1982; Norris, 1980, 1984; Schreiber, 1970). In 1965 the Commission's powers were expanded to permit it to screen individual complaints related to certain articles of the American Declaration of the Rights and Duties of Man. As a consequence, since 1966 the Commission has heard complaints against almost every OAS member state. This constitutes one of the most salient differences between the European Convention and the American Convention. Whereas the right of individual petition is optional under the former, it is automatic under the latter (Driscoll, 1979, pp. 51-52).

Another existing regional institution is The Arab Commission on Human Rights, which was set up by the League of Arab States in 1968. Its main function has been the drafting of agreements to submit to the Council of the League. To date it lacks any power to review complaints from states or individuals (Boutros-Ghali, 1982; Driscoll, 1979, p. 52). {37}

The most recently developed regional body, as of 1988, is the African Commission on Human and Peoples' Rights. The Organization of African

Unity adopted the African Charter of Human and Peoples' Rights in 1981. It entered into force on October 21, 1986, and, according to Article 45, authorizes the African Commission "to collect documents, undertake studies and researches on African problems in the field of human and peoples' rights" (for discussion of the Charter, see Anonymous, 1986b; Anonymous, 1988-89; Gittleman, 1984; Lihau, 1986; M'Baye, 1982; Ndiaye, 1982).

Progress to build an Asian human-rights organization has been slow. Proponents of regional human-rights tribunals attempted to orchestrate a series of seminars in Asia to replicate the successful regional seminars that led to the African Charter, but their efforts met with little success (Tolley, 1987, p. 158).

An advantage of regional human-rights organizations over international ones is that the locally proposed standards can be more compatible with indigenous values. Consequently, implementation of those standards is less likely to be regarded as cultural imperialism. States will be more inclined to comply with rules which are concordant with their political culture.

For those seeking universal human rights, however, this may present a problem. To the extent that regional standards conflict with international ones, claims to universality may be jeopardized. It is precisely this issue which lies at the heart of the entire human-rights movement, namely the tension between universalism and relativism.

CONCLUSION

As the human-rights institutions and instruments have evolved, they have been subject to certain recurring problems. One of the most challenging issues has been the question of how to balance national sovereignty with international human rights. If human rights are to have any significance, they must be transnational in application. This means that states must of necessity relinquish some measure of autonomy.

Another complexity is that states have a peculiar role to play in the field of human rights. Since it is states which most frequently violate human rights, it is an awkward arrangement, to say the least, that states should be designated as the champions of human rights. In the absence of international human-rights machinery, therefore, it is unlikely that those rights will be safeguarded. If states perpetrate human-rights abuses, then a complaints {38} procedure limited to states' submissions will accomplish little. States will not report their own misdeeds. As mentioned previously, states are generally reluctant to report violations in other states because this may sour diplomatic relations. When states do lodge complaints, they are often politically motivated. Thus, when international enforcement does permit individuals to send communications to tribunals, this constitutes a real advance.

Because of governmental pressures to avoid public condemnation, the selection of members of various human-rights bodies has involved a similar concern. Many would have preferred persons serving in their individual capacity to government representatives, because such persons would have been relatively free to investigate alleged human-rights abuses in an independent manner. As the human-rights institutions have become increasingly bureaucratized, though, even the so-called independent experts and individuals not officially representing their governments (as in the case of the Subcommission) have been subject to governmental control.

One of the most serious questions (and one which is rarely discussed in the literature) has to do with the values of actors in international organizations. Do the elites who purport to represent the positions of their nationals do so accurately? Do indigenous perceptions of human rights correspond to the viewpoints expressed by elites in the context of UN debates? If not, then the standard argument advanced by international lawyers, namely that ratification of international instruments indicates universal acceptance of the norms, is false. This would mean that the UDHR, despite nearly unanimous support at the UN, does not necessarily have the support of the peoples of the world. It remains to be seen how many human rights are actually consistent with the diverse value systems across the globe.

2

THE CONCEPT OF HUMAN RIGHTS

THERE IS considerable disagreement among theorists about both the nature and legitimacy of rights. Some of the theoretical issues raised by rights theorists are important for elucidating the notion of a human right. This chapter focuses on the conceptual analysis of rights only insofar as it is relevant for understanding human rights.[5] It will be shown that the case against the doctrine of *logical* correlativity,[6] which associates rights of one person with the duties of another and vice versa, is flawed. If, as will be argued, rights and duties are always correlative, then duty-based moral systems could accommodate human rights, the assertions of some commentators notwithstanding (e.g., Donnelly, 1982b). Next I will argue against some traditional categorizations of rights. Several observations are included, motivated by the desire to expand the standard view of rights. By anticipating possible objections that rights theorists might raise to the assertion of particular universal human rights, I hope to make possible a more solid foundation for a broader range of human rights.

In the second part of the chapter I present some classic definitions of human rights, followed by a discussion of some of the traditional Western sources from which human rights are thought to be derived, which concludes that those sources are lacking. The underlying reasons for their inadequacy are traced back to a deeply rooted belief in the presumed universality of Western moral notions. These same assumptions manifest themselves in some of the international human-rights documents. It is clear from even the most cursory study of other cultures that their value systems differ from those of the West in significant ways, as can be seen in the cases of female circumcision and child labor.

THE NATURE OF RIGHTS

There are almost as many theories of rights as there are rights theorists. It is sometimes said that the only true rights are legal rights (Bentham, 1843, Vol. 2, p. 501, Vol. 3, p. 221; Hart, 1973, pp. 171-201). Other scholars argue for a broader view of rights which would encompass moral rights {40} as well. For the purposes of explaining the general character of rights, it will not be necessary to distinguish between them.

As is typical in the history of philosophy, what was once a simple notion is often transformed into a much more complicated structure. While this is sometimes useful (and indeed necessary) for certain concepts, it can obfuscate the essential features of an idea. Rights theories exemplify this tendency of rejecting more simple accounts in favor of more complex normative structures (Martin & Nickel, 1980, p. 165). Some of the so-called simple characterizations of rights, however, do capture the essence of a right. For many philosophical writers, a right is treated synonymously with a *claim* (Feinberg, 1973, pp. 64-66). The *Oxford English Dictionary* defines a right as a "justifiable claim, on legal or moral grounds, to have or obtain something, or to act in a certain way." A leading proponent of this view is Joel Feinberg, who states that "To have a right is to have a claim to something and against someone, the recognition of which is called for by legal rules or, in the case of moral rights, by the principles of an enlightened conscience" (1980, pp. 159-160).

What distinguishes a right from a demand is that it is justified, either by appeal to preexisting legal rules or to morality. Thus a right is a *valid* claim. H. J. McCloskey prefers to define a right as an entitlement rather than a claim (McCloskey, 1976a). The view that rights can be explained as legitimate or reasonable claims is mistaken, according to McCloskey, because it is based on the premise that rights "are and must always be rights against some other person or persons" (1976a, p. 100). He rejects the duty definition as well: "What is common to all rights is not some duty or duty relationship but an entitlement" (1976a, p. 104).

Whereas the previous characterizations attempt to isolate a single concept underlying the notion of a right, a competing school of thought seeks to encompass all rights within a complex normative apparatus. Wesley Hohfeld's classic work, *Fundamental Legal Conceptions* (1923), laid the foundation for much subsequent philosophical exegesis. He asserted that rights could be understood as belonging to one of four categories: claim, liberty, power, or immunity.[7] Hohfeld's analysis has been used, among other things, to refute the logical correlativity doctrine. His framework has been adopted and extended by a number of philosophers (e.g., Flathman, 1976 and Wellman, 1985).

In contrast to these normative theories are functionalist accounts of rights, the most famous of which is that of Ronald Dworkin (1977; see also Scheingold, 1974). According to this view, what is distinctive about rights is that they function as trumps over collective goals. This would seem to require {41} that rights be individuated in order to distinguish them from what one might call "collective rights" (see Dinstein, 1976; Garet, 1983; and Van Dyke, 1980).

RIGHTS AND DUTIES

The view that rights and duties are correlative used to be the dominant one among philosophers (Lyons, 1970, p. 45; Martin & Nickel, 1980, p. 165). The principal idea is that to say that A has a right to X, is to say that B has a duty to ensure that A can, in fact, obtain X. But further, to say that C has a duty to D with respect to E, is to say that D has a right to E vis-à-vis C. Many rights theorists, including Feinberg, Lyons, Martin and Nickel, and McCloskey, take varying stances against this position. Most of the arguments are based on the four Hohfeldian categories.

Lyons, for instance, contends that one set of rights, "active rights" (rights to do things) does not fit the pattern of correlativity (1970, p.48). The first example he offers involves the right of free speech.[8] Alvin speaks to a crowd from a soap box, decrying U.S. military involvement in Vietnam. During the course of pontificating, he is assaulted by private citizens and removed from his platform. For Lyons, the question is whether Alvin's right to free speech (or the specific right to address the crowd) is "equivalent to the assertion of correlative obligations incumbent on others" (1970. p.50). Lyons wants to say that Alvin's right to free speech does not correspond to any duty: "The constitutional right of free speech is independent of, for example, the obligation not to assault that was breached by those who silenced Alvin" (1970, p.51). According to Lyons, the listeners may be under a duty not to attack Alvin, but not under a duty to respect his free speech. But he goes on to conclude that Alvin's right does not correspond to any duty on the part of Congress either:

> These Constitutional rights exemplify what some jurists call "immunities" for to assert them is to say that protected areas of speech *cannot be taken away*. Alvin's Constitutional right has a conceptual correlative: but it is not an obligation; it is a legislative "disability," the assertion of which says that Congress is not empowered to enact certain laws (1970, p. 51).

The second example offered by Lyons is the right of a California motorist to turn right on a red light. Lyons tries to show that there is no clear duty associated with this right. But in fact he undermines his argument: "it seems {42} more plausible to say that this right imposes obligations on law enforcement officials not to interfere with one's making a right turn (when allowed by the conditions of the right)" (1970, p. 55). He refuses, though, to concede the point: "A policeman may admittedly be under an obligation not to stop or disturb a private citizen without cause—but can we say that that obligation is 'correlative' with my right to make a right turn on a red light in California?" (1970, p. 55).

The crux of the argument against the logical correlativity doctrine seems to derive from the Hohfeldian interpretation of an immunity right, the correlative of which is a disability. According to Hohfeldian scholars, disabilities are associated with the absence of obligations. I would argue that this distinction is merely semantic. It is not simply that Congress is not empowered to enact legislation which restricts freedom of speech but, also, that Congress is under an obligation not to enact such legislation, for to do so would violate the right. Furthermore, one could argue that there is a duty which "stands to" the right of freedom of speech "just as Bernard's obligation to pay Alvin correlates with Alvin's right" in Lyons' paradigmatic example (1970, p. 50). The duty is that of the judiciary to protect the right to freedom of speech. I maintain that in every case in which Hohfeldian language is used, a correlative duty may always be found.[9]

29

McCloskey proposes another type of counterexample to the rights implied duties thesis, namely that of the conscientious objector (1976a, p. 104). He asserts that the right to be a conscientious objector corresponds to no duty on the part of others. His argument revolves around a reformulation of the conflict between the individual and the state in terms of rights language rather than duty language:

> Thus to assert that he has a right here is distinct from claiming that others have a duty to leave him free from interference. One can, with very good sense, assert that the state has a right to punish him for doing that to which he has a moral right (1976a, p. 104).

But if a right to be a conscientious objector is actually recognized as a valid moral right, then it stands to reason that the state has a duty not to interfere. The argument is part of a larger attempt by McCloskey to eliminate claim language in favor of entitlement language, but this program is unpersuasive.[10]

Philosophers have also challenged the logical correlativity doctrine by asserting the existence of duties without corresponding rights. Feinberg, for instance, says that duties of charity which "require us to contribute to {43} one or another of a large number of eligible recipients, no one of which can claim our contribution from us as his due" (1970, p. 244), shows the absence of a correlative right. Hart (1979) and others contend that while we have duties not to mistreat animals and babies, nevertheless, they have no rights against us (in part because they are not moral agents—see Lamont, 1950, p. 93). Still others have claimed that the duty to rescue has no correlative right (Bedau, 1968). It is even sometimes suggested that the man in André Malraux's novel, *La Condition Humaine* (1933), felt he had a duty to give his supply of poison to his fellow prisoners, though they had no right to it (Acton, 1950, p. 108).

There are at least two objections which can be raised to arguments of the kind advanced by the above philosophers. The first is that, in the cases where we would agree that there are such duties, there is also a corresponding right. If society recognizes duties to be kind to animals and babies, for instance, then, indeed, those entities could be said to have rights.[11] The second is that, in those cases in which we are hesitant to assert the existence of a right, it is because the attribution of the duty seems dubious. Unfortunately, many persons do not recognize duties of charity, for example, perhaps because such duties give rise to something resembling economic rights. The reluctance of theorists to acknowledge the existence of rights corresponding to duties held by others may stem from the fear that to do so would cheapen rights language by a proliferation of less significant rights (Hart, 1979). But the problem does not lie in the correlation; it rests in the absence of some mechanism for justifying the assertion of particular rights/duties.

Rights and duties are in fact flip sides of the same coin.[12] Brandt has said that the difference between a right and a duty is similar to the difference between the active and the passive voice (1959, p. 434). While this observation is not a new theory of rights, Waldron regards the simple association of a duty to a right as capable of forming the basis for a "more satisfactory" account than some of the more elaborate ones:

> Thus the right of free speech, for example, is understood in terms of recognition that an individual's interest in self-expression is a sufficient ground for holding other individuals and agencies to be under duties of various sons rather than in terms of the detail of the duties themselves (1984, p. 11).

The importance of demonstrating the logical correlativity of rights and duties does not lie so much in any explanatory power it has for Western rights theories, but rather in the flexibility it affords the formulation of international {44} human-rights standards. Correlativity is crucial because it means that the framing of moral claims in terms other than rights is not necessarily problematic. The recognition of an obligation may well signify the presence of an implicit right.

The misleading separation of rights from duties has led philosophers to make distinctions between right-based, duty-based, and goal-based theories (Dworkin, 1978, pp. 169-173). It is noteworthy that Kant's famous duty based theory has been employed as a basis for theories of rights (Waldron, 1984, p. 13). This suggests that just because a moral theory is couched in the language of duty does not imply that it cannot be a vehicle for the advancement of rights. Mackie (1978) goes so far as to argue that any moral theory is necessarily right-based, even if rights can only be identified as implicit.

OBSERVATIONS ON RIGHTS

Traditional rights theorists have constructed a framework which is unduly restrictive. An examination of some of the common classifications reveals several artificial distinctions. The removal of these conceptual obstacles should facilitate the formulation of a broader and more accurate concept of human rights.

THE DOCTRINE OF MORAL CORRELATIVITY

The idea that to hold rights one must be capable of and willing to perform duties, is known as the doctrine of moral correlativity (Feinberg, 1973, pp. 61-62). It is sometimes asserted that a right, in order to be a right, must be unconditional. But this is demonstrably false. Consider the case of the prisoner, some of whose rights are suspended because he has not fulfilled his duties (Feinberg. 1973, p. 62).[13] Here we would agree that it is appropriate to make rights contingent on duties. One could go so far as to argue that, for adults at least, all rights are contingent on duties. Even the right to life, for example, could be said to be contingent on the duty to respect other lives. On the other hand, if babies and animals have

rights, then they have them irrespective of their capacity to perform duties. So {45} the doctrine of moral correlativity appears to be contingent.
As a consequence, societies in which rights depend on the performance of
duties can still be said to have rights.

Positive Versus Negative

Philosophers have traditionally divided rights into two categories:
positive and negative. If a citizen has a right to freedom of speech, for
example, then the state has a duty of noninterference. This so-called
negative right allegedly imposes no burdensome or costly duty on the
state. The standard view of the positive right holds that welfare rights
require extensive governmental action. It is worth pointing out that the
views discussed above are those of Western philosophers who are sympa-
thetic to civil and political rights but not to economic rights. Therefore,
the positive/negative rights classification simply reflects the values of the
political culture in which the philosophers live.

The allegation that positive rights demand elaborate state action has
been criticized by philosophers such as Sidney Hook (1970) and Henry
Shue (1980). In *Basic Rights*, Shue challenges the premise that only
positive rights require a vast expenditure of funds. Opponents of positive
rights might argue, for example, that providing a food stamp program
would involve a costly and unwieldy bureaucratic network. The right to
food thus appears to be an expensive right.

But some of the "negative" rights—for instance, the right to a trial by
jury—certainly necessitate the existence of an elaborate (and expensive)
criminal justice apparatus. The maintenance of civil and political rights
depends on the existence of police, courts, and a plethora of other institutions. This reappraisal suggests that the emphasis placed on particular
rights is a matter of political preference rather than simple economic
calculations.

Legal Versus Moral

A second distinction that is often drawn is that between moral and
legal rights. Legal positivists claim that a right exists only if it is enforceable. Legal rights which exist by virtue of legislative enactment, common
law, and so on, are, therefore, the only type of rights possible.[14] Other
theorists, such as natural law/rights theorists, hold that moral rights are
prior to and independent of legal rights. {46}

The distinction can be quite crucial when, for example, a legal system
makes no provision for a particular right. The argument that the system
should be modified to incorporate the right will be fortified by the demonstrated existence of a moral right. Without moral rights it would be con-
siderably more difficult to bring about changes in law. The validity of legal
rights can be based partly on the extent to which they correspond to moral
rights.[15]

Individual Versus Group

In the Western political tradition, only individual adult moral agents have been accorded the privilege of holding rights. But there is nothing inherent in the notion of a right which logically requires this restriction. Nonetheless, some Westerners deny the existence of group rights, and their reluctance to grant such rights may stem from a fear that such rights are merely expressions of utilitarian goals. Since one of the main purposes of rights is to limit the arbitrary exercise of governmental power, utilitarian goals masquerading as group rights would perhaps seriously undermine the power of rights as trumps.

Not all group rights, however, need be opposed to individuals' rights, e.g., the right to self-determination. The United Nations has, in fact, recognized community rights, the rights of peoples, and the rights of groups, in addition to the rights of individuals (Ramcharan, 1983, p. 278). The advantage of admitting group rights is that there may be certain rights which people ought to be able to claim, which cannot be easily expressed in individualistic terms. One could make the case, for example, that some of the rights articulated in the African Charter on Human and Peoples Rights, specifically Articles 19-24, which pertain to colonialism, require the language of group rights rather than individual rights (Anonymous, 1983b).

HUMAN RIGHTS AND THE PRESUMPTION OF UNIVERSALITY

The emergence of rights in political thought is generally regarded as a new development. There are those who maintain that rights did not exist in ancient civilizations and those who argue that rights are not to be found in non-Western moral systems. Any historical study of rights reveals how hazy the philosophical charting of the evolution of rights has been. Based {47} on what little evidence is presented, it is astonishing that anyone should offer decisive conclusions about the role of rights in other epochs and cultures. The absence of any consideration of moral notions comparable to rights makes the presumed universality of human rights dubious at best. If we are to save human rights from the charge of cultural imperialism, then it is necessary to reinforce their underpinnings. The remainder of this chapter will identify some of the weaknesses in the foundations of human rights, as put forward by (mostly Western) philosophers.

Definitions

The classic definition of a human right is a right which is universal and held by all persons:

> A human right by definition is a universal moral right, something which all men, everywhere, at all times ought to have, something of which no one may be deprived without a grave affront to justice, something which is owing to every human being simply because he

is human (Cranston, 1973, p. 36).

One of the definitions cited most often is that of Wasserstrom (1964). Any true human right, it is said, must satisfy at least four requirements:

> First, it must be possessed by all human beings, as well as only by human beings. Second, because it is the same right that all human beings possess, it must be possessed equally by all human beings. Third, because human rights are possessed by all human beings, we can rule out as possible candidates any of those rights which one might have in virtue of occupying any particular status or relationship, such as that of parent, president, or promisee. And fourth, if there are any human rights, they have the additional characteristic of being assertable, in a manner of speaking, "against the whole world" (1964, p. 50).

As one can see from the definitions, human rights are presumed to be universal in character. This would not in itself be problematic (indeed it is desirable), except that the philosophical foundations are never adequately demonstrated. The failure to ground human rights, as will be discussed below, has much to do with their historical antecedents, in particular natural law and natural rights, with which human rights are assumed by many philosophers to be synonymous (Donnelly, 1985, p. 10; Pappu, 1969, p. 44; Wasserstrom, 1964). {48}

Traditional Western Sources

For many centuries natural law played a dominant role in Western political theory. Natural law was considered to be the standard against which all other laws were to be judged. To contest the injustice of a man-made law, one could appeal to the higher authority of God or natural law. Eventually natural law evolved into natural rights, which are considered to be the modern manifestations of natural law. The change reflected a shift in emphasis from society to the individual. Whereas natural law provided a basis for curbing excessive state power, natural rights offered a means by which an individual could press claims against the government.[16]

Natural law/rights theorists have asserted the existence of specific rights such as the right to liberty (Hart, 1979), the right to life (McCloskey, 1975), the right to self-preservation (Hobbes), the right to property (Locke), the right to freedom from torture (Nickel, 1982), and the right to participate (Stackhouse, 1984). Because they take the validity of the rights to be a self-evident proposition, there has traditionally been little room for debate. One might expect to encounter difficulties when various proponents defend different and sometimes conflicting rights based solely on the claim that the rights are self-evident. Not surprisingly, philosophers have not welcomed discussions of competing moralities, largely because they take their own values to be obviously correct.[17] Strangely enough, Waldron notes that natural rights "seemed peculiarly vulnerable to ethical skepticism" but concludes that "it would be wrong to suggest that the discussion of human rights has been seriously impeded by these difficulties" (1984, p. 3).

Though the contemporary notion of human rights may be the offspring of natural rights, there are, nonetheless, differences between them. The most important of these is the extent of the moral universe to which they lay claim. Whereas natural rights were not widely contested because they were asserted in a universe of shared values, human rights have been highly controversial. Consider Locke's assertion of the natural right to property, the validity of which was taken for granted in England, but which might require argumentation in some socialist countries (to say the least). The presumption of universality no longer serves "universal" rights well.[18]

In the past, attempts to ground human rights were not successful. The best-known and most celebrated efforts employed the vague concepts of human nature and rationality to establish particular rights. It could be argued that it is nonsensical to separate the two insofar as rationality is, in some regions, regarded as integral to human nature. Other conceptual devices which have provided tentative bases for human rights include: the ability to use language, reciprocity, the capacity to conform to moral requirements, {49} self-motivated activity, self-consciousness, and purposive agency (Husak, 1984, p. 128).

Increasingly, justification for human rights is coming to depend less on human nature and rationality and more on the concepts of basic human needs and human dignity. These strategies, however, are subject to the same weaknesses as their predecessors. How theorists derive specific human rights from needs or dignity remains entirely obscure. Just as some philosophers began to challenge the assumption that human nature could give rise to specific human rights (Blackstone, 1968, p. 624), others (e.g., Donnelly, 1985, pp. 28-30) question the ability of basic-needs theorists to delineate in the abstract those needs which should give content to the idea of human rights. Presumably, adherents to this approach would not advocate the establishment of rights based on all needs. Someone must decide what needs are truly basic, and inasmuch as different judges will perceive different needs as taking highest priority, this approach does not circumvent the challenge of diversity.

The problem with all of these approaches which aim at anchoring human rights by another concept is that they cannot demonstrate their necessary connection to human rights. The interpretation of basic needs, for example, falls prey to the same hermeneutic weakness of natural law/rights. There is no way to prove the validity of any particular interpretation because no procedure is established by which the legitimacy of particular human rights can be judged. Indeed, there is some consensus among philosophers that up until the present, all attempts to provide solid philosophical foundations for human rights have failed (e.g., Feinberg, 1973, p. 90).

In the absence of a satisfactory grounding for human rights, theorists are compelled to fall back upon mere assertions as to the self-evident nature of particular human rights. In view of the diversity of moral systems in the world, it is difficult to understand why the presumption of universality could endure so long without being seriously questioned. The answer lies in the psychological predisposition of human beings to generalize from their own perspective. Western philosophers in particular seem to be prone to projecting their moral categories on others. As a consequence, the presumption of universality is deeply ingrained in Western moral philosophy.

✳ *"Everyone thinks the same"*

Two of the best-known examples of these tendencies are Immanuel Kant (1981) and John Rawls (1971). Their conceptual devices-the categorical imperative and the original position, respectively-presuppose the existence {50} of a set of universal moral principles. Many philosophers employ Kantian notions as a vehicle to advance human rights. As Feinberg has observed, however, the claims that human beings are "ends in themselves" or "sacred" or "of infinite value" are themselves in need of a foundation (1973, p. 92). Kantian moral theory assumes the existence of a single pattern of moral reasoning. The abstract rational process is presumed to bear a single and universal result, irrespective of cultural differences.

The device of the original position developed by John Rawls (1971) provides another illustration of the universalistic premise. The idea is that individuals behind the "veil of ignorance," stripped of their identity, will select principles of justice by which society should operate. One could make a strong case that the contractarian scenario which Rawls has devised is rigged. For example, Rawls requires that persons in the original position be risk-averse and not be envious.[19] By imposing constraints such as these, Rawls ensures that individuals in the original position will agree to the principles he advocates. Thus, the device provides an ex post facto justification for his own personal moral convictions.

It is plausible that individuals from the same culture might agree to the same principles. Americans conceivably would designate Rawls's principles as their own. But if one transposes the scenario of the original position to an international setting (Beitz, 1979), it becomes doubtful whether all the participants will acquiesce. The presupposition is that individuals stripped of their cultural and political heritage would be pure rational beings and would thus dutifully select liberal democratic principles of justice. The premise that individuals could negotiate for fundamental principles in the absence of culture is quite fantastic. And this is precisely the root of the problem: underlying the presumption of universality is the belief that all peoples think in a similar fashion.

The most remarkable example of a scholar assuming that there is a single correct pattern of moral reasoning can be found in the work of Lawrence Kohlberg. His stage theory of moral development is perhaps the most blatantly universalistic moral theory one could imagine. Those surveyed who did not reason according to preconceived styles were considered to have retarded powers of moral reasoning. Among other things, his work has been challenged as failing to take into account gender differences (Gilligan, 1982). Its cross-cultural validity is still hotly debated. But the astounding nature of Kohlberg's presumption of universality is typified by his conclusions in an article about capital punishment (1975). On his view, reaching the highest stage of moral development entails rejection of the death penalty. Even though Kohlberg never reveals his own convictions, it seems clear {51} that these conclusions may reflect his own values. Kohlberg's moral theory represents a classic example of the fallacies which accompany the presumption of universality. Needless to say, in the event one disagrees with Kohlberg, e.g., on the defensibility of the death penalty, one's abilities in moral reasoning are called into question. This kind of thinking typifies the universalist position, namely that alternative patterns of thought are dismissed from the outset.

PROBLEMS WITH INTERNATIONAL HUMAN-RIGHTS DOCUMENTS

Instead of facing the reality of moral diversity from the beginning, those who participated in drafting international human-rights standards avoided the issue. To circumvent fundamental disagreement, the individuals involved took the tack of including a wide range of rights in the Universal Declaration of Human Rights. To have some understanding of the nature of the problem which international human rights have encountered, it is necessary to review briefly the universal rights set forth in some of the main international human-rights instruments.

As should be clear by now, it is only within a universe of shared values that the presumption of universality encounters no difficulties. Various international human-rights instruments have remained controversial, however, precisely because they contain values which are not shared on a worldwide basis. Several provisions from the UDHR should demonstrate the extent to which the presumed universality of some human-rights provisions is called into question.

Article 17 provides that "Everyone has the right to own property alone as well as in association with others" and that "no one shall be arbitrarily deprived of his property." The value underlying this standard is hardly universal. One commentator refers to the problem with Article 17 as one of cultural imperialism because it "...seeks to impose free enterprise and capitalism on the rest of the world" (Zvobgo, 1979, p. 95). Another human-rights analyst rejects the universality of Article 17(1): "The community ideology does not admit of private property, except in consumer goods" (Sinha, 1978b, p. 144).

Some of the articles concerning elections reflect a preference for a particular kind of political system. Articles 18, 19, and 20 provide for rights to freedom of thought, religion, and association. Article 21 guarantees the {52} right to participate in government, equal access to public service, and free elections. In Article 21(3) the ideological basis of the human-right standard is made manifest:

> The will of the people shall be the basis of the authority of govern-
> ment; this will shall be expressed in periodic and genuine elections
> which shall be by universal and equal suffrage and shall be held by
> secret vote or by equivalent free voting procedures.

While these articles clearly embody the preferred set of political devices of Western liberal democratic regimes, the provisions may not be
universally accepted. From the Third World perspective, Article 21 seeks
to "universalize Western-style elections" (Zvobgo, 1979, p. 95), which are
obviously not universal: "Monarchies, dictatorships, single-party rules, or
single-candidate elections are not non-existent in today's world" (Sinha,
1978b, p. 144). Of course, one cannot infer from the existence of these
political regimes that the people themselves prefer them to Western-style
democracies. But it is ethnocentric to assume that Western electoral
procedures are unanimously favored.

It is not only in the political realm that human rights seem not to be
expressions of universal values. Some of the rights concerned with social
life may also be unrepresentative of the entire world. For instance, Article
16 provides for the right to marry and to found a family. Article 16(2)
stipulates that marriages shall be entered into only with the free and full
consent of the intending spouses. And finally, Article 16(3) specifies that
the family is the natural and fundamental unit of society, and is entitled to
protection by society and the state. It is not clear if the fundamental unit is
the nuclear family or whether the article might allow for the kinship group
instead. The phraseology suggests that only the immediate family can be
understood to be the basic unit, which would appear to be insensitive to
the many societies which have different patterns of social organization.
The provision guaranteeing voluntary choice of marriage partners runs
counter to the practice of arranged marriages, which is an integral part of
many value systems of the world. Even the first clause holding that there
is a right to marry and found a family may be problematic when one
considers that there have been many restrictions on the right to marry and
procreate, which were at one time regarded as moral by Americans, e.g.,
compulsory sterilization, prohibition of homosexual marriages, and anti-
miscegenation laws. {53}

Some believe that the reason why many of the values in the UDHR
appear to be Western is that the Third World did not participate in great
numbers when it was drafted. Zvobgo (1979, p. 95) maintains that, were
the Declaration to be debated again in the General Assembly, the final
draft would differ significantly from what was adopted in 1948. Others,
while acknowledging that the UN human-rights debate took place at a
time when the great majority of Third World nations were still under
colonial rule, still maintain that the contribution of the Third World was
"by no means negligible" (Alston, 1983b, p. 61). Among the most active
participants were Chile, China, Cuba, India, Lebanon, and Panama. At the
General Assembly in 1948, Egypt, Ethiopia, Liberia, Afghanistan, the
Philippines, Thailand, India, and Pakistan, as well as all of the Central and
Latin American States were among the 48 voting in favor of the Declara-

tion. Saudi Arabia, South Africa, and the Eastern European nations were the eight abstentions; no one voted against (Alston, 1983b, p. 61).

Since there is still considerable reason to believe that the Declaration bears a Western imprint, this suggests that the role of government elites at international settings may not be indicative of the traditional value systems which they are supposed to represent. The problem with the particular configuration of rights found in the UDHR is that some of the rights may not be compatible with the diverse value systems of the world. Consequently, the promulgation of the UDHR appears to many countries as the imposition of an alien value system:

> Thus, to the extent these kinds of rights are concerned, we have the scenario of one particular culture, or one particular ideology, or one particul.ar political system claiming to be imposed upon the entire world.... It is self-defeating for the human-rights movement to take the latter approach and say, force private property upon the Soviet Union or China, or abolish arranged marriages in India, or force general elections in Saudi Arabia, and then—and here is the greatest danger of all—retire in the smug delusion that having done that, justice has thereby been achieved for the individual (Sinha, 1978b, pp. 144, 159).

Sinha attacks the single catalogue approach because it does not take into account cultural variability. He advocates an approach which is culture based. By making a distinction between the catalogue and the concept of human rights, he wants to allow for the development of particular rights standards for different social systems. Instead of "the catalogue of one particular society being rammed down the throat of another under the crusadic (sic) disguise of human rights" (1978b, p. 159), Sinha prefers to let societies devise their {54} own means of paying homage to human-rights standards. But while his theory is culturally sensitive, it cannot provide any universals. Hence it is no longer a theory of *human* rights but rather a theory of *cultural* rights.

NON-WESTERN CONCEPTIONS OF HUMAN RIGHTS

The international documents are not sufficient, in and of themselves, to resolve the question of whether the human rights which they enumerate are Western or universal. Of course, it is possible that they could contain some rights which are universal and some which are not. To decide which rights are *truly* universal, some have sought to characterize the concept of human rights according to various geographical, cultural, religious, and ideological perspectives. It is important, however, to be aware of the limitations of this literature.

First, there do not even exist articles on the concept of human rights in all societies. Whether those about which nothing is written have well-defined concepts of human rights we do not know. Second, the articles that do exist tend to focus on what is distinctive about the concept in the country or religion in question. So the result may be to afford insight into the distinctive features of the concept rather than to provide any indication about what aspects might be consistent with the values embodied in the international documents. The point is that the emphasis is on what is distinctive rather than what is common. Third, we cannot tell whether or not to rely on the characterizations provided. Analysts, even when speaking of the same culture, sometimes give radically different interpretations to the concept and often formulate conclusions on the basis of misleading evidence. Discussions of human rights in China, for example, tend to focus on what rights Chinese officials have granted rather than on what the traditional values are. Fourth, no systematic comparative analyses of indigenous concepts of human rights have ever been undertaken.

In the process of evaluating non-Western perspectives, one is struck by the lack of appropriate documentation. What there is, is generally not well substantiated and is often so vague that it is not possible to tell whether the society really supports particular rights or not. Moreover, the focus is on legal and religious texts from which we cannot glean the information necessary to tell what the cultural norms are. By drawing almost exclusively from the written materials of the elites, they give us no way of determining whether indigenous perceptions of morality include human rights. {55}

The following is a representative selection of the kinds of articles about non-Western conceptions of human rights which are available at present:

Africa: Adegbite (1968), Akpan (1980), Bello (1981), Cobbah (1987), Gittleman (1982), Haile (1984), Hountondji (1986), Howard (1983, 1984a, 1984b, 1986a), Kannyo (1984), Kunig (1982), Legesse (1980), Marasinghe (1984), M'Baye (1982), Mojekwu (1980), Ndiaye (1982), Neff (1984), Okoli (1982), Turack (1984), Umozurike (1983), Wai (1979), Weinstein (1976), Wiseberg (1976).

Asia: Burks (1986), Chang (1946), Cheng (1979), Edwards (1986), Goldman (1983), Henkin (1986), Hsiung (1986), Huang (1979), Inagaki (1986), Kim (1986), Lee (1986), Leng (1980), Lo (1948), Nathan (1986b), Scobie & Wiseberg (1985), Sutter (1978), Tai (1986), Wilson (1986), Woo (1980), Yamane (1982).

Soviet Union: Anonymous (1986b), Blaser (1984), Blishtshenko (1973), Chalidze (1974), Chemenko (1981), Dean (1980), Kadarkay (1982), Kartashkin (1977, 1982a), Kennan (1980), Koldayev (1976), Kudryavtsev (1986), LaPenna (1977), Lee (1985), Leonidov (1982), Medvedev & Kulikov (1981), Szymanski (1984), Tchechko (1948), Webster (1983).

Soviet/American: Berman (1979), Blaser (1984), Kelley (1984), McWhinney (1962). Somerville (1948).

Socialist: Cavoski (1982), Egorov (1979), Gjoliku (1984), Heuman (1979), Kartashkin (1982a), Kataio (1981), Nielsen (1982b), Patyulin (1981), Przetacznik (1977), Spasov (1981), Tay (1978, 1981a).

Marxist: Buchanan (1981). Hirszowicz (1966), Kolakowski (1983), Lukes (1982), Macfarlane (1982), Markovic (1982).

Islamic: Ahmed (1956), Bassiouni (1982), Coulson (1957), Dudley

(1982), El Naiem (1984, 1987), Gazzali (1962), Hakim (1955), Hassan (1982), Jshaque (1974), Kabir (1948), Khadduri (1946), Malik (1981), Mawdudi (1976), Nasr (1980), Nawaz (1965), Piscatori (1980), Rabbath (1959), Rahman (1978), Said (1979a, 1979b), Said & Nassar (1980), Sinaceur (1986), Tabandeh (1 970), Taperell (1985), Zakaria (1986).

Hindu: Mitra (1982), Puntambekar (1948), Sastry (1966).

Buddhist: Inada (1982), Jayatilleke (1967), Niset (1977).

Judaic: Polish (1982), Sidorsky (1979b).

Catholic: Baum (1979), Hollenbach (1979, 1982a), Langan (1982).

Christian: Abraham (1982), Cahill (1980), Deats (1978), Harakas (1982), Schall (1981).

The best collection of articles on religious perspectives on human rights is found in *Human Rights in Religious Traditions*, edited by A. Swidler (1982). In addition, a number of interesting papers were presented at a conference sponsored by UNESCO (1979). {56}

Miscellaneous: Third World — Arat (1986), Ferguson (1986), Tyagi (1981), Zvobgo (1979); First vs. Third World views — Farer (1979), Hauser (1979); India — Baxi (1978), Buultjens (1980), Johnson (1986), Khanna (1978), Kumar (1981), Nanda (1976), Noorani (1978), Pandeya (1986), Thapar (1978); Latin America — Quesada (1986), Wiarda (1978); American — Henkin (1979b, 1981), Marshall (1968); Human rights and regime type — Berger (1977), Howard & Donnelly (1986), Hoffman (1981); Human rights and capitalism — Rimlinger (1983); Western — Cranston (1973), Raphael (1967); Regional — Hannum (1984); Attempted comparisons — Bozeman (1971), Donnelly (1982b, 1985), Khushalani (1983), Pollis (1982), Sinha (1981), Tomuschat (1981).

THE REALITY OF CULTURAL DIVERSITY

Since it is not possible to conclude that all cultures do share the same concept of human rights on the basis of evidence currently available, this means that cultural differences may raise significant problems. The presumption of universality begins to totter when it confronts divergent interpretations of humanitarian standards. Nowhere is the contrast in values more striking than in the cases of female circumcision and child labor.

The Case of Female Circumcision

There are three types of female circumcision. F. P. Hosken, one of the leading opponents of the practice, offers the typology:

1. Sunna Circumcision: removal of the prepuce and/or tip of the clitoris.
2. Excision or Clitoridectomy: excision of the entire clitoris with the labia minora and some or most of the external genitalia.
3. Excision and Infibulation (Pharaonic Circumcision): This means excision of the entire clitoris, labia minora, and parts of the labia majora. The two sides of the vulva are then fastened together in some way either by thorns

... or sewing with catgut. Alternatively the vulva is scraped raw and the child's limbs are tied together for several weeks until the wound heals (or she dies). The purpose is to close the vaginal orifice. Only a small opening is left (usually by inserting a slither [sic] of wood) so the urine or later the menstrual blood can be passed. (Hosken, 1976, p. 30; see also Huelsman, 1976). {57}

Women who live in societies where the practice of circumcision continues must undergo surgery throughout life. Women who are infibulated have to be opened to permit intercourse and to be cut open further for the delivery of a child (Daly, 1978, p. 157). Sometimes women are sewn up again after delivery, depending on the wishes of their husbands.

Female genital mutilation occurs in certain tribes in the following countires: Kenya, Tanzania, Ethiopia, southern Egypt, Sudan, Uganda, northern Zaire, Chad, northern Cameroon, Nigeria, Dahomey, Togo, northern Ghana, Upper Volta, Mali, northern Ivory Coast, Liberia, Sierra Leone, Guinea, Guinea Bissau, the Gambia, Senegal, and Mauritania (Hosken, 1976, p. 22). Excision in small girls still takes place in Yemen, Saudi Arabia, Iraq, Jordan, and Syria (Groult, 1975, pp. 93-118). The operation is also performed in Europe when members of tribes emigrate (Anonymous, 1984b). It is difficult to pinpoint the precise number of girls who undergo the surgery because the operation is usually performed in secret. The Minority Rights Group report states: "The total number of women affected is in any case unknown, but without any doubt involves several tens of millions of women" (McLean & Graham, 1983, p. 3). A more scholarly article cites figures of between 30 and 74 million women as being currently circumcised in at least 20 African countries (Boulware-Miller, 1985, p. 156). There are various justifications offered for female circumcision. The main one is the preservation of the moral purity of women. The operation supposedly ensures the fidelity of wives. In 1938 Dr. Allan Worsley analyzed the reasons given for the practice: "Although it is often denied, the preservation of virginity lies at the root of this custom" (Worsley, 1938, pp. 686-691). Daly notes that, "A basic belief that justifies all, erasing all responsibility is of course that these rites keep women faithful" (Daly, 1978, p. 160). It complicates the issue further that the operation is performed by women, which might make it appear that men bear no responsibility for perpetuating the practice. In fact, both men and women ensure the continuation of the practice.

In the past, international organizations have been unwilling to get involved because of professed respect for the cultural traditions of others. And perhaps their reluctance is reasonable, since the custom is accepted as moral and legitimate in the societies in which it occurs. Those who do not undergo the surgery are ostracized. No one will marry uncircumcised girls. In one study, conducted by means of a detailed questionnaire administered to 3,210 females and 1,545 males in the Sudan, it was shown that the ratio of those who favored continuing the practice to those who did not was five to one for women and seven to one for men, though the majority was against the most severe Pharaonic type (El Dareer, 1983b). {58}

There is a tendency among current writers to speak of female circumcision not as morally abhorrent or acceptable but rather in terms of the health problems that it causes. Warning that female circumcision may well be hazardous to the health of young girls seems initially to avoid the pitfalls of the moral dilemma. For this reason, this is increasingly the sort of position that international organizations such as the World Health Organization (WHO) and the United Nation's Children's Fund (UNICEF) are taking. Perhaps the best discussion of female circumcision along these lines, within the framework of human rights, is an article by Kay Bouleware-Miller (1985). Here she discusses three major human-rights arguments challenging female circumcision as (1) a violation of the rights of the child, (2) the right to sexual and corporeal identity, and (3) the right to health. Her conclusion is that:

> Although the right to health argument may not bring immediate results, it is likely to have the most success because it considers the practice from the perspective of the Africans ... [it] integrates the issues of physical, mental, and sexual health as well as child development (1985, pp. 176-177).

Unfortunately, the health argument is subject to at least two telling criticisms. First, the peoples whose way of life is criticized, whether on health or moral grounds, may not see a difference between the two types of argument. That is, even if the argument based on health is on its face more sensitive to cultural differences, those practicing the custom may suspect that the real argument is that Westerners object to it on moral grounds. Moreover, the argument is rendered even less effective by the fact that operations of this type are now carried out in hospitals under thoroughly antiseptic conditions. The fact that many women in the society perpetuate the custom is one which must be squarely faced. The presumption of universality cannot alter the reality that the practice is accepted as moral by members of the culture.[20]

The Case of Child Labor

The specter of relativism also rears its head in the case of child labor. Today anywhere from 52 to 150 million children (under age 15) work throughout the world. The conditions are often exploitative and unhealthy. As a consequence, many in the international community have focused their energies toward the complete eradication of all forms of child labor. This {59} goal of abolition is justified in absolutist terms: "a necessary evil" (Blanchard, 1983, p. 23; Boudhiba, 1982, p. 11; Dogramaci, 1985, p. 11; Mendelievich, 1979, p. 55; Rodgers and Standing, 1981, p. v), "an affront to our conscience"(Blanchard, 1983, p. 6), "a scourge" (Valcarenghi, 1981, pp. 12, 23), "unnatural" (Mendelievich, 1979, p. 48), "tragic" (Dogramaci, 1985, p. 10), and "a moral indictment on our society" (Chan, 1980, p. 78). Francis Blanchard, Director General of the International Labor Organization, has said that the goal of the international community should be "ultimately, the elimination of child labor" (1983, p.

6), a position which derives its justification by appeal to "universal values" (1983, p. 20). In its 1984 report on child labor, the Anti-Slavery Society for the Protection of Human Rights acknowledged the Western bias in international legislation but, nonetheless, concluded that UNICEF should make "a specific commitment to the eradication of child labour in all its forms" (Anonymous, 1984, pp. 46, 57). Another glaring example of the universalist presumption is found in the international edition of *Newsweek* in a special report entitled, "All Work and No Play—The World's Youngest Laborers *Sacrifice* their Childhood in Days of *Endless Toil*" (Smolowe et al., 1983—emphasis added). The language and melodramatic tone reflect the deeply ingrained Western way of thinking about childhood. They also convey the message that the proper goal ought to be the complete abolition of child labor.

Despite the presumption that child labor is entirely wrong, it is an economic necessity. In many societies, children are expected to help with the family business or to bring home a substantial portion of the family income. It is an accepted part of the way of life in much of the world, and is perceived as natural and moral.

> In most agrarian societies, children's work is not only highly prized for its economic utility but as representing the highest ideals of the culture, *viz.* obedience, respect or filial piety. Serving those above one in the domestic hierarchy of age statuses is conceptualized as moral duty, often a sacred obligation (LeVine, 1984, p. 3).

The ethnocentric assumption in the literature leads to a narrow-minded solution which is not only unworkable but which is also undeniably a form of cultural imperialism. Since the concept of childhood varies across cultures, as do ideas about work, it is not wise to adopt an absolutist abolitionist approach, even as a long-term objective. Children's work is an essential part of the family's survival; and unless that is taken into account when policies are formulated, the viability of international standards to protect {60} children will be uncertain. By no means does this imply that we should turn a blind eye to the problem. It is simply that outright condemnation is ineffective and, indeed, counterproductive. Greater cultural sensitivity would permit the formulation of more globally acceptable strategies.

CONCLUSION

I have tried to show that, properly interpreted, the concept of human rights is compatible with moral systems that are centered on concepts other than rights. This would remove the objection that duty-based systems cannot accommodate human rights. But even if human rights, in the abstract, may be possible in any moral system, we cannot presume that all moral codes contain the same or similar values. Women's rights and children's rights are problematic because societies do not all believe that these groups deserve special status. So, to assert the existence of universal standards for them is ethnocentric. The recognition of moral diversity calls into question the presumption of universality and leaves human rights vulnerable to the apparent dangers of relativism.

3

RELATIVISM REVISITED

Spix and Martius asked a chief of the Miranhas why his people practiced cannibalism. The chief showed that it was entirely a new fact
to him that some people thought it an abominable custom. "You
whites." said he, "will not eat crocodiles or apes, although they taste
well. If you did not have so many pigs and crabs you would eat
crocodiles and apes, for hunger hurts. It is all a matter of habit.
When I have killed an enemy, it is better to eat him than to let him
go to waste. Big game is rare because it does not lay eggs like tur-
tles. The bad thing is not being eaten, but death, if I am slain,
whether our tribal enemy eats me or not. I know of no game which
tastes better than men. You whites are really too dainty" (Sumner,
1911, p. 331).

THE theory of cultural relativism has been greatly misunderstood and un-
fairly dismissed not only by its critics but also by its proponents. This
chapter attempts to clarify the issues central to the debate and thereby
correct the caricatured picture of relativism. Although the most controversial aspect of relativism tends to be the question of the extent to which
relativists must tolerate intolerance, the crux of the argument should be
whether or not it is possible to establish cross-cultural universals. I begin
by presenting a brief description of the historical circumstances which
gave rise to the theory of cultural relativism. It was in the early stages of
the formulation of the theory that the groundwork was laid for future
misunderstandings. Next follows a conceptual analysis of the theory
paying close attention to rendering the theory coherent by avoiding self-
referential paradoxes. Related to this issue is the question of whether
tolerance is a necessary concomitant of the theory of cultural relativism. I
then discuss the importance of enculturation to the theory and its consequence, namely ethnocentrism or a lack of tolerance. Since tolerance is an
American ideal, American anthropologists have been uneasy about the
implications of embracing relativism completely. This misunderstanding
of the theory as wrongly connected with tolerance is reflected in the
debate surrounding the Universal Declaration on Human Rights in the
1940s. Finally, I conclude that relativism in no way precludes {62} the
possibility of cross-cultural universals discovered through empirical research. The existence of such universals might very well indicate worldwide support for particular human rights.

HISTORICAL OVERVIEW

The doctrine of relativism is not a modern development. The Greeks wrote about its implications and Herodotus (484-425 B.C.) captured its essential insight when he wrote:

> For if one were to offer men to choose out of all the customs in the world such as seemed to them the best, they would examine the whole number, and end by preferring their own; so convinced are they that their own usages far surpass those of all others (1947, Book 3, Chapter 38).

Some maintain that cultural relativism offers nothing new and is basically the same debate that was carried on by the Greek sophists of the fifth century B.C. (Schmidt, 1955, p. 783) and subsequently by Hume (Hartung, 1954, p. 120) and by Montaigne (Geertz, 1984, p. 264). There is, however, something rather distinctive about cultural relativism, particularly as advanced by Herskovits (see also Tennekes, 1971, p. 22). The core of the theory is not just recognition of cultural differences in thought, value, and action. It is a theory about the way in which evaluations or judgments are made. The insight is more subtle and sophisticated. The theory calls attention not only to behavioral differences but to the perceptions of cultural phenomena. Culture is so powerful in the way it shapes individuals' perceptions that understanding the way of life in other societies depends on gaining insight into what might be called the inner cultural logic. This focus on perception and evaluation makes Herskovits's theory markedly different from earlier philosophical treatment of similar ideas.

Cultural relativism emerged in its modern form in reaction to cultural evolutionism. The latter theory was a stage theory which held that human societies progressed from "primitive" or "savage" to "modern." Naturally, Western civilization ranked highest on the scale because the standard for judging was based on Western values. The anthropologists of the nineteenth century who subscribed to evolutionist theory were not aware of their universalistic predilection: {63}

> [They] did not grasp the covert ethnocentric bias, the specific, culturally patterned, informative and normative blend of each perception. Again and again they constructed the antithetic picture of the European and the savage, of culture and nature. Usually it is the advanced and enlightened European who is contrasted with the "savage who delights to torture his enemies, offers up bloody sacrifices, practises infanticide without remorse, treats his wives like slaves, and knows no decency, and is haunted by the grossest superstitions" which made Charles Darwin to say that he would "as soon be descended from that heroic little monkey ... as from a savage who delights to torture his enemies" (Kronenberg, 1984, p. 235).

In the 1800s, anthropological data provided the means to glorify the European way of life by comparison. Various developments at the turn of the century produced "a general sense of disillusionment, anger, and frustration; more generally, the effect was a widespread pessimism" (Hatch, 1983, p. 28). This more gloomy outlook called into question the nineteenth-century idea that human civilization is improving and that European/American civilization stands at the top of the ladder of human achievement. Cultural evolutionism also had objectionable racist overtones: "It goes without saying that the people who were thought to be the least cultured were also thought to be the least intelligent and the darkest in pigmentation" (Hatch, 1983, p. 26). Cultural relativism was introduced in part to combat these racist, Eurocentric notions of progress (Rioux, 1957, p. 65; Spiro, 1978, p. 336; Stocking, 1968, pp. 115-117, 1982, p. 176).

ORIGINAL VERSION OF THE THEORY OF CULTURAL RELATIVISM

A consideration of the original version of the theory of cultural relativism is necessary to elucidate the conceptual problems it subsequently encountered. The individuals largely responsible for championing the new theory were Franz Boas, Ruth Benedict, and Melville Herskovits. Boas was the first real leader of the movement. Born and educated in Germany, he received a doctorate in physics from the University of Kiel. By the time he took up his appointment at Columbia University, he had already shifted from physics to anthropology. Since he had a Ph.D. in physics, it is not surprising that he was greatly influenced by the Einstein revolution in 1905 and the radical new ideas about relativity. {64}

Boas challenged the superiority of modern twentieth-century civilization, arguing that there may be other criteria for measuring progress than those stressed by our society. He believed that our vision is obscured by an emotional, subjective bias:

> It is somewhat difficult for us to recognize that the value which we attribute to our civilization is due to the fact that we participate in this civilization, and that it has been controlling all our actions since the time of our birth; but it is certainly conceivable that there may be other civilizations, based perhaps on different traditions and on a different equilibrium of emotion and reason, which are of no less value than ours, although it may be impossible for us to appreciate their values without having grown up under their influence. The general theory of valuation of human activities, as taught by anthropological research, *teaches us a higher tolerance* than the one which we now profess (1901, p. 11—emphasis added).

Thus it appears from the outset that cultural relativism was cast as a value theory. The ideas contained in this passage, enculturation and tolerance, provided the basis for the early theory of cultural relativism.

As a professor at Columbia University from 1896 until 1937, Boas prepared several of his students, most notably Benedict and Herskovits, to continue the relativistic tradition. Ruth Benedict's *Patterns of Culture* (1934) presents one of the most controversial renditions of the theory of relativism. This is the problematic and much contested "equally valid patterns of life" formulation which appears in the final passage of her book:

> The recognition of cultural relativity carries with it its own values, which need not be those of the absolutist philosophies. It challenges customary opinions and causes those who have been bred to them acute discomfort. It rouses pessimism because it throws the old formulas into confusion, not because it contains anything intrinsically difficult. As soon as the new opinion is embraced as customary belief, it will be another trusted bulwark of good life. We shall arrive then at a more realistic social faith, accepting as grounds for hope and as new bases for tolerance the coexisting and equally valid patterns of life which mankind has created for itself from the raw materials of existence (1934, p. 278).

It is clear that she believes tolerance is part of the theory of cultural relativism (1934, p. 37; but see Hatch, 1983, pp. 99-100, and Williams, 1947).

The formulation for which Herskovits is most known is exceedingly broad and quite radical: "Evaluations are relative to the cultural background out of which they arise" (1950, p. 63, 1972, p. 14). As it stands, this proposition {65} exposes itself to the specter of self-refutation. But further, he maintains that:

> cultural relativism is a philosophy which, in recognizing the values set up by every society to guide its own life, lays stress on the dignity inherent in every body of custom, and on the need for tolerance of conventions though they may differ from one's own. (1950, p. 76)

As with the formulation of Boas and Benedict, this one links tolerance to the theory. It is precisely this association which has left cultural relativists in dire straits. As Bidney observes, their version of cultural relativism reflects their political orientation (1953b, p. 688). In some ways, it is predictable that they should have molded the theory to help advance the cause of tolerance, a value to which they were greatly committed. But in doing so, they committed what has been termed the positivistic fallacy (Bidney, 1944) or the naturalistic fallacy (Frankena, 1939), which is to say that they derived an "ought" from an "is," a subject on which I will elaborate later.

IMPLICATIONS OF THE THEORY OF CULTURAL RELATIVISM

⌈ The most valuable feature of cultural relativism was, and still is, its ability to challenge the presumed universality of standards[21] which actually belong to only one culture: ⌉

> It is aimed at getting people to admit that although it may seem to them that their moral principles are self-evidently true, and hence

seem to be grounds for passing judgment on other peoples, in fact, the self-evidence of these principles is a kind of illusion (Cook, 1978, p. 294).

Others have pointed out how each society will view its own standards as universally valid:

> Social conditions not only enforce particular practices; they also in-culcate the conviction of their rightness.... Our assumption about the rationality and self-evidence of our values is itself, it would seem, a socially bred illusion—dogmatism parading under a veneer of reason (Asch, 1952, pp. 367-368).

This applies equally to our conceptions of normalcy. Benedict, for instance, has argued strongly for the view that "abnormality" and "normali-ty" are {66} culturally defined categories and has given examples in which what we consider to be an abnormality forms the cornerstone of another culture's social structure (1978, p. 285). She contends that whereas a mild mystic is aberrant in our culture, most peoples regard even extreme psychic manifestations "not only as normal and desirable, but even as characteristic of highly valued and gifted individuals" (1978, p. 280).

Likewise, homosexuality among the Greeks was thought to be part of the good life, e.g., as presented in Plato's *Republic* (1968). Among many American Indian tribes one finds an institution called *berdache* (by the French) which Benedict describes as follows:

> The men-women were men who at puberty or thereafter took the dress and the occupations of women. Sometimes they married other men and lived with them. Sometimes they were men with no inver-sion, persons of weak sexual endowment who chose this role to avoid the jeer of women. The berdaches were never regarded as of first-rate supernatural power, as similar men-women were in Si-beria, but rather as leaders in women's occupations, good healers of certain diseases, or, among certain tribes, as genial organizers of so-cial affairs. In any case, they were socially placed. They were not left exposed to the conflicts that visit the deviant who is excluded from participation in the recognized patterns of his society (1978, p. 281).

These data are revealing because they suggest that grounds for con-demning the activities of others may be arbitrary and thus not convincing. The intensity with which one feels opposition to a practice may have little to do with its acceptance in another social context. Benedict's observation of the diversity of customs led her to conclude that "morality differs in every society and is a convenient term for socially approved habits" (1978, p. 286). It is precisely this view which is primarily responsible for the scorn of cultural relativism by philosophers. The relevance of empirical data for normative assertions will be reexamined in Chapter 4.

Cultural relativists sought not simply to demonstrate that standards of morality and normalcy are culture-bound but also to call into question the ethnocentric assumption of Western superiority. So-called primitive societies may be more complex than Western "civilization." Herskovits remarked, for instance, that the Australian aborigines are ordinarily considered to be among the most "primitive" peoples in the world, and yet their kinship system is "so complex that for many years it defied the attempts of students to analyze it" (1972, pp. 26-27). From their vantage point we seem simple since "we do not even distinguish between paternal and maternal grandparents, {67} or older and younger brother, and call literally dozens of relatives by the same word, 'cousin' " (1972, p. 26). The study of anthropology has been called the most liberalizing of all the sciences (De Laguna, 1942, p. 142), principally because through cultural relativism we have come to realize that other cultures have their own inner logic. Even some of those who ultimately reject relativism see the value in it. In a discussion of relativism and human nature Selznick remarks: "To be sure, the diversity of cultures is impressive. It is especially impressive to undergraduates, and is a very valuable antidote for any tendency to guffaw at strange practices and call other people 'gooks'" (1961, pp. 92-93).

Some people take a more disparaging view of relativism.[22] They either equate it with a strong form of skepticism, calling it nihilistic (e.g., Cook, 1978, p. 310; De Laguna, 1942, pp. 142, 146; Hatch, 1983, p. 64; Jarvie, 1983, p. 45; Ladd, 1982, p. 158; Stace, 1962, p.53), or insist that it undermines our ability to condemn repressive practices in other countries. Since anthropologists were writing in the 1940s, it is not surprising that the argument most often advanced was that according to relativism we could not have fought the Nazis because relativism calls for absolute tolerance. Currently, relativism is out of favor mainly because of this view. According to Barnes and Bloor. "In the academic world relativism is everywhere abominated" (1982, p. 21). They suggest that a possible reason why it is intensely disliked is that "many academics see it as a dampener on their moralizing" (1982, p. 47). In speaking of ethical relativism, Hatch notes that philosophers see little virtue in it (1983, p. 12) and that by and large most ethical relativists have been anthropologists and not philosophers (1983, p. 63). Others have also pointed out that philosophers tend to dismiss relativism (Cooper, 1978, p. 99). In a much-cited article, Hartung (1954, p. 118) characterizes cultural relativism as "a peculiarly crude form of ethnocentric morality" and refers to Arthur Murphy's views. Murphy has called cultural relativism "intellectually irresponsible" (1943, p. 152). Hartung himself claims that relativism "is an ethnocentric circumlocution, a round-about way of saying that our liberal tradition is the best tradition, and that all *ought* to follow" (1954, p. 121). In an article entitled "Ethical Relativism and its Irrelevancy for the Issues of a Complex Society," Winthrop blames relativism for all of society's woes (1977). De Laguna remarks that relativism has been around for a long time, which she regards as a perplexing problem because she thinks it is so clearly self-refuting (1942, p. 141). According to Hatch, by the 1970s ethical relativism "was almost universally rejected by the discipline [anthropology]" (1983, p. 103). {68}

Cultural bound
: one set of cultures

It is odd that cultural relativism should evoke such strongly negative reactions if it is so transparently flawed. The relativists who proposed the theory have generally put forward such weak formulations of it, and yet it still appears to touch a sensitive nerve. The absurdity of many of these formulations, both by critics and proponents, will be closely scrutinized in the next section. I hope to show that, if properly construed, relativism can be embraced as: "...certainly harmless, probably true, and if anything a useful corrective to precisely the sort of dangers with which it is often associated" (Unwin, 1985, p. 205).

FORMULATIONS

Up to this point I have intentionally not distinguished among the various ideas which fall under the heading of relativism: linguistic, epistemological, cultural, ethical, and so forth. This was deliberate because these ideas were conflated in historical discussions, which is what accounts for some of the analytic problems. Some of the questions which arise concern the extent to which epistemological relativism underlies all forms of relativism and the relationship between cultural and ethical relativism (see, e.g., Spiro, 1986). In what follows the focus will be on only the types of relativism which bear on the issue of the universality of human rights. Therefore only cursory attention will be given to the debates about epistemological and other forms of relativism.[23] Instead, the focus will be on cultural and ethical relativism and the relationship between them.

According to Herskovits, cultural relativism is based on the proposition: "Evaluations are relative to the cultural background out of which they arise" (1950, p. 63, 1972, p. 14). This idea is not new. One of Kant's greatest contributions to philosophy was the idea that our perception of the world is filtered through our preexisting conceptual categories. But whereas Kant believed in universal categories, Sapir and Whorf were among the first to recognize that these categories reflect linguistic and cultural conditioning (Kay & Kempton, 1984).

The immediate question which Herskovits's formulation raises is the extent to which the word "evaluation" applies. If by evaluations, he means *all* evaluations, that is, evaluations of factual data, then the theory refutes itself. This is because if A is true, then by virtue of the meaning of A, A is contingent (on whether a culture believes A). Hence, A could be false: {69}

> On this interpretation the theory destroys its own basis. It is intended to be an empirical truth of anthropology and sociology holding for all cultures, but it destroys the basis for the objectivity which is required to make meaningful assertions that are cross-cultural. It destroys objectivity because the frame of reference for measurement in each culture is somehow peculiarly "true" for that culture and no over-arching or inter-cultural standard is available to objectively adjudicate inconsistent reports. Thus the cultural relativist cannot have it both ways: he cannot claim that the truth of

> factual judgments is relative to their cultural background and at the
> same time believe in the objectivity of sociological and anthropolog-
> ical investigations (Schmidt, 1955, p. 781).

I reject this extreme interpretation of Herskovits's thesis. Instead, I will
take cultural relativism to mean that⌊some evaluations are relative to the
cultural background out of which they arise.⌉ Studies have shown that
many concepts, such as time and space, standards of beauty, and others,
are relative to their cultural context. I am more interested, however, in
ethical relativism, a subset of cultural relativism, which is of particular
importance for human rights. Many of the debates about cultural relativism are actually about ethical relativism. The problem is that participants
have not used precise terminology. Campbell, for example, implies that
this is so when he comments that cultural relativism has received the most
criticism when applied to ethics and aesthetics (1972, p. xxi). Even
Schmidt, whose lucid analysis is exemplary, uses the term cultural relativism for what is really ethical relativism (1955).

THE THEORY OF ETHICAL RELATIVISM

At least three different theories of ethical relativism appear under
various guises.[24] The first, which I call the theory of apparent ethical
relativism, is the claim that peoples differ in their basic moral beliefs.
Schmidt calls this "the fact of cultural relativism (1955, p. 782), and
Brandt (1967, p. 75) and Frankena (1973, p. 109) call this "descriptive
ethical relativism." The point of contention is that whereas Schmidt (cor-
rectly) takes moral differences among cultures to be a well-established
empirical fact, Brandt, Frankena, and followers dispute this with the same
tired and worn example of patricide.[25] In their view, what seems to be a
moral difference may be nothing more than a discrepancy in factual
information. {70}

Brandt compares the Eskimos and natives of the South Pacific with
the Romans to make the point that what seem to be moral differences are
not. He notes that in some societies, such as that of the Eskimos, patricide
occurs because the old are regarded as a burden on the community (1959,
p. 100). Through the hardships of living, the Eskimos come to view patricide as euthanasia, "the merciful cutting short of a miserable, worthless,
painful old age." The Romans, by contrast, more or less took for granted
the notion that patricide was "murder for gain." Brandt's conclusion is
that, "although the Romans and the Eskimos may use the very same
words to describe a certain sort of act—and then may express conflicting
ethical appraisals of it actually in some sense they have in mind quite
different things" (1959, p. 100). The second example he employs is the
practice of some natives in the South Pacific for whom it was customary
that a son bury his father alive when the father reached a ripe old age
(1959, p. 95). This practice was based on the belief that the father's body
would be identical in the next life. Hence, it was advisable to dispatch him

before he became too feeble. Brandt's claim is that in the absence of such a belief in the afterlife, the son would not kill his father. Like all sons, he respects his father and commits the act in question only out of filial responsibility.

Brandt's point can be easily misinterpreted. He is not claiming that there are no fundamental ethical conflicts even though "no anthropologist has offered what we should regard as really an adequate account of a single case, clearly showing there is ultimate disagreement in ethical principle" (1959, p. 102). Rather, his point is that some apparent ethical conflicts are just that, apparent. They are factual conflicts rather than ethical ones.

This separation of facts and values as ingredients in moral judgments is, for the most part, artificial. All moral judgments depend on factual judgments. These facts are not merely circumstantial but are central to the belief system. If one narrows the scope of the conflict to a factual belief, then one is arbitrarily denying the moral character of the cultural act. By removing the set of facts on which the practice depends, Brandt distorts the value system so that it resembles our own.

Even if one were to concede that the example of patricide does not reveal any ultimate ethical conflict, this does not preclude the existence of other fundamental ethical conflicts. Brandt himself offers the example of various peoples who seem indifferent to the suffering of animals for no apparent "factual" reason (1959, pp. 102-103). He mentions the practice in South America of plucking chickens alive and a custom among the Hopi where pulling off the wings of birds is child's play. From these data he concludes that "there is at least one ultimate difference of ethical principle" (1959, p. 103). {71}

Ironically, whereas his single example in support of fundamental ethical differences is not persuasive, his original example of patricide is. Brandt claims that many peoples (other than our own!) "seem quite indifferent to the suffering of animals" (1959, p. 102), but this is absurd. That we tolerate such practices as leash laws, slaughterhouses, and especially animal experimentation may well suggest that we are as insensitive.

Brandt's example of patricide is often invoked to refute the extreme relativist claim that murder is accepted as moral in some places (Benedict, 1934, p. 45). If we accept Brandt's view of patricide as a form of euthanasia, then he has successfully shown that the custom is not a counterexample to the assertion that murder is universally condemned. By so doing, he has, unbeknownst to himself, traded one ethical disagreement for another. Although euthanasia is considered moral in much of the world, in the United States, for example, it is largely regarded as immoral.

The second theory of ethical relativism is what Schmidt calls the thesis of ethical relativism as descriptive (factual) hypothesis. Since this is the version of the theory which I would like to defend, I will sometimes refer to this theory simply as relativism. This position holds that "·there are or there can be no value judgments that are true, that is, objectively justifiable independent of specific cultures" (Schmidt, 1955, p. 782). Brandt and

Frankena refer to this view as "meta-ethical relativism" by which they mean that "in the case of basic ethical judgments, there is no objectively valid, rational way of justifying one against another; consequently, two conflicting basic judgments may be equally valid" (Frankena, 1973, p. 109).

One should note first that Schmidt's formulation would seem to allow for the possible existence of what he calls "cultural invariants" and what I call cross-cultural universals (1955, pp. 783, 790). (A cross-cultural universal, if it can be empirically shown to exist, is a value which is shared by all cultures in the world.) Schmidt eventually concludes, however, that the thesis of ethical relativism as descriptive hypothesis is false because he is prepared to accept the existence of certain absolute values whose justification lies outside the cultural realm.[26] Brandt and Frankena's view of the theory of meta-ethical relativism is similar to the above formulation in that it also permits cross-cultural universals, but it differs in its unfortunate use of the phrase "equally valid." This phrase has universalistic overtones insofar as it presupposes the existence of some universal standard for measuring validity. Hence, this phrase should be removed from the theory of ethical relativism as descriptive hypothesis.

This theory differs from that of apparent ethical relativism in that it makes a claim about the source of justification for different moralities. Whereas the theory of apparent ethical relativism is a theory about the existence of {72} different moral systems, it says nothing about which ones may be right or wrong. Thus, an individual could subscribe to the first theory and still assert, on the basis of absolutist principles, that all moral systems other than his or her own are wrong. Adherence to the second theory, however, forces one to abandon the ill-conceived notion of an absolute moral scale by means of which some cultures are judged morally superior to others.

The third theory of ethical relativism is the thesis of ethical relativism as prescriptive (value) hypothesis. This is the view that "in every case the rightness of any act or goodness of any thing for a member of culture A is justified by reference to what in fact is considered right or good in culture A" (Schmidt, 1955, p. 786). Brandt and Frankena refer to this view as "normative relativism," by which they mean:

> what is right or good for one individual or society is not right or good for another, even if the situations involved are similar, meaning not merely that what is thought right or good by one is not thought right or good by another (this is just descriptive relativism over again), but that what is really right or good in the one case is not so in another (Frankena, 1973, p. 109).

This is the theoretical position that is commonly ascribed to the extreme relativists, such as Benedict and Herskovits.

A number of observations are in order. First, it is amusing that in this version the theory is practically unintelligible to Western philosophers. This is because Western philosophers presume that the concept of morality makes no sense unless it is universally applicable. For them, morality cannot be "local." So, to say that action A in circumstances C is right for B but not for D is to utter mindless gibberish. Second, as Frankena points out, normative relativism must be interpreted in such a way that it is not identical to the theory of apparent relativism (this is no mean feat). Third, the theory of ethical relativism as prescriptive hypothesis, in order to be a prescriptive hypothesis, must rely on the suppressed value judgment that one ought to do what is considered right by the culture to which one belongs. If this version of the theory is amended in this way, it is susceptible to the charge of self-refutation, for it asserts an absolute prescription that all prescriptions are relative:

> [T]he thesis of cultural relativism taken as a cross-cultural value theory falls as a victim of its own meaning. It has cut down its own claim to objectivity as a prescriptive theory that holds cross-culturally. It holds only for those cultures which contain a majority of persons who assert it. For another culture that denied cultural relativism as a prescriptive theory, the denial would be justified (Schmidt, 1955, p. 786). {73}

TOLERANCE

This form of the theory is often associated with the idea of tolerance. Those who take this view assume that the theory requires them to be tolerant of diverse moral practices. Bagish speaks of relativism as if it forces us to tolerate everything (1983, p. 28). Harrison also believes that a relativist is committed to tolerance "as the one virtue he must accept" (1976, p. 131). Hartung characterizes the plea for tolerance as "unqualified" (1954, p. 122). He continues by pointing out that relativists have provided a useful notion which has served to defend slavery and genocide (1954, p. 123). Kluckhohn also gives an extreme interpretation to relativism:

> If one follows out literally and logically the implications of Benedict's words, one is compelled to accept any cultural pattern as vindicated precisely by its cultural status: slavery, cannibalism, Naziism, or communism may not be congenial to Christians or to contemporary Western societies, but moral criticism of the cultural patterns of other people is precluded (1955, p. 663).

[Diametrically opposed to this view are those who hold unequivocally that ethical relativism does not logically entail tolerance:]

> [T]he two parts of the doctrine are not logically or necessarily interdependent. The first part says that people are brought up to see the value in things that their local experience has suggested. The second part says that we should respect all cultures. But there is no true "therefore" between these two parts. It cannot be proved from the proposition that values are relative, that we ought to respect all sys-

57

tems of values. We might just as well hate them all. (Redfield, 1962, pp. 146-147; see also Barnett, 1948, pp. 352-354; Brandt, 1959, pp. 288-293; Harrison, 1976, p. 134).

Since in my view the normative theory is self-refuting, its connection to tolerance is not an issue. The objection might be raised, however, that tolerance is associated with the theory of ethical relativism as descriptive hypothesis. This would be catastrophic for the theory of ethical relativism as a whole because it would turn a descriptive theory into a prescriptive one and by so doing make it self-refuting for precisely the same reasons as before. The key point is that the theory of ethical relativism as descriptive hypothesis is not a value theory but rather a theory about value judgments.

The theory of ethical relativism is undeniably a useful one to employ for the advancement of the cause of tolerance. It provides a theoretical apparatus {74} which can serve as a vehicle for the dissemination of the idea. This does not mean, however, that relativism depends on the idea of tolerance or in any way implies tolerance. Some claim that without tolerance the theory has no force. Hatch, for example, contends that without it, the question of relativism seems "trivial or esoteric" (1983, p. 65). Ladd agrees with this perspective:

> There are philosophers who say that the paradoxes just mentioned disappear if ethical relativism is viewed as a meta-ethical theory rather than as an ethical theory proper. Meta-ethical theories are by definition applicable only to ethical theories; therefore, ethical relativism, being a meta-ethical theory, is not applicable to itself. Quite apart from the validity of the separation of ethics from metaethics, this argument implies that ethical relativism has no practical significance whatsoever; it does not make any moral difference whether or not it is true. If this is so, the whole point of ethical relativism would be lost, for relativists like Engels, Sumner, and Herskovits are not mere theoreticians, and they are out to change the world. They are using their relativism for moral purpose (1973, p. 8).

But Hatch and Ladd are wrong to conclude that without tolerance the theory becomes unimportant. They fail to see that it is enculturation that forms the basis of the theory. Strange to say, most critics and proponents of relativism have also underestimated this essential ingredient.

ENCULTURATION AND ETHNOCENTRISM

It is crucial to understand the extent to which the theory of cultural relativism is based on enculturation.[27] Enculturation is the idea that people unconsciously acquire the categories and standards of their culture. Campbell provides a rather graphic illustration:

> In much of Africa, including the Arabic cultures, children are sys-
> tematically trained to use their left hands after urination and defe-
> cation, and their right hands for eating. Harsh punishment and
> scandalized rejection may be used in such training, so that absent-
> minded substitution of the wrong hand is entirely eliminated. When
> such a person for the first time sees a European or an American put
> food in his mouth with his left hand, the sight is vividly disgusting,
> fully as revolting as it would be for us, for example, to see someone
> wipe his mouth with dirty toilet paper (1972, p. xviii). {75}

This indicates that culture comes to be built into automatic, uncritical
perceptions. Individuals are largely unaware that these judgments are
culture-bound. As Campbell puts it, "the immorality is seen as a part of
the event, as a part of the real world rather than an observer's judgment"
(1972, p. xviii).

A reformulation of relativism must call attention to the role of both
enculturation and ethnocentrism. Bidney seems to realize this when he
comments that:

> Herskovits does not explain how it is theoretically possible to have
> cultural relativism without ethnocentrism, in view of the fact that
> cultural conditioning necessarily leads the members of any given
> community to prefer their own value system above all others
> (1953b, p. 690).

Herskovits's failure to locate the power of relativism in enculturation has
led to much of the confusion and controversy about the theory. Had he
and his colleagues had insight on this point, they would not have insisted
that tolerance was a corollary of the theory. They would have known that
tolerance followed for Americans but not necessarily for everyone.

Since enculturation leads individuals to prefer their own moral system, the relativist will likewise tend to perceive his own values as superior.
What this means is that the relativist prefers tolerance, the value associated with the liberal, democratic tradition. Were this value not the preemi-
nent one in his culture, the relativist would not have had such difficulty
with this theory. Another consideration which complicates his position is
that the relativist's culture is absolutist. As Bidney says, "It is only in a
puritanical culture such as ours, wherein cultural absolutes are presup-
posed, that cultural relativism is difficult to comprehend" (1953b, p. 690).

Ultimately, then, this conflict is one between a theory of perception
as culture-specific and the American political ideology which is absolutist
and which advocates tolerance. If tolerance is an absolute good, the
relativist is torn. In fact, one could argue that it is because of the theory of
relativism that Americans could reject tolerance. It is simply a value
preference of our culture. Perhaps a commitment to another value, such
as egalitarianism or humanitarianism or some other, should take prece-
dence over tolerance. It is not the theory of relativism which makes
tolerance supreme; it is the uncritical acceptance of this value by Americans.

If relativism is associated with any value, it is ethnocentrism and not tolerance. Hartung, for instance, maintains that "ethnocentrism is a universal culture trait and denies the objectivity and tolerance which cultural relativism {76} is ordinarily thought to imply" (1954, pp. 123-24). At least one major study confirms this (LeVine & Campbell, 1972). It is worthwhile having clearly in mind Sumner's classic definition of ethnocentrism which identifies the self-evident nature of morality for individuals in the many and diverse cultures in the world:

> Ethnocentrism is the technical name for this view of things in which one's own group is the center of everything, and all others are scaled and rated with reference to it.... Each group thinks its own folkways the only right ones, and if it observes that other groups have other folkways, these excite its scorn (1911, p. 13).

One's own ideas are presumed to have a more general validity than they actually possess (Bohannan, 1963, p. 9; see also Sumner, 1911, pp. 12-13; Westermarck, 1924, Vol. 2, p. 170, 1932b, p. 201).

It should be clear that relativism provides insight into the nature of perceptions. The theory points to the degree to which self-righteous attitudes toward internal moral standards are ingrained. Insofar as individuals adopt moral categories uncritically, conflict between cultures will be exceedingly difficult to resolve, as in the case of international human rights. Hence, there is most assuredly reason to take relativism seriously, the allegations of Hatch, Ladd, and others notwithstanding.

RELATIVISM AS A METHODOLOGICAL PRINCIPLE

Some have taken the position that relativism is a prescriptive principle for methodological purposes (Obeyesekere, 1966; Schmidt, 1955). If relativism does not require of all people tolerance, dignity, or respect for other cultures, then it could be interpreted as demanding a neutral stance by scholars of culture. The argument has been biased from the start by the use of the term tolerance. The word tolerance often implies that there is something objectionable in the other society and that the person observing it must suppress his feelings of revulsion. It might be more suitable to insist that relativists be nonjudgmental or noninterventionist. These terms may also be suspect because they imply that the norm is to judge others and to interfere in their internal affairs (see Stein, 1986). Often, relativism is seen as demanding professional objectivity. The anthropologist in the course of carrying out research is expected to dispense with value judgments. {77} The scientific enterprise, at least in the Western world, is built upon a foundation of objectivity. Since anthropologists wish to embark on scientific ethnographic studies of a serious nature, they do well to approach their subject with objectivity. This is not, however, necessarily part of the theory of relativism. To understand the theory and its actual tenets requires that one resist the temptation to tack on extraneous principles and imperatives.

MORAL CRITICISM

If by now one is persuaded that the theory in itself demands neither tolerance nor objectivity, then it must follow that it does not force its adherents to foreswear moral criticism. Relativists, like everyone else, are ethnocentric (which is why the theory was so confused with tolerance!) and remain true to their own convictions. There is no reason why the relativists should be paralyzed as critics have often asserted (Hartung, 1954, pp. 119-125).

There is nothing inherent in the theory of relativism which prevents relativists from criticizing activities and beliefs in other cultures. But relativists will acknowledge that the criticism is based on their own ethnocentric standards and realize also that the condemnation may be a form of cultural imperialism. Under extreme circumstances, meaning that an action in another culture violates one of the relativists' most deeply held beliefs, the relativists may decide that criticism and even intervention are lesser evils than either ethnocentrism or cultural imperialism (Bidney, 1953b, p. 698).

Certainly the moral criticism loses some of its force if it no longer stems from universal standards. Nevertheless, relativists are not prevented from offering criticism, and the force of their argument against a practice may not be uninfluential. In an interdependent world, if culture A objects strenuously enough to a practice in culture B, culture B may fear a loss of foreign aid or other privileges.[28] Thus, it is not obvious that acknowledging that a criticism is ethnocentric renders it impotent. It is better to be honest about the local source of the criticism than to pretend that it is universal.

Of course, there is another way in which a relativist could launch moral attacks. There may be some standards which are universally shared. If cross-cultural empirical data can be adduced to show that there are deeply held and far-reaching universal values, then the relativist can criticize a society {78} for violating a universal standard and, *ipso facto*, its own standard. To this claim the objection might be raised that where there is universal agreement on a specific value, there is little need for criticism. This point is mistaken because it fails to notice that societies may contravene their own standards.

Ultimately three types of moral challenges are possible. First, where the act in question is contrary to the norms of the society in which it occurs, it can be criticized. Second, where the act violates not only the internal standard of the society but a universal standard as well, it can be questioned. Third, where the act is in accordance with the society's internal standard, but violates the critic's own standard (an external one), criticism of an ethnocentric sort is possible. Although it is appropriate to draw a distinction between criticisms corresponding to internal standards, on the one hand, and external ones, on the other, the theory of relativism blocks neither. It says nothing about the desirability of social criticism. It holds that every society will utilize its own standards. Sometimes there

will be a fundamental conflict among the various standards, and sometimes there will be convergence or consensus on standards. What one
makes of the conflicting or consensual standards depends not on relativism but on the role one wishes to play in the international community.
There is nothing in the theory of relativism which requires one posture as
opposed to another.

IN QUEST OF CROSS-CULTURAL UNIVERSALS

Even though relativists have tended to focus on the differences
among peoples, it is important to realize that there may be cross-cultural
universals which empirical research might uncover. By seeking out specific moral principles held in common by all societies, one might be able to
validate universal moral standards.

A number of critics contend that relativism as a philosophical position entails the rejection of the comparative method and renders the
search for cross-cultural universals meaningless (Bidney, 1953b, p. 694;
Hartung, 1954, pp. 120, 122; Howard, 1968, p. 183; Kluckhohn, 1955, p.
673; Sumner, 1911, p. 418). This interpretation of relativism depends on
the false premise that because all moral systems differ, there can be no
convergence. Why opponents have been so eager to dismiss outright the
notion of overlap is hard to say. The crucial point to understand is that
just because there are discrete, separate, and competing moral systems
does not {79} necessarily mean that they do not overlap. The question as
to the extent of their congruence remains to be seen.

If one concedes that there may be cross-cultural universals, then a
further question arises. Are there only general moral categories that are
shared cross-culturally or are there specific moral principles? (Dewey,
1927; Kluckhohn, 1953, 1956b; Linton, 1952, 1954; Murdock, 1945; Parsons, 1964; Redfield, 1957, pp. 150-160). Bidney, for example, takes the
view that there may be specific universal moral principles:

> In all cultures the perpetuation of the society takes precedence over
> the life of the individual, and hence no society tolerates treason,
> murder, rape, and incest. All societies recognize mutual rights and
> duties in marriage and condemn acts that threaten family solidarity.
> Similarly, all societies give recognition to some personal property
> and provide some techniques for the distribution of economic sur-
> plus to the needy. The fact of common cultural values provides a ba-
> sis for mutual understanding between adherents of diverse cultures
> (1968, p. 545).

Although for the past few decades some anthropologists have argued
on behalf of universals, they have undertaken little, if any, comparative
research on morals (Hatch, 1983, p. 111). Most of their arguments take the
form of assertions of universals based on human needs, biology, human
potential, psychic unity, social imperatives, rationality, and human nature.
It is quite possible, however, that all of these concepts are culturally

determined. In particular, studies on rationality and the concept of the person suggest that these may indeed vary by culture (Shweder & Bourne, 1982). What constitutes a good reason in one society may not be considered as good elsewhere. In the realm of morals the concept of rationality would seem especially ill-suited to yield tangible, concrete answers. Moreover, it is not at all clear that any of the above concepts could provide specific universals. One must conclude then that anthropologists, ironically enough, have abandoned their scientific enterprise when they discourse on universals and sound just like philosophers. What is needed are cross-cultural studies of the kind advocated by Bidney:

> [I]f anthropology is to attain the stage of making significant generalizations concerning the conditions of the cultural process and the values of civilization, then comparative studies of cultures and their values must be made with a view to demonstrating universal principles of cultural dynamics and concrete rational norms capable of universal realization (1953b, p. 698). {80}

METHODOLOGICAL CONSIDERATIONS

Linton, another anthropologist interested in universals, suggests a reason why it might have been difficult to pursue the analysis of universals. It is hard to identify universal values because they are often taken for granted in a society, which may mean that they are not expressed in an explicit manner (1954, p. 152). It may be possible, nevertheless, to study the values since "most value concepts find expression in more than one pattern of overt behavior" (1954, p. 150). Locating the universals may require the discovery of the "implicit philosophy" of a people, to use a phrase employed by Kluckhohn (1949, pp. 356-384) and Northrop (1955, pp. 653-654). In theory, this approach should be free from methodological difficulties.

Its purpose is to undertake a comparative analysis of cultural ideals ("oughts"). Lest one become embroiled in the debate referred to variously as the naturalistic fallacy, the positivistic fallacy, the is/ought distinction, and the fact/value distinction, it is imperative that this matter be clarified. If all societies had "explicit" philosophies which conveyed their ideals in a readily accessible form, there would not be any problem. Since, however, some societies do not articulate their moral principles explicitly in the form of a complete, cohesive philosophy, it becomes necessary to draw some inferences. In looking for the implicit philosophy, one must consider empirical data in order to gain insight into the normative principles of the society under examination. Therefore, a consideration of cross-cultural data, for the purposes of elucidating human ideals, need not commit one to the naturalistic fallacy.

UNIVERSALS VERSUS ABSOLUTES

The question as to the possible existence of universals remains an open one. Some preliminary evidence suggests that there is, in fact, convergence on moral values even where the significance of the particular values within the moral systems vary. For instance, one cross-cultural study compared the moral values of students in a Middle Eastern college with students in an American university (Tomeh, 1968). The findings indicated that the Middle Eastern students were significantly more severe in their overall judgment of moral codes than Americans. While the severity of punishments ascribed was quite different, the hierarchical ordering of moral issues was {81} similar in the two cultural groups. Research such as this might have implications for the study of cross-cultural universals because it could reveal what set of core moral values typically tops the lists of all cultural groups. Even if one accepts the proposition that cross-cultural universals are relevant for the study of morality, one should still make a crucial distinction between universals and absolutes:

> *Absolutes* are fixed, and, as far as convention is concerned, are not admitted to have variation, to differ from culture to culture, from epoch to epoch. *Universals*, on the other hand, are those least common denominators to be extracted from the range of variation that all phenomena of the natural or cultural world manifest (Herskovits, 1972, pp. 31-32; see also Rioux, 1957, p. 61).

Some eminent scholars purport to see value in demonstrating the existence of universals but on closer analysis reveal their absolutist predisposition. Kluckhohn, for example, states that the demonstration of empirical universals is "a significant step" but one which does not "settle any question of absolutes or right or wrong" (1955, p. 677). This clearly shows that Kluckhohn holds an external, absolute standard for evaluating what is right or wrong. But he is mistaken. A cross-cultural universal provides the standard for judging right and wrong. Northrop (1955) and Ladd (1973, pp. 121-124) both fall into the same trap when they assert that the final arbiter of what is right or wrong is natural law.

The difference between universals and absolutes permits us to distinguish the relativist approach from that of the natural-law theorist on the important issue of social change. Natural law posits immutable moral principles whose origin resides in nature. By contrast, cross-cultural universals are moral principles whose source is found in cultural ideals which may evolve. There seems to be a deeply felt conviction that moral principles ought to be immutable. This leads many people to reject cross-cultural universals which they regard as ephemeral. Even though there is something grand and appealing about an eternal, objective principle, in reality it is far better for society to be able to adapt to meet newly emergent needs.

The objection might be raised that some cross-cultural universals might be discovered which Westerners would call "inhumane" or that nothing prevents such universals from arising. This is an unlikely possibility. Since the values in question are cultural *ideals*, it would seem most improbable that any "inhumane" ideal would be universal. Even if a universal ideal is found which some would regard as "inhumane," this is a part of morality. It is better to be honest and to admit that it exists than to pretend that {82} it does not. The possibility for change means that concerted effort might lead the international community to reject it. In contrast, the proposed absolutes of the natural-law theorists may also be "inhumane" according to a non-Western standard, and yet they are not supposed to be subject to reform.

Insofar as relativism allows for the possibility of change, it is not, as some have claimed, an inherently conservative doctrine (Hatch, 1983, pp. 128-131). This assertion is based on the misconception that what is currently the accepted value system in a culture will and should remain unchanged. Herskovits explains:

> In recognizing the validity of all ways of life for those who live in accordance with them, cultural relativism does not deny the dynamics of culture by insisting on an unchanging acceptance by a people of their pre-existing ways of life, or by failing to take into account the influence of cultural transmission in making for cultural change (1972, p. 48).

It is perhaps a concession to reality that moral principles must be universal as opposed to absolute. The most that one can claim on the question of the longevity of moral principles is that certain cross-cultural universals perhaps can be shown to have persisted through countless generations. The mere fact that universals are not absolute does not make them trivial:

> [T]he mere existence of universals after so many millennia of culture history and in such diverse environments suggests that they correspond to something extremely deep in man's nature and/or are necessary conditions to social life (Kluckhohn, 1952, p. 105).

ANTHROPOLOGY AND HUMAN RIGHTS

What then are the implications of relativism for universal human rights? In the 1940s the issue of human rights came to the fore, and anthropologists, who were mostly relativists, were compelled to take a stand on the new United Nations Declaration on Human Rights. An examination of the statement issued by the American Anthropological Association on the new international document should be illuminating because the debate reflects many of the issues already discussed. The record of the 1940s debate makes it all the more difficult to understand why the conflict between relativism and universalism has not received wider analytic treatment since then. {83}

The "Statement on Human Rights" was drafted by Herskovits on behalf of the executive board of the American Anthropological Association. It appeared in a 1947 issue of the *American Anthropologist* and was submitted to the United Nations Commission on Human Rights. Although it did not acknowledge its draftsman, the text reflects his style (Bidney, 1953b, p. 693). The Statement begins by noting that the primary task confronting those wishing to draw up a Declaration on the Rights of Man was to resolve the following problem: "How can the proposed Declaration be applicable to all human beings, and not be a statement of rights conceived only in terms of the values prevalent in the countries of Western Europe and America?" (Anonymous, 1947, p. 539).

The statement presents three propositions:

1. The individual realizes his personality through his culture, hence respect for individual differences entails a respect for cultural differences.
2. Respect for differences between cultures is validated by the scientific fact that no technique of qualitatively evaluating cultures has been discovered.
3. Standards and values are relative to the culture from which they derive so that any attempt to formulate postulates that grow out of the beliefs or moral codes of one culture must to that extent detract from the applicability of any Declaration of Human Rights to mankind as a whole.

The problem observed was that: "What is held to be a human right in one society may be regarded as anti-social by another people, or by the same people in a different period of their history" (Anonymous, 1947, p. 542). The Statement recognized that the Declaration would not be persuasive to all cultures if formulated in the conceptual terms of only one nation:

> It will not be convincing to the Indonesian, the African, the Indian, the Chinese, if it lies on the same plane as like documents of an earlier period. The rights of Man in the Twentieth Century cannot be circumscribed by the Standards of any single culture or be dictated by the aspirations of any single people. Such a document will lead to frustration, not realization of the personalities of vast numbers of human beings (Anonymous, 1947, p. 543).

Strangely enough, despite apparent concern about the need to be culturally sensitive, in later passages the Statement reflected an ethnocentric bias. It asserted that where political systems deny citizens the right to participate in their government, or where they seek to conquer weaker peoples, "underlying cultural values may be called on to bring the people of such states to a realization of the consequences of the acts of their governments, {84} and thus enforce a brake upon discrimination and conquest" (Anonymous, 1947, p. 543). It continued by espousing the principle that "man is free only when he lives as his society defines freedom" (Anonymous, 1947, p. 543). This peculiar commitment to a right of self-determination, coupled with freedom of choice, made the statement vulnerable to substantial criticism.

Some have interpreted the last few passages of the statement as contradicting the earlier parts, which championed the theory of relativism. Redfield, for example, referred to the phrase concerning underlying values and called it "to put it bluntly, a weasel; by including it, the declaration was made self-contradictory. You either respect all values or you do not" (1962, pp. 148-149). Such a "brake upon discrimination and conquest" might exist if there are, in fact, underlying cultural values to invoke, but as Redfield asks, "what if the underlying approved values are not there?" (1962, p. 148). Another commentator, Steward, inquires: "What are these 'underlying cultural values' that can be used to suppress intolerance and promote political freedom in cultures which lack economic or social freedom or that can be used to halt conquest in a competitive world?" (1948, p. 351). Herskovits may have been right. There may indeed be cultural ideals which can be called on to challenge repressive practices; but he cannot merely assert this. Since anthropologists interpreted relativism as requiring tolerance, the idea that their professional association should make a formal statement on human rights was troubling. After all, their academic training had emphasized objectivity in the study of other cultures and had encouraged them to refrain from making value judgments about specific practices. Thus, there was not only a reaction to the content of the Statement itself but to the very idea that the Association should make any public statement whatsoever. Anthropologists came to different conclusions regarding the role they should play in the movement to advance universal human rights. One view was that professionals as a group should avoid making value judgments and adhere to science (Steward, 1948). On this account, anthropologists as individual citizens had "every right to pass value judgments," but the Association, as a scientific organization, had "no business dealing with the rights of man" (Steward, 1948, p. 352).

Another position taken was that support of social movements by the Association was permissible as long as those engaged in such activities declared with candor what their position was and abandoned any attempt to justify the stand scientifically. In Barnett's words: "If we must support proposals and movements—and I believe that the Association should at times do just that—then let us admit either tacitly or explicitly, that we have an {85} axe to grind and dispense with the camouflage" (1948, p. 355). The main flaw in Barnett's entire analysis, however, is his assertion that a scientific approach to the question of human rights is not possible. This conclusion is unwarranted since it remains to be seen whether empirical cross-cultural research will yield universals to validate human rights.

A third position was that anthropologists might as well expound their views since they are inevitably actors in society and as such affect life in other societies whether they speak out or remain silent (Bennett, 1949; Redfield, 1962, p. 149). Bennett's view is that the selective presentation of facts is unavoidable. Since science is value-laden, anthropologists might as well not try to be objective and simply try to advance those causes in which they believe. But he exaggerates the extent to which the roles of the anthropologist as scientist and as citizen must merge. There is no reason to think that a person cannot manage two roles simultaneously. Consider, for example, the lawyer who despises violent crime but retains enough objectivity and professionalism to represent the accused (even if he knows his client is guilty).

Bennett's position merits close attention. By taking this view, he appears to authorize scientists to utter statements they know to be unsound in order to reach ends they believe in as citizens (Redfield, 1962, p. 178, n. 20). For instance, Bennett claimed that although anthropologists knew that there were differences among human "varieties," ideologically it served their purposes to deny them (1949, p. 334). Herskovits objected to this and said Bennett's approach was far too cynical for most scientists to embrace (1972, p. 46). When Bennett addressed the question of the legitimacy of the Statement itself, he conceded, readily enough, that it used American values but suggested that that might be desirable:

> Now, it is true that the Statement does just that; uses American values with which to set standards—or if its standards are not American, then they are "Western European democratic." Therefore, applying standards of logical consistency, the Statement is on shaky ground. But perhaps this misses an important point. Perhaps, under current conditions in the United Nations, and in the light of political conflicts now under way, the formulations of the Statement are precisely the ones which will prove effective to accomplish certain ends (1949, p. 332).

He insinuated that the Statement was deliberately drafted in ambiguous language, mostly advocating relativism, but containing an escape hatch or two for uncomfortable universalists to appease the various factions in the Association. {86}

Herskovits's response to the three critiques was woefully inadequate (1951). He offered nothing which would resolve the question as to the proper role of anthropologists with respect to human rights. Since he was largely responsible for the Statement and the theory of relativism on which it was based, it is unfortunate that he could not provide a more satisfactory reconciliation of relativism with human rights. Together with Boas and Benedict, Herskovits cast a cloud of confusion over relativism whose shadow is still felt. It is a great pity that all three presented such a weak formulation of the theory. If only they had realized that relativism does not imply tolerance and does not deny the possible existence of cross-cultural universals, anthropologists might have been spared much anguish. It is quite understandable that the question of tolerance should have preoccupied anthropologists at the time the Statement was released. The horror over atrocities in Nazi Germany made the theory appear untenable when it need not have. So, the anthropologists who faced the Declaration on Human Rights and the Statement on it by their professional Association were torn. Their commitments to both professional and political ideologies appeared to be at odds. They were sensitive to the danger of imposing Western values on non-Western societies, something which is still not widely recognized; but at the same time, they were reluctant to disavow their own liberal, democratic principles. In the 1980s one witnesses increasing attention paid to the possibility that human rights will not prove successful until there is a global consensus which supports them. Forty years earlier anthropologists were grappling with this question. So, although their commentary is replete with misconceptions, at least they showed considerable foresight. If other segments of the American and global communities had heeded their intellectual queries, a firmer basis for human rights might exist today.

CONCLUSION

I have tried to show that because relativism is a meta-ethical theory, it is not self-contradictory. Since relativism does not imply tolerance, moral criticism remains a viable option for the relativist. The major contribution of relativism is not its advocacy of tolerance but instead its focus on enculturation. By calling attention to the power of enculturation, relativism might be used to alleviate but not obliterate prejudice even if tolerance is not an integral part of the theory. But, even if people because of cultural {87} conditioning prefer their own standards, this does not mean there will always be irreconcilable differences. Relativism is compatible with the existence of cross-cultural universals. It remains to be seen if empirical cross-cultural data can be adduced to show that some standards are, in fact, universally shared.

4

A CROSS-CULTURAL APPROACH TO VALIDATING INTERNATIONAL HUMAN RIGHTS

The Case of Retribution Tied to Proportionality

{88}

TO determine whether specific human rights are universal and can thus be measured cross-culturally, one first needs a comparative analysis of broader moral principles. The central question is whether there is any comparable notion, or what has been called the *homeomorphic equivalent*, for human rights in other societies. A study of the principle of retribution may provide a promising starting point for comparative research of this kind. I will show that the principle of retribution tied to proportionality is extremely widespread, if not universal. It serves to limit violence, and, as such, may indicate worldwide support for a principled rejection of arbitrary killing. It would be beyond the scope of this study to do more than offer preliminary discussion of this proposed means of establishing a consensus on particular human rights and of validating international standards.

In this chapter I will begin by advancing an argument on behalf of cross-cultural research in the hopes of showing the relevance of empirical data for normative claims. After reviewing some of the more significant attempts to explore morality from a cross-cultural perspective, a case study will be presented of the principle of retribution tied to proportionality. The forms of retribution to be investigated include *lex talionis*, which follows strict proportionality, and the payment of blood money, which follows general proportionality. Behavioral manifestations of retribution include such practices as the feud, vendetta, and vengeance killings. While there are differences among these retaliatory actions, those are not important for our purposes. As Hoebel points out, blood revenge and vendetta are vernacular synonyms for the feud (1976, p. 504). Finally, this empirical inquiry will be connected to international human-rights standards. {89}

THE RELEVANCE OF EMPIRICAL DATA FOR NORMATIVE INQUIRY

In the quest for structural equivalents for human rights, it is necessary to consider empirical data. This is a difficult undertaking, principally for two reasons. First, there is a widespread philosophical objection to combining empirical and normative analyses. To merge them is to risk confusing an "is" with an "ought" (Hudson, 1969). So, it will be crucial to establish the relevance of empirical findings for normative theory. Second, it is not obvious which data can provide a means to discovering the "true" moral standards of a society. Consulting jurisprudential and theological texts will surely paint a picture of moral standards, but they may be only the ideals of the elites; what we are after are native moral categories. The discipline which has most to offer is anthropology, which is devoted to the study of the worldviews and folkways of other peoples. This analysis draws on the ethnographic materials pertaining to law, dispute settlement, values, and morality. Since anthropologists are trained according to a professional ethic which discourages value judgments, they have seldom focused on morality. Although much of their work is concerned with morals, it rarely speaks to perceptions of morality directly. This conclusion is borne out by a thorough review of the articles in the *UNESCO International Bibliography of Social and Cultural Anthropology* from 1955 to 1981 (Schirmer, Renteln & Wiseberg, 1988a).

In the past there has been some recognition of the relevance of empirical studies for moral claims. For example, as early as 1923 Paul Masson-Oursel tried to explain the importance of comparative philosophy. His 1951 article, "True Philosophy is Comparative Philosophy," describes comparative philosophy as the "general examination of the ways in which human beings of all races and cultures reflect upon their actions and act upon their reflections" (1951, p. 6). In 1946 an entire symposium titled "Is Anthropology Relevant to Ethics?" was sponsored by the Aristotelian Society. Philosophers warned against taking for granted our own moral standards: "...it is not easy to guard against assuming that what happens under the cultural conditions we are familiar with, will happen under different cultural conditions" (Russell, 1946, p. 63). With varying degrees of enthusiasm all three participants in that symposium, L. J. Russell, J. D. Mabbott, and A. M. MacBeath, agreed that anthropology is relevant to ethics. They also noted that a consideration of anthropological evidence need not commit one to a relativist position (Mabbott, 1946, p. 85). {90}

Abraham Edel has tried to demonstrate the interrelationship of anthropology and ethics (1962, 1968). He notes that much of the problem in looking for universals or shared moral principles stems from the "established habit in both disciplines" (1962, p. 55). The philosophers' approach is usually analytic and normative and rarely incorporates social science or the study of culture. Anthropologists treat morality as "enmeshed in one or another of the areas of social or cultural description or dispersed over many" (1962, p. 55). If we are reluctant to accept the Kantian claim for a synthetic *a priori* proposition, Edel recommends following the empirical path (1962, p. 63). Edel is convinced that anthropology is potentially a great tool for ethics: "And in so far as anthropology can furnish wide comparative materials on moralities by more systematic investigations it can contribute markedly to the relevant scientific knowledge" (1962, p.67). Danelski, persuaded that empirical study was particularly germane for human rights, argued in 1966 that there was a need for empirical verification of human rights: "and when that is done, there will be a reliable basis for a profound understanding of such rights" (1966, p. 68).

It still may not be clear why the descriptions of diverse moral systems should be pertinent. Suppose that all cultures were committed to capital punishment. That might not mean that it was a moral practice. There is a real danger when relying on moral systems of assuming that tradition is moral. Just because a type of behavior is conventional hardly makes it right. Having admitted that a simple majority rule principle operating in the international system is not acceptable, one must suggest another way to justify the use of empirical data in an attempt to resolve ethical conflicts.

It might be the case that one society holds a monopoly on moral knowledge. The United States Constitution writ large in the form of United Nations documents (Henkin, 1979b) may reflect true enlightenment. Other cultures may simply lack moral insights. Yet, this cannot be so. Should one say that the cultures which have arranged marriages are wrong, just because the practice contravenes international human-rights standards (Universal Declaration of Human Rights, Article 16(2); International Covenant of Civil and Political Rights, Article 23; International Covenant of Economic, Social and Cultural Rights, Article 10) even if many cultures accept it? If it turns out that most cultures do not believe in a moral principle which the Western world embraces, it might be that they are right. It might also be true that most cultures, including Western and non-Western societies, believe in a certain moral idea or value. That there may be evidence that a majority of countries and peoples are committed to a particular moral standard might indicate their willingness to accept a human-rights standard {91} which is based on the norm. It would be quite significant if there should happen to be convergence among the many moral systems in the world. Such unanimity might provide a stronger foundation for human rights.

There is discussion in the literature of the need to pare down the number of rights from the lengthy, inflated list (Alston, 1984; Nickel, 1982; Pocklington, 1982). Those which should remain are those for which evidence can be marshaled. In the absence of any justification for human rights, other than mere assertions that they are self-evident, inalienable, and other universalistic moral epithets, there is a real need for proof. If one can demonstrate that there is a convergence in traditional belief systems with respect to specific moral principles, then there may be hope that one can prove that there is a consensus. It may be possible to revive languishing human rights. Although empirical findings may not be automatically relevant to ethical inquiry, in the present case, they are vital. Without evidence of support for the values which underlie human rights standards, any claim to universality will fall flat.

PREVIOUS COMPARATIVE ANALYSES OF MORALITY AND HUMAN RIGHTS

There have been previous attempts to analyze ethical issues on a cross-cultural basis and to evaluate human rights from the viewpoint of specific cultures. For instance, there exist several comparative studies of freedom (Boas, 1940; D'Angelo, 1973; Haldane, 1940; Nielsen, 1964; Shih, 1940). Laurie Wiseberg and Harry Scobie provide a survey of scholarly attempts to undertake systematic comparative research on various aspects of human rights (1981). Interestingly enough, they begin their discussion by focusing on the definitional problem, after which they mention some criticisms of the allegedly narrow conceptualizations of particular human-rights nongovernmental organizations (1981, p. 150). Their thoughtful study evaluates the concepts utilized by Amnesty International, Freedom House, the United States Department of State Reports on Human Rights, and the Physical Quality of Life Index of the Overseas Development Council. One of their conclusions is that, "There is extant today no single social accounting scheme that is adequate—both conceptually valid and quantitatively reliable for monitoring the status of human rights the world over" (1981, p. 167). The problem is that the measuring tools are culture-bound. They maintain that the scheme of, for instance, Freedom House "is so partisan {92} and culture-bound that it would be intellectually and politically dangerous to rely upon it" (1981, pp. 167-168).

Even the book entitled *Comparative Human Rights* fails to avoid cultural bias. First, the collection contains essays which compare at most several countries, all of which are in the Western world. Its greater failure is its lack of any comparative analytic framework within which to study human rights. Nor is there any systematic investigation of any single human right or principle throughout the world. Recognizing that the term "human rights" is confusing, the editor, Richard Claude, can say only that it is "as convenient a generic term as is available to embrace the whole universe of civil rights, civil liberties, and newly emerging social and economic rights which enjoy or are moving toward legal sanction from country to country" (1976, p. x). Whether social and economic rights are "new" depends on one's cultural outlook. This presents no problem for Claude, however, since his discussion draws largely, but not exclusively, upon historical developments in France, Great Britain, and the United States. These three systems supply the framework for what he calls the "classical model" of development (1976, pp. 6-7). It is probably not necessary to point out that the standards which he uses cannot be universal by any stretch of the imagination. In effect, he circumvents the conceptual issue, though he does acknowledge it: "If we set our sights on a world perspective, the narrow bases of the model and derivative hypothesis should be apparent. The model is rooted in the experience of liberal democratic systems" (1976, p. 43). Most strange is the complete disregard for conceptual analysis of human rights in Chapter 15, "Comparative Rights Research: Some Intersections Between Law and Social Sciences." Focusing on institutional description, policy analysis, and behavioral explanation, Claude neglects to address the need for consensus on the standards by which human rights phenomena may be empirically measured.

Another attempt to find a standard which would apply cross-culturally is by Ivo Duchacek (1973). He provides a comparative study of political, economic, and social rights and liberties expressed in national constitutions of the Western, Communist, and Third worlds. The analysis considers over a hundred bills of rights. Unfortunately, however, a study of this kind can demonstrate at best only what the elites believe. Even that may not be possible. Almost all countries put human rights in their constitutions, not necessarily because the elites believe in them, but because human rights are fashionable. Although one may be able to ascertain the assumptions of the drafters of the constitutions, there is little chance of determining what the traditional moral codes are like. Another problem with the analysis is {93} that, with the exception of Chapter 3, "Right to Economic and Social Progress," the book is largely an elaboration of civil and political rights, the mainstay of the West.

A particularly interesting example of comparative rights analysis is found in the introduction to Lawrence Beer's book, Freedom of Expression in Japan (1984). He tries to work out a transcultural standard and seems committed to using empirical data: "More attempts should be made to bring philosophy and empirical findings under one analytic roof" (1984, p. 27). He acknowledges the tendency in comparative law studies to focus on Western legal cultures and to pay relatively little attention to non-Western legal systems. He also discusses the need to come up with a broader formulation of the concept of freedom and one that could provide a basis for a critique of nation-state practices (1984, p. 26). Most importantly, he is conscious of the need for a culturally unbiased human-rights theory:

> To develop human rights theory that is sensitive to ambiguities, respectful of empirical differences among cultures, and responsive to principle is a tremendous challenge. Human rights theory is needed to buttress activism on behalf of human rights, but state or private human rights advocacy does not imply there is good reason to care about human rights. Questions of seminal theory are sometimes wrongly shunted aside, but the issue is critically real: does the moral sensitivity manifested by commitment to human rights make any intellectual sense? (1984, p. 27).

Although Beer does identify many of the significant and nagging problems that plague comparative analysis of rights, he does not offer much in the way of an approach to avoid them. Not only does he fail to define freedom or freedom of expression in a value-neutral manner, but his foundation for a general human-rights theory is highly ethnocentric. He offers only a standard Kantian approach which begs the question. A person "is a kind of being that has an intrinsic value intellectually and morally justifying his/her treatment as an end in himself/herself" (1984, p. 30). "I owe respect to others for the reasons they owe me respect" (1984, p. 31). Beer's philosophy presupposes a Western ethical foundation based on individualism.

Beer also asks how freedom of expression fits into a general scheme of human needs and human rights. He answers with the work of Christian Bay who claims (conveniently) that freedom of expression is the ultimate public value for a democracy. Whether or not that is true for democracies, a human-rights theory must take into account systems other than democracies. Otherwise a theory of human rights cannot be distinguished from {94} theories of democracy. It is reasonable to think that human rights can be safeguarded in societies which are not democratic. Moreover, the way in which democracy is defined will vary by ideological system.

If the value chosen for comparative analysis is freedom and that value is presumed to be the "ultimate," or "best," or most important value, then the Western ethnocentric bias has hardly been avoided. This is precisely the value held in highest esteem in the West. Whether it or some other value might be more cherished is not considered. The very choice of which value to compare may reflect more cultural presuppositions than has been hitherto acknowledged.

In *Creeds, Society, and Human Rights: A Study in Three Cultures* (1984), Stackhouse examines human-rights issues in the context of three world "religions," Christianity, Marxism, and Hinduism (1984, p. 10). At first he appears to find the idea of identifying points of agreement among different religions appealing. Ultimately, he rejects the idea because he believes that the content of the principle in different settings makes this approach questionable:

> The apparent agreements among all peoples regarding certain "universal" ethical normals suggest that there are such things as universal principles, but the disagreements as to their contexts force us to carefully examine and judge between the basic background beliefs by which they are understood and between the functioning of these norms in social practice (1984, p. 269).

Stackhouse says that we can only find human rights by seeking the "truth," and he seems to view human rights as its own religion. Human rights only have justification insofar as we are willing to make a leap of faith (1984, pp. 270-271). In the end, he claims that human rights are most secure under his own religion:

> As a convert to the Liberal-Puritan synthesis and through that to ecumenical Christianity, I have become convicted [sic] that the last of these three views (treated first in this book) is the truest description of human condition. This view preserves freedom and is rational; it is potentially universal and practically creates in particular settings the social space whereby the concrete social structures are opened up so that most basic human needs are likely to be met over time with a minimum of destructive violence (1984, p. 272).

It is not surprising that Stackhouse adopts the values of his own culture and religion: freedom, rationality, and minimizing violence. These are Western values. If they are potentially universal, he must show this. {95}

After the consideration of these works, it should be clear that to date negligible progress has been made in the direction of establishing that human rights are universal or even that certain moral principles are widely shared. The studies raise important questions, indicate the need for empirical data, and reflect a feeling of dissatisfaction with the present state of human rights.

THE PRINCIPLE OF RETRIBUTION: A CASE STUDY

The principle of retribution was selected for comparative study not only because there are available empirical data on this subject but also, and more importantly, because there is reason to believe that this principle may be universal: "Retribution is a universal phenomenon and experience among primitive as well as among civilized people, in ancient Greek drama, in the Old and New Testaments" (Hall, 1983, p. 294). Some have noted that it is prevalent among "primitive" peoples. Herbert Spencer acknowledges that this principle is widespread: "The principle requiring 'an eye for an eye and a tooth for a tooth' embodies the primitive idea of justice everywhere" (1900, p. 528). Edward Westermarck speaks of "jus talionis, or rule of equivalence between injury and retaliation, which is characteristic of savage justice" (1932, p. 95). In his brilliant analysis of the principle of retribution, Hans Kelsen states that it is the most fundamental principle of social order for "primitive man" (1946, p. 64). In a 1983 popular work on retribution, *Wild Justice: The Evolution of Revenge*, Susan Jacoby refers to "the ineradicable impulse to retaliate when harm is inflicted..." (1983, p. 5). Also calling it ineradicable, Westermarck says, "The retributive desire is so strong, and appears so natural, that we can neither help obeying it, nor seriously disapprove of its being obeyed" (1924, p. 91). Dautremer, in his analysis of legal revenge in Japan, claims, "The desire for revenge is indeed an innate sentiment in man, and in all the primitive civilizations we find personal revenge existing as a prescriptive right" (1985, p. 82). Posner has claimed that there is a "vengeful component in our genetic makeup" (1980a, p. 79).

Some may wonder about the choice of retribution as a topic for comparative study. One of the three main justifications for punishment (the other two are deterrence and rehabilitation), retribution is generally regarded as the least worthy (Grande, 1983). This is because retribution is viewed basically as another term for the instinct of revenge. In the West there has been a tendency to deny the legitimacy of retribution or revenge. Jacoby {96} points out that while justice is a legitimate concept, vengeance is not (1983, p. 1). She explains that:

> The very word "revenge" has pejorative connotations. Advocates of draconian punishment for crime invariably prefer "retribution"—a word that affords the comfort of euphemism although it is virtually synonymous with "revenge" (1983, p. 4).

Some, for example Percy (1943), have distinguished between revenge (personal gratification) and retribution (impersonal and impartial action).

But even retribution has fallen out of favor and has come to be associated with cruel punishment (Poupko, 1975, p. 541). The eminent moral philosopher Sidgwick wrote that he had "an instinctive and strong moral aversion to it [retribution]," and that "it is gradually passing away from the moral consciousness of educated persons in the most advanced communities..." (1962, p. 281). He did admit, however, that "it is still perhaps the more ordinary view" (1962, p. 281).

Even though Western philosophers and theologians may advocate forgiveness in lieu of retribution, their position is not shared by most of the world. Hall maintains that retribution is a part of every legal system:

> It is implied or expressed in every legal system, even in those that explicitly reject it and then go on to impose punitive sanctions on criminals in proportion to the gravity of the harms they commit.... The plain fact, like it or not, is that retribution, crude or refined, has been and is *inevitable*. Responsibility will vary from collective to individual, or both may coexist, but retribution is constant (1983, p. 294).

TWO CONCEPTUAL CLARIFICATIONS

Two conceptual clarifications are in order. First, the distinction between justice and revenge is arguably false. Vengeance is inevitably the basic element of punishment (Durkheim, 1966, p. 89; Margolin, 1933-34, p. 767). In the absence of state punishment, people who want to see justice done may turn to vigilantism. This may indicate that one of the strongest justifications for punishment is actually retribution (Blau, 1916, p. 4; Jacoby, 1983, p. 10). Throughout the world people equate justice with vengeance, even if not consciously. There is a deeply rooted belief in the just-deserts doctrine that holds that criminals should receive the punishment they deserve. {97}

Just as theorists have insisted on a distinction between justice and vengeance, they have argued that retribution and forgiveness are diametric opposites. Westermarck, however, denies that the rule of retaliation and the rule of forgiveness are so radically opposed to each other (1932b, p. 75). His argument depends on showing that deterrence and rehabilitation (which he calls reformation) are offshoots of retribution (1932b, pp. 80-88). Deterrence cannot justify punishment because punishing an innocent person might result in greater deterrence. There must be a notion of just deserts in the punishment. Thus, punishment requires a retributive justification even if it has the socially beneficial and desired effect of deterrence. Westermarck links rehabilitation to repentance. For it is only through repenting that criminals can come to realize that their actions were wrong. When they become remorseful, their characters are reformed. Inherent in the idea of rehabilitation is the principle of retribution. What the reformed or rehabilitated criminal must know is that the victim did not deserve the act; and, therefore, that the criminal does deserve to be punished. Without the recognition of just deserts, rehabilitation would not make sense.

If Westermarck's reasoning is correct, then he has gone beyond Kelsen. Kelsen demonstrated that the principle of retribution is the fundamental principle of social order for "primitive man." Westermarck, if his analysis is to be believed, has proved that the principle of retribution necessarily underlies all forms of punishment:

> Thus the theories both of determent and of reformation are ultimately offspring of the same emotion that first induced men to inflict punishment on their fellow-creatures. It escaped the advocates of these theories that they themselves were under the influence of the very principle they fought against, because they failed to grasp its true import (1932b, p. 83).

The ethnographic data suggest that the purpose of taking revenge is ultimately to restore social order and to maintain social cohesion. It is only through the process of retributive action that both sides can forgive each other. It may not make sense or be at all helpful, then, to characterize revenge and forgiveness as polar opposites.

A DEFINITION

It is time to consider the definition of retribution. Retribution means a recompense for, or requital of, evil done; return of evil (*Oxford English Dictionary*, 1933, p. 581). {98} The etymological derivation of the word is from the Latin *retribuere*, meaning restore or give back. There is a clear indication that at its root is the idea of compensation (repayment, recompense). This will be important later in the discussion of blood money.

There are a few important aspects of retribution worth emphasizing. Retribution makes no sense unless it involves an act taken in response to a first act. It presumes that the original act was wrongly committed (Kelsen, 1946, p. 50). In Japan, for instance, the taking of revenge was moral unless the victim was killed for having committed a crime, i.e., not wrongly killed (Mills, 1976, p. 530). The idea of equivalence or proportionality is central to the principle of retribution. A clear philosophical definition of retribution tied to proportionality is provided by John Rawls:

> What we may call the retributive view is that punishment is justified on the grounds that wrongdoing merits punishment. It is morally fitting that a person who does wrong should suffer in proportion to his guilt, and the severity of the appropriate punishment depends on the depravity of his act (1955, pp. 4-5).

Kelsen explains this in psychological terms:

> The substantializing tendency of primitive thinking makes man— even civilized man—believe that the evil which one sustains and the evil which one must inflict according to the principle of retribution

can and shall be "equal"—equal in both a quantitative and a qualita-
tive sense (1946, p. 59).

Often the language of balance and equilibrium is invoked, which suggests that there is an underlying reciprocity behind the idea of retribution.
Pilling reports that the Australian aborigines explain the resolution of
conflict as "square now" (1957, p. 241). "Square" means that the dispute is
over (1957, pp. 312-317). Boehm describes the feud by reference to the
analogy of scorekeeping (1984, p. 218). Kelsen says that equilibrium is the
"specific function of retribution which balances punishment against
wrong and reward against merit, as on scales" (1946, p. 236). The language of balance, equilibrium, and geometry pervade analyses and descriptions of retribution.

Implicit in balance is reciprocity, which is frequently expressed in the
form of the traditional *lex talionis,* an eye for an eye and a tooth for a
tooth. The presumption is that the appropriate social response to a breach
of a norm is a response in kind. The determination of what constitutes
equivalence between crimes and punishments generally varies cross-
culturally. But what is clear is that the principle of retribution is tied to a
principle {99} of proportionality. The linking of these two concepts is
arguably universal. Even if the proportion is measured differently in
various societies, there is a discernible scaling between crime and punishment.

LEX TALIONIS

Lex talionis is defined as the principle or law of retaliation, that the
punishment inflicted should correspond in degree and kind to the offense
of the wrongdoer, as an eye for an eye, a tooth for a tooth (*Oxford English
Dictionary,* 1933, p. 234).

There is an intriguing debate in the *Rivista Internazionale di
Filosofia del Diritto* (Mitias, 1983; Primorac, 1979, 1984) about the question of whether a retributive theory of punishment, necessarily requires
the *lex talionis.* Primorac defines *lex talionis* as the doctrine that the
punishment should fit the crime, that its severity should be proportionate
to the gravity of the crime. The source of disagreement between Primorac
and Mitias appears to be over the breadth of interpretation of the *lex
talionis.* The real principle necessary for the theory of retribution is
proportionality.

Mitias claims that asking why a criminal should be punished and
what and how much suffering a criminal should endure are two different
types of questions (1983, p. 216). His thesis is that the question of the
measurement of punishment is not logically entailed by the question of
why the criminal should be punished. Mitias says that although the
concept of crime entails punishment, there is no direct, logical, organic
relationship between any specific crime and any specific punishment. This
means that the question of proper punishment is logically independent of

the question of its justification. Mitias wants to say that the retributive theory of punishment does not, in fact, require that the punishment fit the crime, but only "that justice be done, both to the criminal and to the injured person or persons. Each one of them should receive what he deserves" (1983, p. 218).

Primorac responds to this argument by demonstrating that in giving a criminal his or her just deserts, one must ensure that the punishment fits the crime. That is, the severity ought to be proportionate to the gravity of the misdeed:

> When we say of a criminal that he has been punished in a way which does not reflect his deserts, that his punishment is accordingly not just, what do we mean but either that the punishment is disproportionately harsh or, alternatively, that it is disproportionately mild, and that in either ca.se it does not fit the crime committed? {100} If this is not obvious, consider the statements "X was given a punishment which does not fit his crime because it is too harsh compared to the seriousness of the deed, yet he was punished according to his deserts and justly," and "Y got a punishment which does not fit his crime because it is too lenient compared to the gravity of the deed, yet he was punished according to his deserts and justly." Both statements are contradictions; which goes to show that the notion of just and deserved punishment, which Mitias is willing to accept, is just the notion of punishment which fits the crime in that its gravity is proportionate to that of the crime, which he repudiates (1984, p. 84).

Mitias and other retributivists who question the necessity of *lex talionis* generally raise two objections. First, they say it is impractical to try to find an exactly equivalent response. This objection depends on the second which is that the *lex talionis* is repressive because it does not take into account varying circumstances. According to Primorac, this argument hinges on an overly literal interpretation of *lex talionis*. He tries to refute this by explaining that the retributivist applying *lex talionis* would consider the context of the crime and resolve to impose a punishment equivalent to it:

> The main point is that there are differences in gravity due to differing motivations, which a retributivist applying the *lex talionis* would consider differences of deserts, on account of which justice demands punishments of differing severity (1984, p. 87).

Lex talionis requires the full measure of what is proportionate to the gravity of the offense if the perpetrator is fully responsible for his or her act, i.e., if no mitigating circumstance exists.

Mitias also seems confused about what the *lex talionis* requires. He thinks it requires a specific punishment that is universally applicable. Primorac responds by pointing out that just because societies and cultures differ in their hierarchization of crimes and punishments does not mean that there exists any real difficulty for retributivism and *lex talionis*:

> To demand that punishments be measured out justly, according to deserts, i.e., that they should be proportionate in severity to the gravity of crimes, does not commit oneself to the idea of there being only one framework for carrying out this demand, valid throughout history (1984, p. 90).

A retributivist need not insist upon a transcultural and transhistorical system of crimes and punishments. It may be that every society is committed to retribution tied to proportionality but utilizes its own scale. {101}

In some ways the debate is a peculiar one. Both sides seem to ignore the possibility that *lex talionis* does require a literal interpretation, i.e., an eye for an eye, etc. Even though they both agree that just punishment should be based on a principle of proportionality, they still appear to disagree. Mitias's main conceptual error lies in his failure to realize that punishment may always be proportional even if its specific form and duration vary cross-culturally. Primorac, on the other hand, confuses *lex talionis* with proportionality. Retribution cannot always be applied according to *lex talionis* because there is not always an exact equivalent for a crime. The underlying principle of *lex talionis* is proportionality, and this is what Primorac really means to say is essential for the retributive theory of punishment. The reason why the debate is confused is that the writers have wrongly equated *lex talionis* with the principle of proportionality.

There is a debate in the literature about whether *lex talionis* must be interpreted literally. For the purposes of this analysis the outcome of this hermeneutic controversy is not crucial. Proportionality tied to retribution is pervasive. It does not matter if we call it *lex talionis* or not. It turns out, however, that in the case of homicide, there is widespread consensus on the applicability of the *lex talionis* and on the specific punishment that is appropriate. The idea that a life must be paid for with a life is remarkably prevalent throughout the world. Even though the practice of blood money is accepted in many societies, there is still recognition of the basic norm of equivalence.

INTERPRETING ETHNOGRAPHIES

Before examining the ethnographic data, a few warnings about interpretation are in order.[29] Since it is not feasible for any one individual to collect field data on all peoples throughout the world, it is necessary to rely upon the research of others. In the case of anthropological research there is a danger that the limitations of fieldwork may lead to distortions in the interpretations of aspects of the culture. There is always the question whether the categories and notions used by the investigator are held by the people. There is also the possibility of misinterpretation. For example, when Colin Turnbull writes about the way of life among the Ik in the Mountain People (1972), he describes a systematic plan to starve certain segments of the society {102} to death.[30] The conclusion he draws is that this society is devoid of a moral sense, i.e., is amoral. First of all, his assumption that withholding food from some members of the community demonstrates the absence of morality must be challenged. Among the Eskimos, for instance, infanticide and senilicide are considered moral (Boas, 1884-85, p. 580). It is by no means clear that the denial of food is universally regarded as immoral. In the United States the debate about this subject takes place in the context of euthanasia. Second, Turnbull visited the Ik during one year. Presumably this was a lean year. It is crucial to know how food is distributed during a year of plenty in order to justify the extreme conclusion that the Ik are an amoral people (Lear, 1984, p. 150).

In the case of retribution there is a particular danger that projection may occur. The scholars who write about retribution tend to think, naturally enough, in retributive terms. It must be admitted that there may be a possibility that by seeking out the principle of retribution and the *lex talionis*, the anthropologist, through this determination, may make sure to find it. Kelsen, in a discussion of vengeance among animals, recounts an extraordinary example of projection. It is Westermarck citing the following case from Palgrave's report of a journey through central and eastern Arabia as proof of "animal revenge":

> One passion alone he [the camel] possesses, namely revenge, of which he furnishes many a hideous example, while in carrying it out he shows an unexpected degree of far-thoughted malice, united meanwhile with all the cold stupidity of his usual character. One instance of this I well remember. It occurred hard by a small town in the plain of Ba'albec, where I was at the time residing. A lad of about fourteen had conducted a large camel, laden with wood, from that very village to another at half an hour's distance or so. As the animal loitered or turned out of the way, its conductor struck it repeatedly, and harder than it seems to have thought he had a right to do. But not finding the occasion favourable for taking immediate quits, it "bode its time"; nor was that time long in coming. A few days later the same lad had to reconduct the beast, but unladen, to his own village. When they were about half-way on the road, and at some distance from any habitation, the camel suddenly stopped, looked deliberately round in every direction to assure itself that no one was within sight, and, finding the road far and near clear of passers-by, made a step forward, seized the unlucky boy's head in its monstrous mouth, and lifting him up in the air flung him down again on the earth with the upper part of skull completely torn off, and his brains scattered on the ground. Having thus satisfied its revenge, the brute quietly resumed its pace towards the village as though nothing were the matter, till some men who had observed the whole, though unfortunately at too great a distance to be able to afford timely help, came up and killed it (Kelsen, 1946, p. 51-52).
> {103}

Kelsen wonders whether to be more amazed by the camel with its sense of justice and its clever cautiousness or by the men who were so far away that they could not come to the boy's rescue but could watch the strange behavior of the camel and observe its motives and intentions exactly (1946, p. 52). There is the same danger that in interpreting human behavior the anthropologist may project unjustifiably the principle of retribution on the societies he or she is studying.

THE ETHNOGRAPHIC MATERIAL

The discussion of retribution will proceed in the following manner. After a consideration of some of the ethnographic material on the *lex talionis*, evidence will be presented of its existence in some of the major religious texts in the world. After this demonstration of the geographical distribution of the *lex talionis* formulation will be an analysis of the feud as a logical development of it. The feud, it will be argued, occurs wherever there is a lack of agreement about proportionality. After linking *lex talionis* and feud; the case of blood money will be discussed in order to show how retribution with general proportionality operates. Next is the consideration of the virtues of retribution. Here the need to avoid three basic misconceptions will be explained. Finally, the section on retribution closes with an analysis of how retribution functions as a form of what might be called negative reciprocity.

There are very few cross-cultural studies of retribution (Kelsen, 1946; Posner, 1980a; Westermarck, 1924). The most brilliant analysis of the principle of retribution is found in Hans Kelsen's book, *Society and Nature: A Sociological Inquiry* (1946), particularly in Chapter 3. This impressive work furnishes many examples of cultures which follow the principle under consideration. This study draws heavily from the sources Kelsen cites and adds others.

The Australian aborigines "carry out the principle of retaliation, not only as a dictate of passion, but as an ancient and fixed law" (Ridley, 1975, p. 159). Among the natives of Central Africa, it is said that "revenge is a ruling passion, as the many rancorous fratricidal wars that have prevailed between kindred clans, even for a generation, prove. Retaliation and vengeance are, in fact, their great agents of moral control" (Burton, 1860, Vol. 2, p. 329). The inhabitants of South Africa believe in the "intrinsic justice of retaliation" (Kidd, 1969, p. 84). {104}

In addition to general accounts of retaliation existing among many peoples, there are specific examples of the *lex talionis* formulation. As there are many such examples, several illustrations will have to suffice. Thomson observed that: "The great principle of justice upon which the [Maori of New Zealand] acted was an eye for an eye and a tooth for a tooth, and the object of their punishments was to obtain compensation for injuries, not to prevent crimes" (1970, Vol. 1, pp. 98-99). A 1709 report of a Jesuit missionary describes the principle among the Hindus of the district of Madura in India:

> These Indians observe the Law of Retaliation very strictly. If there happens to be a quarrel, and one of the Parties pulls his own eye out, or is guilty of suicide; the other party must inflict the like punishment upon himself, or on some of his Relations (Lockman, 1743, Vol. 2, p. 410).

Of the American Indians it has been said that "there never was any set of people, who pursued the Mosaic law of *retaliation* with such a fixt eagerness as these Americans" (Adair, 1930, p. 157).

Possibly the most precise formulation is found in Rafael Karsten's monograph *Blood Revenge, War, and Victory Feasts Among the Jibaro Indians of Eastern Ecuador*:

> The Jibaro Indian is wholly penetrated by the idea of retaliation; his desire for revenge is an expression of his sense of justice. This principle is an eye for an eye, tooth for tooth, and life for life. If one reprehends a Jibaro because he has killed an enemy, his answer is generally: "He has killed himself."
>
> When a murder committed by one's own tribesman is to be avenged, the social morals of the Jibaros require that the punishment shall be meted out with justice, in so far that for one life which has been taken only one life should be taken in retaliation. Thereupon, the blood guilt is atoned (tumashi akerkama) and the offended family is satisfied. Consequently, if a Jibaro Indian wishes to revenge a murder of his brother, it may well happen that he, in case the slayer himself cannot be caught and punished, will assassinate his brother or father instead of him, but he does not take the life of more than one member of the family, even if he has an opportunity of killing more (1923, pp. 10, 11, 13).

Karsten presents evidence of the *lex talionis* formulation, collective responsibility, and the clearly understood limit to the retaliatory act. It is permissible among many peoples to take revenge not necessarily on the offender but on any member of his family or clan. Although this may strike Westerners as strange, this surely provides a deterrent to violence. What {105} is most important to understand is that the practice of vengeance killing is not comparable to uncontrolled warfare. The principle of *lex talionis* as expressed here provides a limit to action. Karsten elaborates on this point: "This principle, which requires that there shall be justice in the retaliation so that life is weighed against life, of course, in itself has a tendency to limit blood revenge" (1923, p. 13).

In Japan a victim could be avenged only once (Mills, 1976, p. 534). Retribution in China also conformed to the principle of a life for a life (Meijer, 1980, pp. 203, 214). Among the Bedouin of Cyrenaica, a district in North Africa which is now part of Eastern Libya, E. P. Peters reports that the *lex talionis* is found: "A life had been taken for a life and the way is now open for the restoration of normal peaceful relationships" (1967, p. 265). Evidently, it is a common practice among this people to hold a peace meeting at which time "it is accepted that the killings have cancelled each other out" (1967, p. 265). This notion of cancelling out the original wrong is perhaps what makes the *lex talionis* so widely appealing. Here Peters provides substantiation for the argument that retribution and forgiveness are not diametrically opposed.

It is important to evaluate evidence to the contrary. In Albania, when a murder occurred, the injury would be avenged; and the vengeance generally took the form of a life for a life (Hasluck, 1967). In a few cases, however, the formula of "one for one" was disregarded. In Lume, a district which prided itself on its "spirit," the formula of "two for one" was the rule when a man killed his social superior. This might not represent a real deviation from the *lex talionis* insofar as the social superior might be worth two of his offender, that is, worth twice as much. In other words, this version of the rule still appears to acknowledge the basic norm. When a man suffered the loss of his wife, child, or guest, he might take "double" or even "triple" vengeance. This phrasing permits one to draw the inference that the basic vengeance was one life.

Another society in which the *lex talionis* may not be found is the Huli of New Guinea. Robert Glasse asserts that:

> The Huli concept of revenge, however, is not one of only equivalent return: they seek to inflict a more grievous injury than they have received, even though this usually results in counter-action in return. If a pig is stolen, a dozen of the thief's pigs will be taken in return if his identity is discovered; if a kinsman is killed, the dead man's relatives will seek to kill four or five enemies in return. There is no precise scale as to the amount of vengeance which ought to be exacted for each offence: but the principle is clear: to inflict greater damage than was received (1959, p. 283). {106}

It is possible that Glasse has misunderstood the practice of vengeance killing among the Huli. It is also conceivable that the Huli informed Glasse that they try to retaliate in such a way as to inflict greater damage than was sustained. Whether they actually do this is not clear. Glasse provides no illustrative cases or substantiation of any kind for his allegation. Even the language he uses implies that the principle of inflicting greater damage is ideal culture and not actual practice. He says they "seek to kill" and they "seek to inflict a more grievous injury than they have received." Whether this is based on what he was told or on what he observed is not made clear. The more revealing comment is that they seek to inflict greater injury than they received, even though "this usually results in counter-action in return." This indicates that the failure to give an equivalent return does not function as retribution. It simply starts a new feud. Implicit in the passage is that retribution will restore the equilibrium only if an equivalent response is made. In the case of homicide, this means a life for a life and not five for one. Even if Glasse's assertion is correct, the Huli might be the only culture which exceeds the *lex talionis*. In any event, there is a clear connection between punishment and the principle of proportionality.

There is further reason to suspect that the Huli follow the principle of proportionality and one tied to equivalence. In warfare when there is a negotiation of a truce and the fight has been a large one, Glasse says the two sides may exchange an equivalent number of pigs. These pigs are known as "pigs to make the war sleep" (1959, p. 287). It would be unlikely that equivalence would matter between peoples in the context of warfare but not for members within the group in the context of a feud.

The third and final counterexample is the Gamo of Ethiopia: "[T]he concept of vengeance does not exist in their vocabulary" (Bureau, 1979, p. 93). Although the sketchy article makes the claim that the Gamo lack vengeance, they do not lack the desire for it: "Indeed, the desire for vengeance and the pleasure one takes in its satisfaction are not foreign to the Gamo" (1979, p. 93). Thus, vengeance is not entirely absent despite the mechanisms established to prevent it from taking its course. Moreover, one might interpret the punishment for murder in such a way as to render it consistent with *lex talionis*. According to Bureau, banishment of the murderer is an immediate consequence of the act (1979, p. 103). Since the family of the murderer essentially loses one of its members, the victim's loss has been balanced. The main problem with Bureau's account of homicide among the Gamo is the dearth of information and evidence. Based on what he says, it is quite difficult to tell whether or not vengeance exists {107} among the Gamo. If one decides to accept Bureau's interpretation, then at best the Gamo lack vengeance when the social mechanisms function properly. When they do not, presumably the psychological need for vengeance prevails.

These three ethnographic examples are the only ones encountered in which the principle of proportionality was apparently absent. Where the *lex talionis* is not found, one would expect to find a different proportionality tied to retribution. For example, blood money serves as a substitute for *lex talionis*. It is worth emphasizing that the claim is not that *lex talionis is* universal but that it is extremely widespread and represents a form of the principle of retribution tied to proportionality.

THE CONCEPT OF EQUIVALENCE

The idea of equivalence is of central importance in understanding retribution in many societies. According to Radcliffe-Brown, in order for a violent revenge to be considered a justifiable act, its magnitude should be valued as an equivalent to the injury suffered (1940, p. xx). He says that "the *lex talionis* requires that the damage inflicted shall be equivalent to the damage suffered" (1952, p. 215). In some cases, the requirement of equivalence is strictly followed. For example, if X murders Y who has a much higher status than X does, then X will not be killed in response. The appropriate person would be a member of X's clan who has the status equivalent to Y's. When Y's clan avenges his death by killing this person, balance is then restored. An example of strict observance of the rule of equivalence can be taken from the Quianganes of Luzon, an island of the Philippines, who:

> are themselves carefully on their guard against hurting the feelings of another, and demand that others shall do the same with them. Blood vengeance is a sacred law with the Quianganes. If one plebeian is killed by another, the matter is settled in a simple manner by killing the murderer or some one of his family who is likewise a plebeian. But if a prominent man or noble is killed by a plebeian, vengeance on the murderer, a mere plebeian, is not enough; the victim of the sin-offering must be an equivalent in rank. Another nobleman must fall for the murdered noble, for their doctrine is, what kind of an equivalent is it to kill some one who is no better than a dog? Hence the family of the slain noble looks around to see if it can not find a relative of the murderer to wreak vengeance {108} upon, who is also a noble; while the murderer himself is ignored. If no noble can be found among his relatives, the family of the murdered man wait patiently till someone of them is received into the noble's estate; then, the vendetta is prosecuted, although many years may have elapsed (Blumentritt, 1891, p. 390).

The need to take revenge on a person of precisely the appropriate status may justifiably delay the vengeance killing. One imagines that this must discourage aspirations to higher social status in some societies.

Equivalence may refer not only to status but also to gender and age. Among the Nuba of Sudan, equivalence is so specific that a man must be killed for a man, a woman for a woman; and the age of the person killed in revenge is supposed to approximate that of the original victim (Nadel, 1947, p. 151). These sorts of strict requirements are customary among many peoples.

A question might arise as to who determines the equivalence. The equivalence is generally understood by those who belong to the society. Pospisil explains:

> Who, however, determines the equivalent? Implied in the writings of Radcliffe-Brown and Nadel is the notion that the criteria for equivalence are sufficiently objective, i.e., part of a general custom known to all, so that it is often unnecessary for a specified authority to deliver an opinion on the balance between the injury and revenge (1968, p. 389).

Kelsen furnishes us with a striking example of a society which followed the principle of retribution linked to equivalence. Even the cannibalistic natives of British New Guinea did not kill or eat their victims indiscriminately:

> [P]risoners taken in warfare were brought alive to the hamlet-group, where they would be tortured before being killed and eaten. This apparently occurred *only when* a prisoner was to be killed in payment for the death of a member of the captor's community, and in spite of the pleasure to be derived from a cannibal feast it was

clear that commonly prisoners would only be tortured and killed in such numbers that their deaths made the score even between their community and that of their captors (Seligman, 1910, Part 2, pp. 569-570—emphasis added).

Even cannibals do not exceed the bounds of equivalence. This suggests that the commitment to one for one may be shared on an extremely wide basis. {109}

ANIMAL VENGEANCE

The principle of retribution is highly important to "primitive man" according to Kelsen. Sometimes the death of a human caused by animals is interpreted as an act of vengeance:

> Hence the death of a human being caused by elephants, lions, tigers, or bears is often regarded as an act of vengeance of the animal or its kind. Indeed, it is a widespread primitive inclination to interpret a human death inflicted by an animal as an act of vengeance for some committed wrong (Kelsen, 1946, p. 83).

This may in part be derived from the belief that animals carry the spirits of ancestors. The killing of certain animals is often permitted only if the animal or its relatives have committed a wrong. The Kenyahs, for example, regard the crocodiles infesting their rivers as more or less friendly. Sometimes the attribution of friendliness leads to the death of one of them. It is believed that the person taken in some way offended or injured one or all of the crocodiles or that he was carried off by a stranger crocodile. At any rate, "it is considered that the crocodiles have committed an unjustifiable aggression and set up a blood-feud which can only be abolished by the slaying of one or more of the aggressors" (Hose & McDougall, 1901, p. 186).

The Dayak of Borneo kill an alligator only if it has killed a man. The natives of Madagascar never kill such an animal, "except in retaliation for one of their friends who has been destroyed by a crocodile. They believe that the wanton destruction of one of these reptiles will be followed by the loss of human life, in accordance with the principle of *lex talionis*" (Frazer, 1935, p. 214). This principle is important to the Batak of Sumatra, who regulate their behavior toward tigers according to the following formulation: "He who owes gold must pay gold: he who owes breath (that is, life) must pay breath" (1935, p. 216). The Kookies of the mountains to the northeast of the Chittagong province appear to be guided by the principle:

> The Kookies, like all savage people, are of a most vindictive disposition: blood must always be shed for blood; if a tiger even kills any of them near a *Parah*, the whole tribe is up in arms, and goes in pursuit of the animal; when if he is killed, the family of the deceased gives a feast of his flesh, in revenge of his having killed their relation. And should the tribe fail to destroy the tiger, in this first gen-

eral pursuit of him, the family of the deceased must still continue to {110} chase; for until they have killed either this, or some other tiger, and have given a feast of his flesh, they are in disgrace in the *Parah*, and not associated with, by the rest of the inhabitants. In like manner, if a tiger destroys one of a hunting party, or of a party of warriors, on a hostile excursion, neither the one nor the other (whatever their success may have been), can return to the *Parah*, without being disgraced unless they kill the tiger (Macrae, 1801, p. 189).

In the case of manslaughter, it is necessary among some peoples to perform a purification rite. An analogous purification is necessary when a man has killed certain animals, e.g., a lion. Killing an animal is considered as equal to the murder of a man by the natives of the Congo. The slaying of an elephant entails a sham prosecution of the successful hunter to avoid the vengeance of the slain beast. They also observe the usual identification rites customary for murdered enemies (Kelsen, 1946, p. 82).

The relationship of "primitive man" to plants is also determined by the principle of retribution. Kelsen explains: "Should one 'kill' them, that is cut them down, because they are necessary for the satisfaction of one's needs, then one must expect retribution" (1946, p. 93). The East Semang (Pangan) on the Malayan Peninsula believe that there is a "birth-tree" which is sympathetically connected with the life of a man. If the tree dies first, that is interpreted as a sign that the owner's death will follow. When one Semang kills another, except in war, he avoids the "birth-tree" for fear it will fall on him. The tree is considered the abode of the man's avenging spirit: "The real authority of retribution is the human death soul which is reincarnated in the plant" (Kelsen, 1946, p. 97).

Even natural disasters, accidents, illness, weather, misfortunes, and other phenomena are interpreted according to the principle of retribution (Kelsen, 1946, pp. 97-118).The Bakairi in central Brazil trace evil, especially illness and death, to the magical influence of members of other tribes (1946, p. 98). The Bororo Indians in central Brazil interpret death and illness as retribution exercised by slain animals of hunters. The Waspisianas in British New Guinea believe that a person never dies a natural death and would be eternal were it not for the kenaima or evil spirits which kill him or her (Farabee, 1967, p. 87). In South America, any sickness or deformity among newborn children is considered the result of supernatural influence (Kelsen, 1946, p. 99). When parents fall ill in the Fiji Islands, children sacrifice a finger joint because they believe that they will satisfy the desire for retribution of the superhuman authority who imposed the illness as punishment (Kelsen, 1946, p. 103). {111}

RETRIBUTION IN MAJOR WORLD RELIGIONS

It may appear that the only examples cited are from smaller-scale societies and that the principle of retribution might not be applicable to so-called modern societies. But since the major religions of the world, whose influence extends throughout the globe, contain provisions for *lex talionis*, there is reason to believe that the principle of retribution is shared by countries which follow these religious tenets as well.

The Judeo-Christian religious traditions take much from the Bible. There are numerous places in the Old Testament where *lex talionis* is mentioned. One of the most famous texts on retribution tied to equivalence appears in Chapter 21 of Exodus which has been extremely influential for both Christian and Jewish law:

> And if any mischief follows,
> then thou shalt give life for life,
>   Eye for eye, tooth for tooth,
> hand for hand, foot for foot,
>   Burning for burning, wound for
> wound, stripe for stripe.

(Exodus, 21:23-25, Holy Bible, King James, 1952).

Throughout the Bible there are references to the idea of blood guilt. After Cain killed Abel, God told him: "The voice of your brother's blood is crying to me from the ground" (Genesis 4:10). The idea that a wrong act sets something wrong in the universe which then clamors for vengeance is found in many religious systems. Also in Genesis one finds: "Who so sheddeth the blood of man, by man his blood shall be shed" (9:6). In Leviticus it says, "And he that killeth the life of a man shall surely be put to death" (24:17). The *lex talionis* formulation appears in one form in Deuteronomy: "And thine eye shall not pity; but life shall go for life, eye for eye, tooth for tooth, hand for hand, foot for foot" (19:21). For the subtleties in the interpretation of *lex talionis*, the reader should consult David Daube's meticulous study in *Studies in Biblical Law*, Chapter 3 (1969). There are certainly many passages in the Old Testament which support the principle of retribution. The *lex talionis* is intended to be applied at least in the case of murder. (For other Biblical references, see Jackson, 1973.) {112}

There may be a conflict between the Old and New Testaments on the interpretation of *lex talionis*. Fisher contends that there is no real issue since Judaism never favored a literalist or vindictive application of it (1982, p. 582). He maintains that the talion in a nonliteral sense of moral equivalency "has considerable force in the Hebrew scriptures and the New Testament alike" (1982, p. 585). Fisher takes talion to be a "general principle of moral equivalency" or proportionality. So, the two are not in conflict. Since, however, the talionis applied literally in the case of murder, at least according to the Old Testament, it remains unclear what position Christians would take on the death penalty. It is not obvious, especially because, even if humans are expected to turn the other cheek, this does not mean there will not be divine retribution. That is, human forgiveness does not preclude the possibility of divine vengeance. The point to be stressed is that the principle of retribution tied to proportionality is recognized in some of the major religious traditions in the world.

For the most part, it is applied literally in the case of murder, the debates about literal interpretation notwithstanding.

The right of retaliation appears in the Koran in Surah V, 49:

> Therein have we prescribed (as a law) for them: "A life for a life, an eye for an eye, a nose for a nose, an ear for an ear, a tooth for a tooth, and wounds are (an occasion for) retaliation"; so if anyone remit it as a gift, it is an expiation for him, but whoever does not judge by what Allah hath sent down—they are wrong-doers (R. Bell, 1960, Vol. 1, p. 100).

The last phrase expresses a prohibition against inflicting a punishment greater in magnitude than the crime. There is some evidence that Mohammed sought to substitute the custom of blood money for the *lex talionis*. Hardy (1963, p. 32) says that Mohammed wanted to emphasize the desirability of being merciful:

> O ye who have believed, retaliation in the matter of the slain is prescribed for you, the free for the free, the slave for the slave, the female for the female; ... In retaliation is life for you, O ye of insight: mayhap ye will show pity (Surah II, 173 and 175; R. Bell, 1960, Vol. 1, p. 24).

The Prophet tried to limit the retaliation to the payment of compensation in another passage (Surah IV, 94, 95). The desire of Mohammed to limit the use of the *lex talionis* may be commendable, but it is simply one attempt by the religious elite to displace traditional notions. Even Hardy recognizes that Mohammed could not hope to remove the *lex talionis*: {113}

> [W]hatever Mohammed's own wishes may have been (and it is clear enough that he encouraged clemency and the taking of blood money, particularly between believers) there is in fact little evidence that he actually tried to abolish the old procedures (Hardy, 1963, p. 29).

Presumably he did not seek to discard them because the belief in *lex talionis* was too deeply rooted.

Robert Roberts analyzes the murder provisions in the Koran and concludes that "...there seems to be no reason for taking the expression (*lex talionis*) either in the Qoran or in the Old Testament, other than in its strict literal sense as teaching perfect retaliation" (1971, pp. 87-88). He does applaud Mohammed for taking a step in the right direction, meaning his attempt to "abolish the cruel custom of retaliation" (1971, p. 89). He is impressed by the extent to which blood money exists. Following Mohammed's lead, a number of jurists tried to extend gradually the sphere in which there was a legal obligation to pay blood money in order to curtail private vengeance taken by the next of kin (Hardy, 1963, p. 325). The "unfailing obstacle" was the clear language of Surah XVII, 35, which sanctioned the avenger's right to exact punishment:

> Do not kill the person whom Allah hath made inviolable except with justification; if anyone is killed wrongfully, we give to his next-of-kin authority, but let him not be extravagant in killing; verily he has been helped (Bell, 1960, Vol. 1, p. 26).

The extravagance here refers to the limit of vengeance, taking only one life for one.

ANCIENT LAW

In ancient law there is evidence of the pre-Biblical importance of *lex talionis* and of blood money (Alt, 1934; Blau, 1916; Cohn, 1971; Daube, 1969; Dembitz, 1895; Diamond, 1957; Doron, 1969; DuCros, 1926; Finkelstein, 1936; Frymer-Kensky, 1980; Harris, 1924; Kugelmass, 1981: LaGrange, 1916; MacCormack, 1973; Tower, 1984; Weingreen, 1976). There is strikingly little said of homicide in the Code of Hammurabi (Driver & Miles, 1952, Vol. 1, p. 314). Nevertheless, it is worth considering this ancient code because it demonstrates how longstanding the acceptance of {114} *lex talionis* actually is. Despite the tendency in historical jurisprudence to ignore the Laws of Hammurabi, it is undeniable that they are an "original source of unique value" and trustworthy insofar as the actual monument on which they were inscribed by Hammurabi's order (ca. 1750 B.C.) has been preserved (Driver & Miles, 1952, Vol. 1, p. 56). In their marvelously detailed *Legal Commentary*, Driver and Miles state that in Assyria, as among the Hebrews, one who killed a man was subject to the blood feud, which presumably means that another life would have to pay for the loss of the first (1952, Vol. 1, p. 314). They say further that homicide in Babylonia might have given rise to a blood feud. Even though the laws are silent for the most part on the question of how to treat a homicide, there are three reasons to suspect that retribution followed *lex talionis*. First, there is little doubt that the blood feud was in force in Babylonia at some time partly because the practice existed in Assyria, in Palestine, and among the Arabs. Second, the entire system of punishment, according to Driver and Miles, "was based on talion, which is itself nothing but a legalized limitation of the vengeance of the blood-feud" (1952, Vol. 1, p. 60). Third, there is fragmentary evidence that a life paid for a life. An accuser who failed to prove his charge was supposed to be put to death immediately: "If a man has accused a man and has charged him with manslaughter and then has not proved (it against) him, his accuser shall be put to death" (Driver & Miles, 1956, Vol. 2, p. 13). It is not obvious why the accuser must be killed. Driver and Miles explain the logic:

> At first sight it is somewhat surprising to us that the law should punish an accuser with death if he fails to convict the accused: but, as said above, the penalty is merely a logical application of the rule of talion. The false accuser has sought the death of the accused and he therefore suffers "as he had thought to have done to his brother" (1952, Vol. 1, p. 62).

In section eleven, one who brings a false accusation of theft is liable for the penalty of theft, which is death. This does not appear to fit the usual interpretation of *lex talionis* since a life not actually lost is then repaid by another. Nevertheless, Driver and Miles claim these provisions prove that the Babylonians followed the *lex talionis*.

The stronger evidence which demonstrates the principle of retribution is found in Sections 229 and 230:

> (229) If a builder has built a house for a man and has not made his work sound, and the house which he has built has fallen down and so caused the death of {115} the householder, the builder shall be put to death.
>
> (230) If it causes the death of the householder's son, they shall put the builder's son to death (Driver & Miles, 1952, Vol. 1, p. 83).

These are clearly examples of the payment of one life for a life lost. Here also is acceptance of the strict proportionality which requires that the life taken be of a person of equivalent status, age, and gender. Another example of the law providing for life with life is Section 210. If a man strikes the daughter of a (free) man and causes her to lose the "fruit of her womb," Section 209 provides that he shall pay ten shekels of silver for the fruit of her womb. Presumably the fruit is not regarded as "human," or else a life would have to be paid for its loss of life. But if the man by striking the woman kills her, then they shall put his daughter to death. Section 210 exemplifies the requirement of taking a proportional revenge.

Sections 196 and 197 appear to be based on talion: "If a man has put out the eye of a free man, they shall put out his eye. If he breaks the bone of a (free) man, they shall break his bone" (Driver & Miles, 1956, Vol. 2, p. 77). There appears to be a class bias in the provisions for *lex talionis* in the code of Hammurabi. If a member of the upper class injured a servant, the offense was considered a violation of property rights. The payment of a monetary fine, presumably to the owner of the injured slave, was the normal punishment. If the violence involved two equal members of the ruling class, then strict physical talion was the rule (Fisher, 1982, p. 583).

There is great interest in identifying the origin of the *lex talionis*. Scholars have noted that the talion can be found in ancient law codes predating the Bible by many centuries. In Blau's comparison of the Mosaic and Hammurabi codes, he concludes that the Mosaic Code was not derived from the Babylonian Code. Both, he claims, were derived from a common ancient Semitic source "of which the Mosaic Code preserved much more in the original form than the Hammurabi Code" (Blau, 1916, p. 13). Some have claimed that the talion is cited and applied literally in the Mesopotamian law codes of Eshnunna (ca. 2000 B.C.), Lipit-Ishtar (ca. 1860 B.C.), and Hammurabi (1750 B.C.) (Fisher, 1982, p. 583; Frymer-Kensky, 1980, p. 231). Frymer-Kensky, relying on a growing body of evidence, argues that many of the ideas previously considered Babylonian may have had their origins not in Sumer or Akkad but in the traditions of the West Semites who migrated into Mesopotamia beginning around 2000 B.C. The argument is that the talionic principle may have been introduced by West Semites to Mesopotamia and not vice versa. {116}

The ancient data are important because they demonstrate that the *lex talionis* has been influential through history and also because it reveals that it was not the only sanction. Blood money also existed. For example, the Laws of Eshnunna provided that for all personal injuries short of death, the sanctions were pecuniary (Sections 42-48, Diamond, 1957, p. 151). Section 42 states that, "If a man bites the nose of another man and severs it, he shall pay one mina of silver. For an eye, one mina; for a tooth one-half mina; for a slap in the face ten shekels of silver" (Fisher, 1982, p. 583). Monetary substitution, that is, payment of claims and damages, existed along with physical retribution. There was a clear standard of proportionality reflected in the various fines imposed.

The fact that compensation is also of ancient origin is significant because it contradicts claims that there is a progression in law that is universal (Diamond, 1957, p. 153). David Daube has said that revenge and compensation existed at the same time, despite claims about historical stages with corresponding punishments. Daube rightly challenges the presumption that revenge and compensation are antithetical notions by pointing out that compensation was not a later achievement than punishment in criminal law (1969, p. 130). Compensation served as a form of punishment, and retaliation was regarded as restitutive: "Punishment constitutes compensation in both directions: the criminal, by suffering punishment, is making restitution to the offended party, and again, in suffering punishment, receives his due"(1969, p. 146). Daube suggests that the sources confirm how general and deep-rooted the idea was that criminals must pay for their deeds. Compensation for having committed a wrong is also an ancient idea.

Geoffrey MacCormack in "Revenge and Compensation in Early Law" (1973) agrees with Daube. He concludes that there is no evidence that societies in general, and their law, progressed from a stage characterized by revenge to a stage characterized by the payment of compensation. Nor is there proof that societies passed through a stage in which all wrongs were redressed by the exaction of revenge (1973, p. 83). Most societies appear to have had either revenge or compensation or both. What determines the type of redress is the relationship between the parties. Revenge is most frequently found in connection with killing. Others have noted that the *lex talionis* is literally applied in the case of homicide (Blau, 1916, p. 23; Harris, 1924, p. 7; Diamond, 1957, p. 151).

Since it seems clear that compensation was an established practice in earlier periods, Posner's claim that blood money was not used must be wrong. He asserted that in human history compensation was not used because "people probably lacked sufficient wealth, at least in transferable form" (1980a, p. 77). {117} This is highly unlikely since there was always some means of barter, e.g., cows and goats.

The main point is that retribution, both in the form of *lex talionis—*

strict proportionality—and in the form of blood money or compensation— general proportionality—existed in ancient civilizations. Daube extrapolates from the data on punishment and compensation, concluding that they are fundamental to any social order:

> The two notions are so frequent, they appear in sources so different in all other respects, they underlie terms so ancient ... and, it may be added, they are of so universal a nature, occurring in the ancient and modern literatures of all nations, that we must assume their existence right from the beginnings of any social life (1969, p. 146).

Kelsen holds that blood revenge is the manifestation of the "most ancient social norm; he who kills must be killed" (1946, p. 54). Even though it is often called the Mosaic formulation, the *lex talionis* appears to be widely shared:

> It has been pointed out long ere this that this law is far from being typically Jewish. It is rather human. There is not a race on earth that has not, in one form or another, practiced *Talio*. The Egyptians, the Babylonians, the Chinese; many primitive races and tribes; later on the Greeks and the Romans all accepted the *Talio* as the basis of their dealing with human wrongdoing. They applied it to all manner of offenses against property and persons. It therefore harks back, no doubt, to the primitive promptings of revenge whose gesture is the upraised fist. But who shall say that even the fist of vengeance was not raised to something higher than itself; that even in those early promptings there was not a dawning sense of justice, of that intolerance of evil which later made possible the rise and growth of social order (Blau, 1916, p. 4).

THE FEUD

The existence of *lex talionis* in many of the world's traditions is clearly found in the preceding ethnographic and religious data. In addition, this principle can be shown to underlie several major social processes. Although for this study it does not matter much what terms are used to describe the processes, the disagreement about terminology is somewhat important for the subsequent discussion of prevailing misconceptions about retribution. {118} There is considerable debate in the literature about what constitutes a feud and how it is to be distinguished from vengeance killing and warfare.

Pospisil reviews the basic definitions of the feud (1968, p. 389) and says that any violence between intimate groups cannot be regarded as a feud. Specific characteristics of the feud are: that the hostilities are prolonged and intermittent, that the two groups fighting each other must be related (intertribal, organized violence is war), and that it is allegedly "extra-legal." The main point is that a single fight cannot be defined as a feud. Pospisil claims that it is not justifiable to use the term feud unless there are more than two acts of violence. His reasoning is that it is only when the revenge is not equivalent to the initial injury that a feud is instigated. According to Pospisil:

> Hostile acts consisting of an injury and of an equivalent revenge that is accepted as final by both parties do not merit the term feud and should more properly be called self-redress. The nature of self-redress is, in most cases, basically different from the prolonged violence called feud (1968, p. 390).

In effect, the feud begins after the two killings when both sides do not perceive equivalence. This means the feud depends on the failure to satisfy *lex talionis*. Consequently, the feud is evidence for a commitment to the principle of *lex talionis*. In Europe the feud exists in Turkey (Stirling, 1960), Montenegro (Boehm, 1984), Albania (Elezi, 1966; Ellenberger, 1981; Hasluck, 1967), Corsica (Bisque, 1920; Ellenberger, 1981; Wilson, 1988), and Sardinia (Di Bella, 1980). Marc Bloch discusses how well established the feud was in medieval Europe: "No moral obligation seemed more sacred than this" (1961, p. 126). At every level of society the same custom prevailed: "Blood thus called for blood" (1961, p. 127). Since the whole of feudal Europe contained groups founded on the blood relationship, it is likely that retaliatory killings were pervasive in much of what is now divided up into nation-states, e.g., France, Germany, and Italy.

In Africa the custom of blood revenge has been studied among the Lendu, a Congolese people (Southall, 1956, p. 160), the Bedouin of Libya (Peters, 1967), the Acioli of Uganda (Boccassino, 1962), the Nuer of Sudan (Evans-Pritchard, 1963), the Nuba of Sudan (Nadel, 1947), the Tonga of Northern Rhodesia (Colson, 1953), natives of Central Africa (Kelsen, 1946, p. 56), the Kabyles of Algeria and the Jbala of Northern Morocco (Westermarck, 1924, Vol. 1, p. 484), the Moundang of Chad (Adler, 1980), the Massa and Moussey of Chad and Cameroun (Garine, 1980), the Bulsa of Northern Ghana (Schott, 1980), the Kabiye of Togo (Verdier, 1980), the Beti {119} of Cameroun (LaBurthe-Tolra, 1980), and the Damara mountain hunters of Southwest Africa (Thurnwald, 1930).

In Asia retaliatory killings have been documented in Japan (Dautremer, 1885; Mills, 1976), in China (Dalby, 1981; Meijer, 1980), and in Islamic South Asia (Dupree, 1980—specifically in Afghanistan and Pakistan).

Black-Michaud focuses on feuding in the Middle East and in the Mediterranean (1975). Another study of the Middle East which discusses conflict-resolution mostly in the context of blood money is Hardy's (1963). There are also data on blood revenge among the Bedouins of Jordan (Chelhod, 1980). In some Kurdish areas of northern Iraq there is evidence of the retaliatory principle at work (Barth, 1953).

Other societies in which the principle of retribution operates include the Australian aborigines (Hoebel, 1954, pp. 302-303; Pilling, 1957), the Huli of New Guinea (Glasse, 1959), the Tauade of New Guinea (Hallpike, 1977), the Kutubu of Papua (Kelsen, 1946, p. 61; Williams, 1941), the

Kalingas of the Philippine Islands (Gluckman, 1966, p. 22), the Quianganes of Luzon (Biumentritt, 1891), the Maori of New Zealand (Kelsen, 1946), the Brazilian aborigines (Westermarck, 1924, Vol. 1, p. 478), the Chorti Indians of Guatemala (Wisdom, 1940), the Eskimos (Boas, 1884-85), and the Hindus of India (Kelsen, 1946). "Feuding similar to the vendetta has been reported as being frequent among the Chukchi, Papago, Tallensi, Tlingit, Jivaro and Marshall Islander" (Anonymous, 1970b, p. 945). Westermarck, in a footnote, mentions a number of ethnographies which document blood revenge as a duty among such peoples of the Kandhs of India and the Feloops bordering on the Gambia (1924, Vol. 1, pp. 480-481, n. 10). The analysis of Karsten proves that the principle is certainly found among the Jivaro Indians of eastern Ecuador (1923).

The feud also existed in the United States in the recent past (Ayers, 1984; MacClintock, 1901 ; McCoy, 1976; Mutzenberg, 1916). One celebrated feud involved a Kentucky family named McCoy and another called Hatfield from nearby West Virginia and lasted from 1882 to roughly 1900 (Anonymous, 1970b; McCoy, 1976; Mutzenberg, 1917). There were numerous vendettas in Texas since the 1840s (Sonnichsen, 1971). Sonnichsen wants to dispel the stereotype of the feud in the South. He claims that feuding was not limited to the South and West (1951, p. xv). Rather, its occurrence was widespread across the United States. It occurred in border states, e.g., Arkansas, Alabama, Kansas, and California (1951, p. xviii). Thus, it appears that the feud is not an exotic custom practiced only in remote lands.

The feud is often, and perhaps wrongly, associated with "primitive societies." Keith and Charlotte Otterbein, in an article entitled "An Eye for an Eye, A Tooth for a Tooth: A Cross-Cultural Study of Feuding" (1965), {120} challenge the proposition that societies with a high degree of political complexity lack feuding. Their analysis, utilizing ethnographic materials from the Human Relations Area Files (HRAF), found no support for the hypothesis that the higher the level of political complexity, the less frequently feuding occurs (1965, p. 1476). Hoebel challenges their methodology by focusing on the problem of conceptual analysis of the feud (1976, p. 504). The methodological problems which he identifies bear on the question of the frequency of the feud but do not shed light on the issue of the psychological need for a response. Hoebel is convinced that there is a need: "But if we have strong grounds for doubting that feud occurs with anything like the frequency we have been led to believe, there is no question but that the folk belief in feud as a cultural expectancy, both as ideal and presumed behaviour, is widespread" (1976, p. 511).

It is interesting to see how the attempt to deny legal status to institutions in non-Western societies serves to denigrate their way of life. The presumption that only "primitive" societies have retribution, revenge, and feuds is reflected in the debate about the legal status of the feud. Many anthropologists claim that the feud lies outside of law. Hoebel takes this view (1976, pp. 500-501). Bohannan calls the feud "a faulty jural mechanism" because it does not lead to a final settlement (1963, p. 290). Radcliffe-Brown refuses to consider the feud law because it lacks "the exercise of recognized authority in settling disputes" (1940, p. xx). Pospisil claims that the feud does not fit the four attributes which he believes characterize law (1956). All of these explanations of the feud stem from the same misconception. Just because such action is considered "lawless" does not necessarily mean that the carefully controlled mechanism of the feud may not represent a legal system to peoples who do not have a centralized political authority.

BLOOD MONEY

Whereas the feud is an example of strict proportionality, the practice of paying blood money is an instance of general proportionality. The idea is that the punishment need not fit the crime identically. An equivalent penalty is considered sufficient to achieve retribution. It is worthwhile identifying the place in which the custom has been studied and then commenting upon some of the conditions under which it occurs.

Blood money is known to exist in the Middle East (Hardy, 1963), in such countries as Somalia (Contini, 1971), the Tonga of northern Rhodesia (Colson, 1953, p. 202), {121} the Bedouins of Libya (Peters, 1967, pp. 265-266), in Europe in Montenegro (Simic, 1967, p. 91), in Albania (Hasluck, 1967, p. 395), among the Australian aborigines (Pilling, 1957, pp. 148-149), among the Tauade (Hallpike, 1977, pp. 190, 212-230) and Huli (Glasse, 1959, p. 277) of New Guinea, the natives of New Caledonia (Leenhardt, 1930, p. 46), and the Jivaro Indians of eastern Ecuador (Karsten, 1923, p. 11). Westermarck discusses the practice in *The Origin and Development of the Moral Ideas* (1924, Vol. 1, pp. 477-496) in Chapter 20, "Blood Revenge and Compensation-the Punishment of Death": "custom allows the acceptance of compensation as a perfectly justifiable alternative for blood-revenge, or even regards it as the proper method for settling the case" (1924, Vol. 1, p. 488).

The Indians of western Washington and northwestern Oregon recognize the principle of life for life but still opt for material damages in some cases. Among the Tlingit, a certain number of blankets will atone for the murder of a relative. Blood money is expected to compensate for the murder of a relative by the California Karok. The Kuchin begin by demanding blood money for a slain kinsman, but avenge his death if compensation is denied. Among the Kandhs of rural Bengal, the custom of blood revenge has been modified to permit money compensation. The practice also exists among the Bedawee tribes in Egypt, the Aenezes, and the Wadshagge, among whom it is obligatory. Since among the Irish the village would not compel payment by the guilty party, failure to do so could result in the injured party' s avenging the wrong by reprisal. The practice of paying blood money presumably exists elsewhere but may not have been studied. There is no way to tell if it is mentioned in ethnographies since there is no index to this. It probably receives at least cursory treatment there. It appears, nevertheless, to be found in many parts of the world.

Often there is a choice between blood revenge and blood money. In general, blood money is regarded as an alternative to the *lex talionis:*

> Thus the exaction of life for life. from being a duty incumbent on the family of the dead, becomes a mere right of which they may or may not avail themselves, as they please, and is at last publicly disapproved of or actually prohibited (Westermarck, 1924, Vol. 1, p. 489).

Among some peoples, blood money is considered dishonorable. In parts of Albania this is the case (Hasluck, 1967, p. 395; Westermarck, 1924, Vol. 1, p. 487). It is also true of the Konso of Ethiopia (Hallpike, 1975, pp. 114-115) and the Beni Amer, Marea, the Kabyles, and Jbala (Westermarck, 1924, Vol. 1, p. 457). In Montenegro, although the pacification {122} of feuds might depend on the payment of blood money, when this occurred, it was considered to be a painful loss and a dishonor to have stopped before blood retaliation had taken place (Boehm 1984, pp. 106-107).

Several examples of scales should indicate the range of proportions which exists. Hardy explains how jurists determined the appropriate amount of blood money in the Middle East. The three modes of payment of *diya* or blood money were camels, gold, or money. The amount of *diya* at the time of Caliph Omar was one thousand gold dinars or ten thousand dirhem, the approximate cost of the alternative one hundred camels (1963, p. 37). Other modes of payment included cattle, sheep, or clothes. Among the Nuer of Sudan forty to fifty heads of cattle are paid, at least in theory (Evans-Pritchard, 1963, p. 153). In practice only twenty are handed over following the ceremonies of atonement. In the case of injuries rather than loss of life there are also specific proportionalities. Evans-Pritchard says that it is possible to obtain from the Nuer a list of compensations for injuries to the person: ten heads of cattle for a broken leg or skull, ten heads of cattle for the loss of an eye, two heads of cattle for a girl's broken teeth, and so on. Interestingly, there is no compensation for a flesh wound unless the man dies. Evidently, the compensatory standards vary in different parts of Nuerland (1963, p. 167).

The Mae Enga of the central New Guinea highlands place the value of life at forty pigs. Since, however, the Mae Enga clan often had numerous transactions underway, the compensation of pigs was renegotiated, stalled, or avoided rather than paid in full promptly. As with the Nuer, the ideal compensation might not be paid (Boehm, 1984, p. 213). Among the Huli, also of New Guinea, a thief who steals a pig has to repay the owner five or six pigs in compensation (Glasse, 1959, p. 286). Death payments vary between 30 and 150 pigs depending upon the circumstances (1959, p. 277).

Another noteworthy proportionality concerns the value of woman as compared with man. In some societies the value of the female is precisely half that of the male (Albania—Hasluck, 1967, p. 395; Middle East—Hardy, 1963, p. 39; Libya—Peters, 1967, p. 270). At the same time that proportionality is affected by gender, it remains, in some places, unaffected by age. Payment for an eighty-five-year-old man and a young man were the same in Albania (Hasluck, 1967, p. 395).

There are some practices which differ from the standard payment of blood money. For instance, among the Berbers of Southern Morocco, a man who commits a murder must flee to another tribe and place himself under its protection. His relatives pay blood money to the family of the victim to ensure that the offended party does not take revenge on them. This does {123} not, however, entitle the murderer to return. If he does, he is liable to be killed (Westermarck, 1924, Vol. 1, p. 488).

Occasionally, the payment takes the form of a person. Sometimes, instead of being killed, the murderer is adopted as a member of the family of his victim. This is known to occur among the Kabyles of Algeria (Westermarck, 1924, Vol. 1, p. 484). In another variation, the murderer will persuade the victim's clan not to retaliate by giving the avenger his sister or daughter in marriage. This custom has been noticed among the Jbala, the Beni Amer, and the Bogos. Among the Nuba of Sudan one finds the institution called *nmar*. The kin group avoids blood revenge by offering one of its own members to the victim's clan to take the victim's place. The person surrendered has to correspond in sex and age to the victim (Nadel, 1947, p. 152). If the exchanged man is married, he must leave his wife and must not visit his former family. If the exchanged person does not behave, the adoptive parents can complain to the chief who might summon the man to warn him to fulfill his obligations (1947, p. 153). Sometimes the victim's family also demands blood money, i.e., three or four cows, in addition to the *nmar* exchange.

Among certain North American Indians the feelings of a desolate mother whose son had been brutally murdered were assuaged by adopting the murderer in place of her slain son (Krappe, 1944, p. 183). Providing a spouse to the widow was another practice. According to one account, a widow whose husband had been murdered might be consoled by marrying the murderer (Krappe, 1944, p. 183). Among the Habe hillmen of the French Sudan, a murderer was expected to supply the family of the victim with a woman from his own family. When she bears a son, he is given the name of the murdered man; and then the two families "are once more on the best of terms" (Krappe, 1944, p. 184). Sometimes the offender's family gives slaves to the relatives of the slain to atone, i.e., to compensate, for the guilt (Westermarck, 1924, Vol. 1, p. 484).

One might well wonder what the effect of blood money is. One view is that it provides a deterrent to murder. Hasluck writes of the practice in Albania: "The fear of having to pay a large sum in blood money was therefore a considerable deterrent against murder" (1967, p. 395). The opposite view is that compensation actually encourages violence. In his conclusions about the Tauade of New Guinea, Hallpike maintains that compensation promotes killings:

> While compensation put an end to particular sequences of vengeance killings, or prevented them from starting, it must also have

produced a greater *total* incidence {124} of homicide, since a killer knew that he would be able to "buy off" the relatives of the victim.so that even his kin and neighbours would not have to suffer as a result of his action (1977, p. 230).

The basic notion is that collective responsibility in the case of *lex talionis* ensures that members of the community monitor each other to prevent killings for which any one of them might be killed in response. When the retribution is simply money or beasts, the group need not supervise the activities of its members as closely.

The dominant view in the literature seems to be that the payment of blood money restores the balance in society which was upset. Peters refers to the purpose of blood money as being "restoring peaceful relationships" (1967, p. 267). Among the natives of New Calendonia, the peace concluded after a battle is only complete when "the old balance of life is reestablished between the victor and vanguished" (Leenhardt, 1930, p. 46). Every life lost in the battle is replaced by money representing the dead man. After the two parties count their dead and exchange money, order is restored.

Retribution, according to Kelsen, means punishment and reward (1946, p. 60). So, restitution is one form of retribution and as shown above is tied to a principle of proportionality. Although in theory retribution is distinguished from restitution because it is offender-oriented whereas restitution is victim oriented, restitution is retributive. Therefore, blood revenge and blood money are both retributive.

THREE MISCONCEPTIONS

This section will address three objections to the foregoing analysis. There is a danger that the reader may suffer from three basic misconceptions. First, the meaning of "innocence" in connection with the doctrine of collective responsibility will be explained. Second, the limiting nature of the *Lex talionis,* the feud, and blood revenge will be discussed to show that they preserve order and are highly controlled social mechanisms. Third, there will be a brief reminder that blood money represents a form of retribution tied to proportionality.

Collective Responsibility

It is crucial to understand the doctrine of collective responsibility. As should be clear from the examples already cited, when a person is killed, {125} the principle of retribution requires that someone of equivalent stature, age, and the same gender be killed. This means that the group to which the original offender belongs is collectively responsible for the act and must be prepared to suffer retaliation. In addition, the original act is regarded as an injury to the whole group to which the victim belongs (family, clan, or village), and so the members of the victim's group have an obligation to avenge the injustice. This means that collective responsibility attaches to both the offender's and the victim's groups.

Several examples should give some indication of how far-reaching this doctrine is. Among the Nuba of Sudan, Nadel reports:

> The duty to avenge the death devolves, not on an individual, but on the whole clan.... Again, the revenge is not directed against an individual—the murderer himself—but against any member of the enemy clan who satisfies the conditions of this law of revenge (1947, p. 151).

In Albania, "...expiation might be made by any male who lived in the same house as the murderer and was in either the actual or classificatory sense his 'father,' 'brother,' or 'son' " (Hasluck, 1967, p. 393). The rule had several important reservations. The man killed in the stead of the murderer could not be too old, feeble-minded, or physically frail because such men counted as women. Unless a man of equivalent stature was killed, the feud would not be closed (1967, p. 393). The Tauade of New Guinea hold this view of responsibility:

> When a member of one tribe was killed, no attempt was made to retaliate upon the murderer in person, however long a period of time elapsed before vengeance was taken. It was sufficient that any member of the killer's tribe paid with his life, and in some cases the injured tribe was satisfied if their victim came from the general area of the killer's tribe (Hallpike, 1977, p. 198).

Interestingly, there is considerable social pressure to accept compensation in lieu of vengeance killing. Since the relatives of the killer are at risk, as will be the relatives of the victim if the vengeance killing is of someone of high status, there is great interest in seeing the matter settled through the payment of blood money (1977, p. 192).

Some explanation must be offered for the doctrine of collective responsibility. Otherwise some might mistakenly be under the impression that retribution, as it is practiced in the cultures considered, undermines the presumption of innocence which is held in high esteem in the West. Hall is guilty of this misinterpretation. In a discussion of the universality of collective {126} responsibility in the past, he claims that it resulted in the punishment of the innocent:

> Because collective responsibility means strict liability, the punishment of innocent persons, it is abhorrent to the modern mind.... Nevertheless, the universality of collective responsibility in past ages, the group mind-set rather than individualism (although alleviated from early times by pleas to spare the innocent), the likelihood that a deterrence was also advanced by the threat to punish a wrongdoer's family, clan or nation—these and other factors described above made acceptance of the concept of collective responsibility natural and normal (1983, pp. 290-291).

From his Western perspective, collective responsibility does violate the idea of punishing only the person who committed the act in question. But it must be recognized that from the point of view of other societies the entire group is considered guilty or responsible. It is important to acknowledge this different understanding of responsibility. The vengeance killing is not, therefore, regarded as arbitrary so long as it is accepted that the first offense was actually committed by a member of the group which must suffer the retaliatory killing. Thus, since the membership of the offender's group is not innocent, this way of looking at responsibility, as exemplified by Hall, must be considered ethnocentric.

It is quite possible that collective responsibility not only satisfies the need for revenge but also provides an immensely powerful deterrent to violence. The group will try to restrain its own members in order to avoid retaliatory action. If a person harms someone in another group, the entire community could be put in jeopardy. If the person engages in this sort of action frequently, he or she may eventually be ostracized. The group forswears responsibility for the individual's sporadic, violent acts. Collective responsibility serves to limit the extent to which individuals become embroiled in violent activities.

The Function of Retribution

One of the most important features of retribution, which is often overlooked, is its function as a limit to violence. In fact, *lex talionis* ensures that one life is taken for one life (Margolin, 1933-34, p. 758; Posner, 1980a, p. 82). Blau interprets the *lex talionis* in this "limiting sense of '*only one* life for a life'—no more; '*only one* eye for an eye'—no more" (1916, p. 8). {127} Fisher agrees: "*only* an eye for an eye, *only* a tooth for a tooth" (1982, p. 583). Director of the Institute of Judeo-Christian Studies at Seton Hall University J. M. Oesterreicher adds:

> The principle's demand for punishment commensurate to the crime makes it look like the codification of vengeance. In reality, it seeks to restrain humans' insatiable thirst for retaliation: Take a tooth and be done with it (1980, p. 16).

The original intention behind the talion was "to limit the escalating cycle of the practice of blood vengeance clans and families" (Fisher, 1982, p. 583). Evidently, the ancients viewed the principle as a means of preventing greater penalties than would be just.

The reference to blood vengeance just mentioned by Fisher could be misleading since he implies that it is out of control. Moreover, the feud attempts to achieve *lex talionis* which, as just shown, is a limit. The feud is a device for preventing violence. One should recall the important point made earlier which is that when both sides perceive the first killing and the counterkilling as canceling each other out, violence ceases. The feud exists and continues only so long as the parties involved fail to achieve mutual agreement that the principle of *lex talionis* has been observed.

The aim of the feud has been described as "limited destruction: retribution for a specific injury" (Glasse, 1959, p. 285). Boehm's analysis of the Montenegrin feud includes what he calls two critical elements of conflict management: the deliberate limitation of conflict and a deliberate attempt to resolve the conflict (1984, p. 87). Boehm characterizes the blood feud as "highly patterned" and not willful and random manifestations of violence (1984, p. 152). This "controlled activity" depends on a basic acceptance of the loss of life and an attempt to limit it (1984, pp. 142, 189). Karsten's perceptive analysis of blood revenge among the Jivaro Indians of eastern Ecuador emphasized that the punishment should be meted out with justice "in so far that for one life which has been taken only one life should be taken in retaliation" (1923, p. 13). Even if the opportunity for killing more presents itself, the Jivaro Indian kills only one member of the murderer's family, if not the murderer. Thus, the standard serves as a restraint. As noted earlier, this norm is clearly understood by the community and tends to limit retaliatory practices, as it requires taking only one life in exchange for another.

Many writers pinpoint the reasons why the feud discourages violence. It drives parties to seek peace (Boehm, 1984, pp. 207, 140), and collective responsibility creates a deterrent (Simic, 1967, p. 91). Evans-Pritchard says {128} that the fear of incurring a blood feud is the most important legal sanction within a tribe and the main guarantee of an individual's life and property (1963, p. 150).

Feuds are highly structured, rule-based conflicts and are, therefore, not unlimited. Boehm, for example, describes the Montenegrin feud as the acting-out of homicidal conflict on the basis of cultural rules (1984, p. 53). Moreover, he insists from the outset that not only do the Montenegrins follow rules for revenge killing, but also that they understand their own feuding behavior quite well (1984, p. xi). A consideration of several procedures should reveal the limitations inherent in the feud.

A vengeance killing ordinarily occurs only between two groups. For if there were a counterkilling within the group, it would suffer a double loss instead of one death balancing out another (Boehm, 1984, p. xii; MacCormack, 1973, p. 81). Karsten reports this perception of the Jivaro Indians: " 'It is enough that one member of our family has died,' they say, 'why should we deprive ourselves of one more?' " (1923, p. 13). There are sometimes rules providing that certain persons are exempt from retaliatory killings, e.g., guests (Boehm, 1984, p. 153) and women (Ellenberger, 1981, p. 126). There are often rules about who specifically may avenge the death of the victim. Sometimes it is the father or older brother, but never a woman. Mills, in an article about premodern Japan, provides an example of specific rules as to who may avenge a death. In the matter of vengeance, the son might avenge his father and a younger brother his elder brother, but it was not considered proper for an elder brother to avenge his younger brother nor for an uncle to avenge his nephew (1976, p. 536). In Albania, a murdered man would be avenged by his brother. If his father was not too old and his son not too young to bear arms, then they shared the duty with the brother (Hasluck, 1967, p. 382—who explains other, more complicated rules about who could and could not avenge a death). It is generally accepted that the person killed in retaliation should be the murderer or a close kinsman (MacCormack, 1973, p. 80—see n. 44; Colson, 1962, p. 106; Contini, 1971, p. 78; Karsten, 1923, p. 11). A woman could not be killed in retaliation (except for a slain woman) because she was valued only at half and would, therefore, not provide the proper proportionality. Ellenberger presents the fundamental traits of the vendetta and emphasizes the degree to which the vendetta is rule-bound (1981, p. 126). For example, "one does not avenge the death of a total stranger" or "a murder committed within the family" (1981, p. 126). Not only are there rules about whose deaths shall be avenged but there are rules about who may avenge the deaths: "The method of designating avengers follows well defined rules" (1981, p. 126). {129}

In some societies, such as Japan, the avenger had to request permission (Dautremer, 1885, p. 84; Mills, 1976, p. 536; Westermarck, 1924, Vol. 1, p. 471). Sometimes there is a requirement that the revenge be taken within a certain time period. Pilling describes a rule among the Australian aborigines that resembles a statute of limitations (1957, p. 105). The reaction to an offense normally occurred within a year. Four years was considered "too far," and the offense would not be punished. Where the line was drawn between one and four years is not clear. Nevertheless, there is a rule or understanding about how much time could elapse before punishment would cease to be legitimate. Societies have various restrictions concerning lime. In Albania, for instance, there was the rule of "boiling blood." This means that any member of the victim's tribe had twenty-four hours to kill a man from the murderer's tribe. Some societies make a distinction between taking revenge for injuries and other offenses, and for homicide. DiBella explains the practice in Sardinia among the Barbagia: "Vengeance must be taken within reasonable time limits with the exception of a blood offense for which there is never a prescribed limit" (1980, p. 41). A proverb expresses this: "A death is never forgotten, not even in a hundred years" (1980, p. 42). There are other sorts of limitations on taking revenge. For example, in Albania a murderer must not rob his victim. The killing was to defend the original victim's honor and not to enrich his family (Hasluck, 1967, p. 389). There was one exception to this rule. A murderer could ordinarily take the victim's rifle to prove he had "really trodden in his blood," but afterward he had to return the weapon to the victim's family.

Not only is blood revenge viewed as a sacred duty, but it is part of filial piety. Moreover, the process of taking revenge, in fact, leads to mutual forgiveness. Colson observes that the point is not to punish but to restore harmony (1953, p. 204). Furthermore, it is specifically retaliation which makes forgiveness possible. Admittedly, the standard meaning of forgiveness implies forgiving the act just committed without retaliating (as in turning the other cheek). But forgiveness in other social contexts requires action. Boehm, for example, comments that retaliatory killing is morally necessary (1984, p. 89). After the death is canceled out by another death, there is a particular ceremony of pacification. Following the ceremony the parties express "full forgiveness of the past" (Boehm, 1984, p. 136).

Other societies likewise have a ceremony which leads to forgiveness, e.g., some in the Middle East (Hardy, 1963, p. 87). Among the Bedouins there is a ceremony after a peace meeting is held to acknowledge the acceptance that the killings have canceled each other out. The meeting deliberations are followed by a meal at which all present eat from one bowl. When the meal is over, {130} they pray together. "A life had been taken for a life and the way is now open for the restoration of normal peaceful relationships" (Peters, 1967, p. 265). The Iroquois have a custom whereby the murderer sends white wampum to the family of his victim. If it is accepted, then the memory of the deed is wiped out forever. It is described as a "petition for forgiveness" (Westermarck, 1924, Vol. 1, p. 485). The Albanian feud involves a process of peacemaking (Hasluck, 1967, pp. 404-405). Peace is seldom made unless the same number has been killed on both sides. It is generally made through an intermediary since the enemy might otherwise arrogantly refuse the request. He cannot ignore the pleadings of friends. Among the Eskimos a feud may be settled by mutual agreement. Boas reports that as a sign of reconciliation both parties touch each other's breasts and say "Il-aga" (my friend) (1884-85, p. 582).

Even if the process of taking revenge strikes one as abhorrent, it is undeniably an effective mechanism for restoring social cohesion. Among the Nuba of Sudan it is only when the same number of individuals has been killed that "the account is squared on both sides." At that point, the balance is considered to have been reached and the feud lapses. Until then the two clans cannot drink beer together, in their homes or elsewhere, lest leprosy befall them (Nadel, 1947, p. 151).

Those who believe that the feud is simply spontaneous violence are misinformed. Virtually every scholar who has investigated the feud comments on the specific formalities, procedures, and rules which govern the feud. Boehm maintains that "...revenge killing is controlled as carefully as possible" (1984, p. 229).

Interpretation of Blood Money

The third misconception concerns the interpretation of blood money. It is arbitrary to insist that compensation is conceptually distinct from punishment. With the victim's rights movement there is growing awareness that requiring a criminal to pay restitution to his victim constitutes punishment for him. Restitution is a form of retribution. The practice of blood money does not show that *lex talionis* has been discredited historically or otherwise. The empirical data reveal that the decision to apply the *lex talionis* or to require the payment of blood money depends on the context. When the case involves unintentional homicide, compensation is quite often regarded as sufficient. When the two sides grow weary of battle, even where *lex talionis* is the norm, the agreement to accept blood or wound money {131} is appropriate to achieve reconciliation. So there is no necessary dichotomy between the *lex talionis* and blood money. Both are forms of retribution tied to proportionality, strict proportionality for *lex talionis* and general proportionality for blood money.

THE PRINCIPLE OF RETRIBUTION AND
RESPECT FOR HUMAN LIFE

Some might take the view that the feud, vendetta, vengeance killing, and other retaliatory killings reflect a lack of respect for human life. This is perhaps not the correct interpretation of these practices. One could just as well advance the argument that it is precisely because human life is sacred that a group has the duty to avenge the death of one of its members. If life were not valued highly, then there would be little reason to bother with revenge. Some might try to refute this contention by arguing that it is purely fear which motivates the group to retaliate. Although there may be some kernel of truth to this claim, it does not refute the original proposition that human life is sacred. If the group taking revenge were only interested in terrorizing the other group to ensure that it not attack again, it would have no reason to limit the counter-act to one life. The context is not warfare but the feud. It should be noted that even in warfare among some peoples there must be an exact balance in the numbers of dead on each side. Peace cannot be restored until compensation is paid to even the score. The application of the *lex talionis* of a life for a life is not a bloodthirsty rule. It epitomizes the supreme value of life.

Sally Falk Moore has astutely remarked that all societies have doctrines of restraint. They have clear limits on violence:

> I have no doubt that there is some form of restraining doctrine in all societies. Even in self-help systems, there are clear limitations on sanctioned violence. One must not harm except to right a wrong, or even a score, and then only in prescribed ways and circumstances (1972, p. 67).

Although her analysis is devoted to distinctions among different types of legal liability, she is generally persuaded that violence is not the creed of any society.

This point is also made by Kelsen who states that no tribes permit indiscriminate killing: "The social order of primitive man normally {132} guarantees, with all the means at its disposal, the preservation of human life within the community. This is true even of the most primitive community" (1946, pp. 53-54). Kelsen draws on the work of Tylor and Westermarck. Tylor remarked that "no known tribe, however low and ferocious, has ever admitted that men may kill one another indiscriminately" (1873, p. 714). Westermarck is in agreement with this proposition:

> It is commonly maintained that the most sacred duty which we owe our fellow-creatures is to respect their lives. I venture to believe that this holds good not only among civilised nations, but among the lower races as well; and that, if a savage recognises he has any moral obligations at all to his neighbours, he considers the taking of

their lives to be a greater wrong than any other kind of injury inflicted upon them (1924, Vol. 1, p. 328).

If the interpretation of the data is accepted and the views of these eminent social theorists are compelling, then there is reason to believe that most peoples in the world reject arbitrary, indiscriminate killing. MacCormack states that the "taking of revenge is understood in a rather restricted sense" (1973, p. 80). Based on descriptions of homicide in African societies, he concludes that, "There is nothing indiscriminate or vindictive in the reaction by the kin of a person who has been slain.... On the contrary, there prevails what may be called a principle of equilibrium" (1973, p. 80). Pollis and Schwab also believe that no cultural or ideological system condones "arbitrary and indiscriminate destruction of life or incarceration" (1979b, p. 15). (If their claim is based on any empirical research or observations, this is not made clear.)

Westermarck provides an interesting twist to the discussion. When comparing the punishments of "civilized" and "savage" peoples, one finds, says Westermarck, that "Wanton cruelty is not a general characteristic of their (savage) public justice" (1924, Vol. 1, p. 188). He notes that among several "uncivilized" peoples capital punishment is unknown or almost so (1924, Vol. 1, p. 189). To support this claim, he presents ethnographic materials on a number of cultures. If anyone has violated *lex talionis*, it is the "civilized" peoples: "We find that among various semi-civilised and civilised peoples the criminal law has assumed a severity which far surpasses the rigour of the *lex talionis*" (1924, Vol. 1, p. 186). While few crimes are punishable by the death penalty among the "savages," in Europe numerous offenses were capital. One might consider England, for example:

> From the Restoration to the death of George III—a period of 160 years—no less than 187 such offences, wholly different in character and degree, were added {133} to the criminal code; and when, in 1837 the punishment of death was removed from about 200 crimes, it was still left applicable to exactly the same offences as were capital at the end of the thirteenth century. Pocket-picking was punishable with death until the year 1808; horse-stealing, cattle-stealing, sheep-stealing, stealing from a dwelling-house, and forgery, until 1832; letter-stealing and sacrilege, until 1835; rape, until 1841; robbery with violence, arson of dwelling-houses, and sodomy, until 1861. And not only was human life recklessly sacrificed, but the mode of execution was often exceedingly cruel (1924, Vol. 1, pp. 187-188).

The Maoris were horrified by the English method of executing criminals, first telling them they are to die and then letting them lie for days and nights in prison until finally leading them slowly to the gallows. "If a man commits a crime worthy of death, " they said, "we shoot him, or chop off his head; but we do not tell him first that we are going to do so" (1924, Vol. 1, p. 190).

It seems that all cultures have mechanisms which are intended to limit violence and to prevent needless killing. But if any comparison is to be drawn, then it is the "modern" societies which have tended to have more repressive punishments than the "savages." Westermarck's data contradict the historical state theory put forward by such scholars as Diamond and Durkheim. In fact, smaller-scale societies are much more likely to accept restitution for a crime that could bring the death penalty than are larger nation-states.

RETRIBUTION AS NEGATIVE RECIPROCITY

It may not be obvious why the principle of retribution tied to proportionality should be so important to most, if not all, human societies. Perhaps a consideration of retribution as a form of negative reciprocity will shed light on this. Some have claimed that reciprocity is a fundamental characteristic of all societies (Malinowski, 1949; Mauss, 1954). Howard Becker, for example, entitled one of his books *Man in Reciprocity* (1956) and called the human species *Homo reciprocus*. Hobhouse also claimed that "reciprocity ... is the vital principle of society" (1915, p. 12) without which the formation of rules would not be possible. Since society could not exist in the absence of rules, reciprocity yields social stability. Thurnwald believed that the principle of reciprocity was of central importance and "pervades every relation of primitive life" (1930, p. 106). Simmel emphasized the {134} significance of the principle not only for "primitive" societies but for all human civilizations: "All contacts among men rest on the schema of giving and returning the equivalence" (1950, p. 387). Social equilibrium and cohesion would not be possible without "the reciprocity of service and return service" (1950, p. 387).

Although reciprocity has been discussed in the positive sense, e.g., gift exchange, only a few scholars have noted that its negative dimension is retribution (Brown, 1986; Hallpike, 1975, p. 117; Kelsen, 1946, p. 63). Frans de Waal, for example, has commented on the failure of scholars to analyze negative reciprocity: "Negative behaviour hardly enters into the theories about reciprocity which anthropologists and sociobiologists have developed" (1982, p. 205). He highlights the importance of reciprocity in both its positive and negative forms and concludes that: "Whether what is involved is the returning of a favour or the seeking of revenge, the principle remains one of exchange (1982, p. 206). The reciprocal basis of human exchange appears to be a basic characteristic of society. It should not be surprising, therefore, that the principle of retribution is global since it is one type of reciprocity.

Kelsen certainly agrees that reciprocity and retribution are dominant features of social life. He disagrees, however, about which is prior. He appears to claim that the principle of retribution is more fundamental than that of reciprocity:

The idea of an equivalence between the wrong sustained and the wrong to be inflicted is characteristic of the principle of retribution. This makes retribution appear a kind of exchange, although it is more correct to consider exchange a special kind of retribution (1946, p. 60; 1941, p. 534).

Indeed, Kelsen is so convinced of the fundamental character of the principle of retribution that he even believes that the notion of causality is based on retribution (1941). Whether one considers retribution primary and making up reciprocity through negative and positive forms or whether one sees reciprocity as prior and retribution as the negative form only, it seems clear that the two are inextricably linked.

In a classic article on reciprocity as a moral norm and one of the universal principal components of all moral codes, Gouldner distinguishes between two types of reciprocity (1960, p. 172). Heteromorphic reciprocity means that the things exchanged may be concretely different but should be equal in value. Homeomorphic reciprocity means that exchanges should be concretely alike or identical in form. Gouldner's two types of reciprocity {135} may be applied to blood money and *lex talionis*, respectively. In fact, he identifies homeomorphic reciprocity with the talionic formulation:

> Historically, the most important expression of homeomorphic reciprocity is found in the *negative* norm of reciprocity, that is, in sentiments of retaliation where the emphasis is placed not on the return of benefits but on the return of injuries, and is best exemplified by the *lex talionis* (1960, p. 172).

In an intriguing article on the idea of justice, Krappe also remarks on the relationship between *lex talionis* and reciprocity: "In the main ... the *ius talionis* is merely the expression of the same conception as absolute reciprocity" (1944, p. 184). He further notes that a striking example of the reciprocity he associates with justice is furnished by intertribal slayings (1944, p. 182). Finally, he suggests that reciprocity is the essential ingredient of justice:

> [W]e may recall that the symbol of justice is the balance, a form of symbolism which may or may not be older than the rise of trade in the great river valleys. At all events. it expresses the idea of reciprocity and seems to indicate that reciprocity is an essential, perhaps the most essential, element in the complicated concept of justice (1944, pp. 180-181; see also Kelsen, 1941, p. 537).

CONCLUSION

Some may ask what the precise relationship is between principles and rights. There is no necessary connection. But where it is possible to demonstrate acceptance of a moral principle or value by all cultures, it will be feasible to erect human-rights standards. The reality of universality depends on marshaling cross-cultural data.

The question remains as to which specific human rights can be derived from the apparently universal principle of retribution. If the present interpretation of the principle is accepted, namely that cultures are committed to limits on arbitrary killing and violence, then what are the practical implications for universal human-rights standards? It is not claimed that the principle will clarify all moral debates about killings. For instance, it will not resolve the arguments about infanticide and abortion, for some societies view these acts as arbitrary, unjustified killings while others will take the opposite view. {136}

Nevertheless, the demonstration of a principle is not an empty gesture. Worldwide support for the principle indicates that were we to hold a global referendum on international human rights, all societies, if they were to vote according to their own ideals, would unanimously favor certain standards. In particular, they would endorse the principle that "No one shall be arbitrarily deprived of his life" (Article 6(1), International Covenant of Civil and Political Rights). (This is not to say that they would subscribe to the other provisions of this article, e.g., the inherent right to life.) It would follow that they would also agree with Article 6(3) of the Covenant and the Convention on the Prevention and Punishment of the Crime of Genocide, both of which condemn the arbitrary deprivation of life that is genocide.

The use of the term "arbitrary" in international documents may strike some as unhelpful for the simple reason that different societies will have different ideas about what constitutes arbitrariness. Nonetheless, in some instances cultures will share an understanding that specific acts are arbitrary. When it comes to genocide, this is universally regarded as wrong. No society believes in the *ideal* of genocide.

Any form of killing which lacks justification, e.g., summary executions, would be contrary to the universal principle of retribution. The principle depends on the notion that an act occurs in response to a prior wrongful act. In the absence of the prior wrong, no society tolerates killing. I would go so far as to argue that some forms of arbitrary violence might also be contrary to the principle of retribution inasmuch as they lack justification. Retribution does not apply to killings only. The infliction of punishment for no crime, e.g., torture, would arguably violate the notion of retribution.[31]

According to the principle of retribution, a victim has the right to seek redress of grievance, whether the perpetrator of the act is a private citizen or the state. Since the principle requires that wrongful acts be punished, this entails punishment for officials of the state who commit crimes. That is, in cases where the state causes individuals to vanish or uses torture as a method to extract information, punishment should be imposed. A universal right to retribution would strengthen the demand by citizens that dictators suffer the consequences for harming innocents. Of course, some governments may try to manipulate statutes which classify virtually anyone as an enemy of the state. But generally speaking, those who disappear have not committed an act that the society to which they belong would consider a crime. Just because political elites use transparent and retroactive laws to justify their ruthless means, this does not undercut the power of a right to retribution. Those responsible for the actions of the state should be punished according to the right to retribution.

Ultimately, the search for cross-cultural universals must be realistic. Even the discovery of a moral principle embraced on a universal basis may not be translated easily into particular human rights. But this approach offers the possibility of grounding international human rights in reality instead of naturalistic abstractions. By identifying principles that are shared, we can construct standards which could be implemented because they are based on values meaningful in all cultural contexts. So, while infanticide remains debatable, the plight of the disappeared, the victims of death squads, etc., can be the legitimate focus of international concern. Despite striking cultural diversity, there are some areas of moral agreement.

The present argument holds that negative reciprocity or retribution tied to proportionality in its various forms serves two main purposes. It constitutes an essential ingredient in most peoples' conceptions of justice and as such is ubiquitous, and these social processes, if properly interpreted, reflect a profound commitment to a limitation on violence. If there is universal support for a principle based on the idea that arbitrary, indiscriminate killing is indefensible, then this may provide a foundation for human rights, in particular those against torture and arbitrary killing. It also suggests that there may be hope that cross-cultural empirical research may reveal other universally shared moral principles.

5

CONCLUSION

{138}

IN THIS work I have attempted to reconcile the apparently conflicting positions of the universalist and the relativist. Since proponents of universal human rights generally assume that human rights are self-evident, they cannot respond to the objection that some moral systems do not center on rights at all. But even if other societies are duty-based, for example, rather than rights-based, this does not mean that rights cannot be accommodated within their worldview. It may be that in a given society all the members have a duty to care for the elderly. Whether one says that the elderly have a right to care is largely semantics. The point is that the traditional value system could accept a human-rights standard which provided a right to care for the aged.

Since relativists believe that cultural diversity precludes the possible existence of universal standards, they cannot accept human rights. The theory of relativism, however, has been much misunderstood by relativists and universalists alike. In fact, it does not present any insurmountable barrier to universal human-rights standards. A reinterpretation of the theory shows that it is, indeed, compatible with cross-cultural universals. There may well exist considerable convergence in moral systems, but this remains an open question until such time as cross-cultural empirical research provides the answer.

The quest for cross-cultural universals will require substantial empirical research. Human-rights activists may not be amenable to this approach because it will, of course, take time. But if it is possible to identify values on which a worldwide consensus exists, this means human-rights standards could be based on them. Unanimity will surely provide a stronger foundation for human rights than exists currently. By anchoring human rights via cross-cultural universals, the standards are more likely to be accepted and taken seriously.

As an example of this approach, I presented a case study of the principle of retribution tied to proportionality. This principle, I contend, serves to limit violence and represents a worldwide commitment to doctrines of restraint. It may indicate that all peoples would support limits on arbitrary violence. Although what is considered arbitrary violence may vary from culture to culture, as in the case of infanticide, this study may provide a foundation for a standard prohibiting genocide. {139}

Some believe that with the technological dissemination taking place today, research of the kind suggested here may not be necessary. Remarkable innovations in the fields of transportation and communication promote the diffusion of Western values. Their argument is that it is possible that Western notions of human rights may be more widely embraced as time marches on. But this presumes that other cultures will willingly discard their time-honored customs. Despite the transfer of technology to the far reaches of the globe, many customs have, in fact, not changed. Furthermore, perhaps it is the West whose culturally imperialistic values ought to be changed.

We must search for cross-cultural universals to buttress human-rights standards for which a universal consensus *already* exists. All cultures may now share some ideals. We must harness these ideals as a means by which to ground human-rights standards. As a consensus develops with respect to other values, for whatever reasons, other, new standards can be advanced based on them.

The study of diverse moral systems is of paramount importance, particularly because many Western philosophers presume that morality must be universal in application. It is worthwhile knowing the contours of moral thought in different worldviews. The comparative analysis of human rights affords insight into the nature of morality in the world and increases our moral knowledge in general. For purely academic reasons, research of this kind is greatly needed.

But it is not solely because of intellectual curiosity that the present study was undertaken. There are practical implications to research. The United Nations, for example, can more readily and justifiably criticize the behavior of other nations if truly universal standards exist. Instead of chastising nations for violating standards which they have not ratified or which they have but do not care about, the United Nations could condemn them for ignoring their *own* standards. Comparative research greatly strengthens the foundation of human rights and thereby empowers international criticism. In addition, incorporating human rights in national foreign policies becomes possible when there are clear standards which have been promulgated. By clarifying the concept of human rights internationally, we can avoid the vagaries of foreign policy rhetoric and the schizophrenic changes which have occurred, for instance, between the presidential administrations of Carter and Reagan (see Petro, 1983).

In the end we must resist the temptation of believing that all people share a single moral conception. This is contrary to reality. But at the same time we need not abandon the search for universals. Diversity does not preclude the possibility that there may be convergence in the many moral systems of the world. The question which remains to be answered is what particular {140} moral standards all societies hold in common. The presumption of universality, a common Western intuition, must be shed. The way will then be clear to discover cross-cultural universals. There remains hope that the ideals of all cultures contain some commonalities. Greater specificity is needed if we are to rescue human rights from their precarious position. It is my hope that by taking the approach set forth in this study we will come to know what moral principles are shared across the globe, and thereby what international human rights are possible.

NOTES

[1] This brief historical overview relies heavily on the following excellent reviews to which the reader is directed for more detail: Driscoll (1979), Farced (1977), Humphrey (1984), Schwelb & Alston (1982), Szabo (1982), and Tolley (1987).

[2] NGOs have played an extremely important role in the development of international human-rights law. The reader interested in exploring the literature might begin with the bibliography of Livezey (1988), the book by Chiang (1981), and the analysis by Kamminga and Rodley (1984).

[3] Article I of the UN Charter sets out the fundamental purposes of the Organization, one of which is to "achieve international cooperation in promoting and encouraging respect for human rights and for fundamental freedoms for all without distinction as to race. sex, language or religion." Article 55 provides that the UN promote "universal respect for, and observance of, human rights and fundamental freedoms." And Article 56 stipulates that member states "take joint and separate action in cooperation with the Organization for the achievement of the Purposes set forth in Article 55." (For a legislative history of Articles 55 and 56, see Humphrey, 1967.)

[4] The Covenants provided for the creation of two watchdog committees comprised of members serving in their individual capacity to monitor compliance by states parties. Though the Covenants entered into force in early 1976, the Committee on Economic, Social, and Cultural Rights (designed to monitor compliance with the ICESCR) did not come into existence until May 1986 (for details of the workings of this committee. see Alston, 1987). By contrast, the Human Rights Committee of the ICCPR was created almost immediately after the Covenant entered into force in September 1976 (for details of the workings of this committee, see Fischer [1982], Jhabvala [1984], and Schwelb [1977]).

[5] For a more detailed exposition of rights theories, see Dworkin (1977), Feinberg (1973), Flathman (1976), and Wellman (1978).

[6] As opposed to the doctrine of *moral* correlativity—see below (p. 44).

[7] For cross-cultural research, Hohfeld's intricate typology may have limited applicability. S. F. Moore advises legal anthropologists to read Hohfeld and then "...cheerfully do without him" (!) (Moore, 1969, p. 343).

[8] This particular example was introduced at least as early as 1956 by Glanville Williams.

[9] See also Brandt (1959, p. 434), Braybrooke (1972), Hudson and Husak (1980), Singer (1972), and Waldron (1984, p. 11).

[10] McCloskey's formulation has been criticized elsewhere as being "...not particularly illuminating or informative" (Martin & Nickel, 1980, p. 170).

[11] Hart's argument against babies as right-holders follows a discussion of third-party rights. He observes that simply because someone stands to benefit from the carrying out of a duty by another does not mean that the beneficiary has a claim against that person. But imagine the case in which Hart stumbles across a starving baby (assume there was no preexisting agreement between Hart and the baby's parents). If Hart is under a moral duty to assist the baby, then the baby could be said to have a moral right against Hart.

[12] Western theorists sometimes assert that a right is prior to a duty (Lamont, 1950, p. 94). Others, however, have defended the "...logical priority of duties over rights" (Pappu, 1982, p. 24).

[13] Some might argue that the prisoner is not deprived of rights but only privileges. But among the most fundamental rights is (supposedly) the right to liberty (Hart, 1979).

[14] Of course, it is still possible to identify a legal right even if it is not enforced.

[15] Other factors are relevant, such as whether the legal right was promulgated according to correct procedure. Ultimately, however, the content of the right should resonate with prior moral rights if it is to be regarded as legitimate within the society in question.

[16] For detailed accounts, see Donnelly (1985), Roshwald (1958-59), Strauss (1953), and Tuck (1981).

[17] See Chapter 3. There is a tendency among human-rights scholars to reify their own conceptions (Murphy, 1981).

[18] Another major difference between natural law and human rights is that, according to international human-rights lawyers and the United Nations community in general, human rights accommodate other types of rights in addition to civil and political.

[19] The reason for the risk-averse requirement is that otherwise people might prefer less egalitarian distributive principles. Because they are risk-averse, they worry that without such principles they might end up as the poor. The explanation for the nonenvy requirement has to do with the avoidance of socialism. Since Rawls allows for some inequalities through the difference principle. the existence of envy might lead the participants in the original position to prefer a more strictly egalitarian system.

[20] For an interesting defense of the practice, see Jomo Kenyatta, *Facing Mount Kenya: The Tribal Life of the Gikuyu* (New York: Vintage Books, 1965), pp. 124-148.

[21] The key word here is presumed. I defend the view that relativism is compatible with cross-cultural *universals* but that it denies absolutes (see Friedman, 1986, p. 766; see also p. 80 of the text).

[22] Geertz's article "Anti Anti-Relativism" is almost entirely devoted to the presentation of caricatured arguments about relativism (1984). Some of the more extreme of the various derogatory remarks refer to relativism as "one of the scabbier whores" (1984, p. 266) and as "the inferno" which accounts for the whole modern disaster (1984, p. 267). In a most sardonic tone, Geertz observes that "Cultural relativism causes everything bad" (1984, p. 267). He also calls it "the relativist Dracula" (1984, p. 272) and "the anti-hero with a thousand faces" (1984, p. 273). For critiques of Geertz, see Nisim Sabbat (1987) and Washburn (1987).

[23] The reader interested in these debates should consult the following: linguistic—Kay & Kempton (1984); Rosch (1974); epistemological—Hollis & Lukes (Eds.) (1982); Krausz & Meiland (Eds.) (1982); Lucy & Shweder (1979); Overing (Ed.) (1985): Popper (1966): Schoeck & Wiggins (Eds.) (1961); and Winch (1964). The work of Foot (1979, 1982), Harman (1975, 1978a, 1978b), Lyons (1976a), Westermarck (1932b), Williams (1972, 1974-75), and others will not be discussed. Their concern is the source of justification for moral beliefs.The present focus is on the conflict between moral systems rather than that between individuals. The sorts of questions they are interested in are: How can one person believe that abortion is wrong and another

person in the same society think it right? Should there not be one moral principle that can decide the question; and if so, how can we find it?

[24] In what follows I concentrate primarily on the arguments of the eminent philosophers Schmidt, Brandt, and Frankena. Although my views differ from theirs, their distinctions provide a useful framework for analysis. For an interesting overview of types of relativism, see Spiro (1986).

[25] Philosophers seem to be especially obsessed with the example of patricide (Lean, 1970; Peterson, 1985, pp. 888-894; Taylor, 1958, p. 36; Unwin, 1985, p. 205).There are at least three possible explanations for this. The first is that philosophers never read the anthropological literature (see Westermarck, 1924, Vol. 1, pp. 386-390) and are consequently condemned to repeat the examples of their predecessors. Amazingly enough, even Edel, who is familiar with ethnographies, also focuses on patricide (1982, p. 83). The second possibility is that philosophers now have longer life spans and are worried about their relationships with their sons. The third interpretation, based on Freudian theory, would explain the philosophers' preoccupation in terms of the Oedipal complex.

[26] A slight source of confusion is Schmidt's use of the term invariant when he really means absolutes (1955, p. 790).

[27] Herskovits is generally thought to have developed the idea of enculturation (1964, pp. 326-329). For a review of the concept, see Shimahara (1970). As there is some degree of overlap between enculturation and socialization, the reader might wish to consult Merelman (1986) which contains many references on political socialization.

[28] There are numerous examples which would substantiate this point. One is the decision by the Agency for International Development to withhold its twenty-five-million-dollar contribution from the UN Fund for Population Activities because of the practice of coerced abortion in China. This contribution represents roughly twenty percent of the UN fund's budget (*Los Angeles Times,* August 28, 1986, p. 8).

[29] The reader interested in questions of interpretation may want to read the important 1986 work entitled *Writing Culture: the Poetics and Politics of Ethnography,* edited by James Clifford and George E. Marcus.

[30] Turnbull's work has been severely criticized in a number of comments which appeared in *Current Anthropology* in the 1970s. The first critique was by Frederik Barth (1974), followed by several other papers by Wilson, McCall, Geddes, Pfeiffer, and Boskey (1975). Turnbull wrote a reply to these papers (1975).

[31] There are other provisions in the international instruments which might win universal approval. Among those which all might support are: Article 9 of the Universal Declaration of Human Rights—"No one shall be subjected to arbitrary arrest, detention or exile," and some version of Article 12—"No one shall be subjected to arbitrary interference with his privacy, family, home or correspondence, nor to attacks upon his honour and reputation." Although the phraseology might have to be modified, the underlying notion that arbitrary acts against individuals or groups are wrong and, therefore, contrary to law might be embraced by all peoples.

APPENDIX

Appendix A
United Nations Structure Regarding Human Rights • 1988

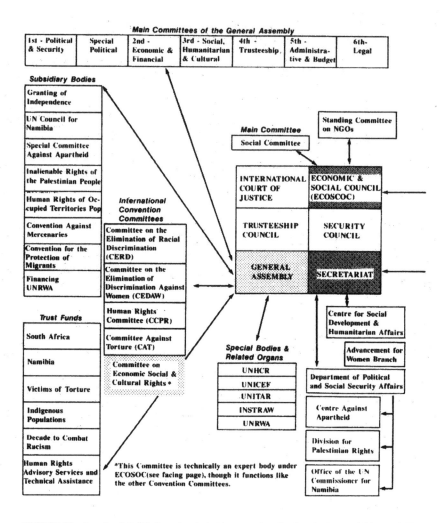

Main Committees of the General Assembly

1st - Political & Security	Special Political	2nd - Economic & Financial	3rd - Social, Humanitarian & Cultural	4th - Trusteeship	5th - Administrative & Budget	6th- Legal

Subsidiary Bodies

- Granting of Independence
- UN Council for Namibia
- Special Committee Against Apartheid
- Inalienable Rights of the Palestinian People
- Human Rights of Occupied Territories Pop
- Convention Against Mercenaries
- Convention for the Protection of Migrants
- Financing UNRWA

Trust Funds

- South Africa
- Namibia
- Victims of Torture
- Indigenous Populations
- Decade to Combat Racism
- Human Rights Advisory Services and Technical Assistance

International Convention Committees

- Committee on the Elimination of Racial Discrimination (CERD)
- Committee on the Elimination of Discrimination Against Women (CEDAW)
- Human Rights Committee (CCPR)
- Committee Against Torture (CAT)
- Committee on Economic Social & Cultural Rights *

Main Committee
Social Committee

Standing Committee on NGOs

INTERNATIONAL COURT OF JUSTICE

ECONOMIC & SOCIAL COUNCIL (ECOSOC)

TRUSTEESHIP COUNCIL

SECURITY COUNCIL

GENERAL ASSEMBLY

SECRETARIAT

Centre for Social Development & Humanitarian Affairs

Advancement for Women Branch

Special Bodies & Related Organs

- UNHCR
- UNICEF
- UNITAR
- INSTRAW
- UNRWA

Department of Political and Social Security Affairs

Centre Against Apartheid

Division for Palestinian Rights

Office of the UN Commissioner for Namibia

*This Committee is technically an expert body under ECOSOC (see facing page), though it functions like the other Convention Committees.

SOURCE: Meselson, Sarah & Wiseberg, Laurie S. "United Nations Bodies with Responsibility in the Field of Human Rights," Human Rights Internet Reporter. Vol. 2, no. 3 (Spring/Summer 1988) pp. 70-71.

NOTE: This graphic has since been superseded but is retained from the original publication of this book. Please see Appendix B for the current arrangement.

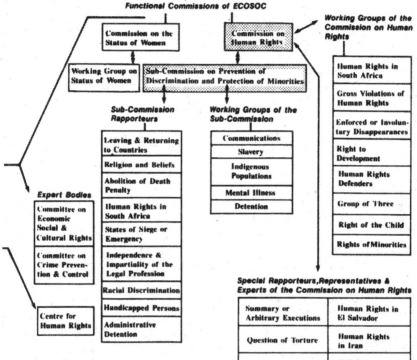

Functional Commissions of ECOSOC

Working Groups of the Commission on Human Rights

Commission on the Status of Women

Commission on Human Rights

Working Group on Status of Women

Sub-Commission on Prevention of Discrimination and Protection of Minorities

Sub-Commission Rapporteurs

Working Groups of the Sub-Commission

Human Rights in South Africa
Gross Violations of Human Rights
Enforced or Involuntary Disappearances
Right to Development
Human Rights Defenders
Group of Three
Right of the Child
Rights of Minorities

Expert Bodies

Leaving & Returning to Countries
Religion and Beliefs
Abolition of Death Penalty
Human Rights in South Africa
States of Siege or Emergency
Independence & Impartiality of the Legal Profession
Racial Discrimination
Handicapped Persons
Administrative Detention

Communications
Slavery
Indigenous Populations
Mental Illness
Detention

Committee on Economic Social & Cultural Rights
Committee on Crime Prevention & Control

Centre for Human Rights

Special Rapporteurs, Representatives & Experts of the Commission on Human Rights

Summary or Arbitrary Executions	Human Rights in El Salvador
Question of Torture	Human Rights in Iran
Human Rights in Chile	Religious Intolerance
Human Rights in in Afghanistan	Human Rights in Haiti**
Use of Mercenaries	Human Rights in Guatemala**
	Human Rights in Equatorial Guinea**

**Under the Programme of Advisory Services

United Nations bodies with Responsibility in the Field of Human Rights

Appendix B
United Nations System Chart • 2011

Published by the United Nations Department of Public Information DPI/2470 rev.2—11-36429—October 2011

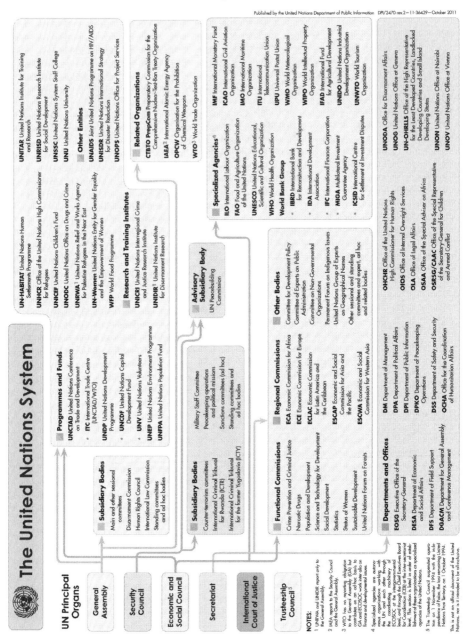

NOTES:

1 UNRWA and UNIDIR report only to the General Assembly.

2 IAEA reports to the Security Council and the General Assembly.

3 WTO has no reporting obligation to the General Assembly (GA) but contributes on an ad hoc basis to GA and ECOSOC work inter alia on finance and developmental issues.

4 Specialized agencies are autonomous organizations working with the UN and each other through the coordinating machinery of ECOSOC at the inter-governmental level, and through the Chief Executives Board for Coordination (CEB) at the inter-secretariat level. This section is listed in order of establishment of these organizations as specialized agencies of the United Nations.

5 The Trusteeship Council suspended operation on 1 November 1994 with the independence of Palau, the last remaining United Nations Trust Territory, on 1 October 1994.

This is not an official document of the United Nations, nor is it intended to be all-inclusive.

Appendix C

Universal Declaration of Human Rights

Resolution 217(A)(III) of the General Assembly, December 10, 1948

PREAMBLE

Whereas recognition of the inherent dignity and of the equal and inalienable rights of all members of the human family is the foundation of freedom, justice and peace in the world,

Whereas disregard and contempt for human rights have resulted in barbarous acts which have outraged the conscience of mankind, and the advent of a world in which human beings shall enjoy freedom of speech and belief and freedom from fear and want has been proclaimed as the highest aspiration of the common people,

Whereas it is essential, if man is not to be compelled to have recourse, as a last resort, to rebellion against tyranny and oppression, that human rights should be protected by the rule of law,

Whereas it is essential to promote the development of friendly relations between nations,

Whereas the peoples of the United Nations have in the Charter reaffirmed their faith in fundamental human rights, in the dignity and worth of the human person and in the equal rights of men and women and have determined to promote social progress and better standards of life in larger freedom,

Whereas Member States have pledged themselves to achieve, in cooperation with the United Nations, the promotion of universal respect for and observance of human rights and fundamental freedoms,

Whereas a common understanding of these rights and freedoms is of the greatest importance for the full realization of this pledge.

Now, therefore,
The General Assembly,

Proclaims this Universal Declaration of Human Rights as a common standard of achievement for all peoples and all nations, to the end that every individual and every organ of society, keeping this Declaration constantly in mind, shall strive by teaching and education to promote respect for these rights and freedoms and by progressive measures, national and international, to secure their universal and effective recognition and observance, both among the peoples of Member States themselves and among the peoples of territories under their jurisdiction.

ARTICLE 1

All human beings are born free and equal in dignity and rights. They are endowed with reason and conscience and should act towards one another in a spirit of brotherhood.

ARTICLE 2

Everyone is entitled to all the rights and freedoms set forth in this Declaration, without distinction of any kind, such as race, colour, sex, language, religion, political or other opinion, national or social origin, property, birth or other status.

Furthermore, no distinction shall be made on the basis of the political, jurisdictional or international status of the country or territory to which a person belongs, whether it be independent, trust, non-self-governing or under any other limitation of sovereignty.

ARTICLE 3

Everyone has the right to life, liberty and the security of person.

ARTICLE 4

No one shall be held in slavery or servitude; slavery and the slave trade shall be prohibited in all their forms.

ARTICLE 5

No one shall be subjected to torture or to cruel, inhuman or degrading treatment or punishment.

ARTICLE 6

Everyone has the right to recognition everywhere as a person before the law.

ARTICLE 7

All are equal before the law and are entitled without any discrimination to equal protection of the law. All are entitled to equal protection against any discrimination in violation of this Declaration and against any incitement to such discrimination.

ARTICLE 8

Everyone has the right to an effective remedy by the competent national tribunals for acts violating the fundamental rights granted him by the constitution or by law.

ARTICLE 9

No one shall be subjected to arbitrary arrest, detention or exile.

ARTICLE 10

Everyone is entitled in full equality to a fair and public hearing by an independent and impartial tribunal, in the determination of his rights and obligations and of any criminal charge against him.

ARTICLE 11

1. Everyone charged with a penal offence has the right to be presumed innocent until proved guilty according to law in a public trial at which he has had all the guarantees necessary for his defence.

2. No one shall be held guilty of any penal offence on account of any act or omission which did not constitute a penal offence, under national or international law, at the time when it was committed. Nor shall a heavier penalty be imposed than the one that was applicable at the time the penal offence was committed.

ARTICLE 12

No one shall be subjected to arbitrary interference with his privacy, family, home or correspondence, nor to attacks upon his honour and reputation. Everyone has the right to the protection of the law against such interference or attacks.

ARTICLE 13

1. Everyone has the right to freedom of movement and residence within the borders of each state.

2. Everyone has the right to leave any country, including his own, and to return to his country.

ARTICLE 14

1. Everyone has the right to seek and to enjoy in other countries asylum from persecution.

2. This right may not be invoked in the case of prosecutions genuinely arising from non-political crimes or from acts contrary to the purposes and principles of the United Nations.

ARTICLE 15

1. Everyone has the right to a nationality.

2. No one shall be arbitrarily deprived of his nationality nor denied the right to change his nationality.

ARTICLE 16

1. Men and women of full age, without any limitation due to race, nationality or religion, have the right to marry and to found a family. They are entitled to equal rights as to marriage, during marriage and at its dissolution.

2. Marriage shall be entered into only with the free and full consent of the intending spouses.

3. The family is the natural and fundamental group unit of society and is entitled to protection by society and the State.

ARTICLE 17

1. Everyone has the right to own property alone as well as in association with others.

2. No one shall be arbitrarily deprived of his property.

ARTICLE 18

Everyone has the right to freedom of thought, conscience and religion; this right includes freedom to change his religion or belief, and freedom, either alone or in community with others and in public or private, to manifest his religion or belief in teaching, practice, worship and observance.

ARTICLE 19

Everyone has the right to freedom of opinion and expression; this right includes freedom to hold opinions without interference and to seek, receive and impart information and ideas through any media and regardless of frontiers.

ARTICLE 20

1. Everyone has the right to freedom of peaceful assembly and association.

2. No one may be compelled to belong to an association.

ARTICLE 21

1. Everyone has the right to take part in the Government of his country, directly or through freely chosen representatives.

2. Everyone has the right of equal access to public service in his country.

3. The will of the people shall be the basis of the authority of government; this will shall be expressed in periodic and genuine elections which shall be by universal and equal suffrage and shall be held by secret vote or by equivalent free voting procedures.

ARTICLE 22

Everyone, as a member of society, has the right to social security and is entitled to realization, through national effort and international cooperation and in accordance with the organization and resources of each State, of the economic, social and cultural rights indispensable for his dignity and the free development of his personality.

ARTICLE 23

1. Everyone has the right to work, to free choice of employment, to just and favourable conditions of work and to protection against unemployment.

2. Everyone, without any discrimination, has the right to equal pay for equal work.

3. Everyone who works has the right to just and favourable remuneration insuring for himself and his family an existence worthy of human dignity, and supplemented, if necessary, by other means of social protection.

4. Everyone has the right to form and to join trade unions for the protection of his interests.

ARTICLE 24

Everyone has the right to rest and leisure, including reasonable limitation of working hours and periodic holidays with pay.

ARTICLE 25

1. Everyone has the right to a standard of living adequate for the health and well-being of himself and of his family, including food, clothing, housing and medical care and necessary social services, and the right to security in the event of unemployment, sickness, disability, widowhood, old age or other lack of livelihood in circumstances beyond his control.

2. Motherhood and childhood are entitled to special care and assistance. All children, whether born in or out of wedlock, shall enjoy the same social protection.

ARTICLE 26

1. Everyone has the right to education. Education shall be free, at least in the elementary and fundamental stages. Elementary education shall be compulsory. Technical and professional education shall be made generally available and higher education shall be equally accessible to all on the basis of merit.

2. Education shall be directed to the full development of the human personality and to the strengthening of respect for human rights and fundamental freedoms. It shall promote understanding, tolerance and friendship among all nations, racial or religious groups, and shall further the activities of the United Nations for the maintenance of peace.

3. Parents have a prior right to choose the kind of education that shall be given to their children.

ARTICLE 27

1. Everyone has the right freely to participate in the cultural life of the community, to enjoy the arts and to share in scientific advancement and its benefits.

2. Everyone has the right to the protection of the moral and material interests resulting from any scientific, literary or artistic production of which he is the author.

ARTICLE 28

Everyone is entitled to a social and international order in which the rights and freedoms set forth in this Declaration can be fully realized.

ARTICLE 29

1. Everyone has duties to the community in which alone the free and full development of his personality is possible.

2. In the exercise of his rights and freedoms, everyone shall be subject only to such limitations as are determined by law solely for the purpose of securing due recognition and respect for the rights and freedoms of others and of meeting the just requirements of morality, public order and the general welfare in a democratic society.

3. These rights and freedoms may in no case be exercised contrary to the purposes and principles of the United Nations.

ARTICLE 30

Nothing in this Declaration may be interpreted as implying for any State, group or person any right to engage in any activity or to perform any act aimed at the destruction of any of the rights and freedoms set forth herein.

Hundred and eighty-third plenary meeting, 10 December 1948

References

Abi-Saab, G. (1973). The Third World and the future of the International Legal Order. *Revue Egyptienne de Droit International, 29*, 27-66.

Abraham, K. C. (1982). Human rights—Indian Christian expressions. *Religion and Society, 29*, 2-12.

Acton, H. B. (1950). Rights. *Aristotelian Society*, Suppl. Vol. 24, 95-110.

Adair, J. (1930). *Adair's History of the American Indians* (S. C. Williams, Ed.). Johnson City, TN: Watauga Press. (Original work published 1775).

Adams. E. M. (1982), The ground of human rights. *American Philosophical Quarterly, 19*, 191-196.

Adede, A. O. (1983). The minimum standards in a world of disparities. In R. St. J. MacDonald & D. M. Johnston (Eds.), *The structure and process of international law: Essays in legal philosophy, doctrine and theory* (pp. 1001-1026). The Hague: Martinus Nijhoff.

Adegbite, L. O. (1968). African attitudes to the international protection of human rights. In A. Eide & A. Schou (Eds.), *International protection of human rights* (pp. 69-81). New York: Interscience.

Adler, A. (1980). La vengeance du sang chez les Moundang du Chad. In R. Verdier (Ed.), *La vengeance*, Vol. 1 (pp. 75-89). Paris: Editions Cujas.

Ahmed, M. K. (1956). Islamic civilization and human rights. *Revue Egyptienne de Droit International, 12*(2), 1-21.

Akpan, J. E. (1980). The 1979 Nigerian constitution and human rights. *Universal Human Rights, 2*, 23-41.

Albright, J., & Kunstel, M. (1987). *Stolen childhood*. Austin, TX: Austin American-Statesman.

Al Ghunaimi, M. T. (1968). *The Muslim conception of international law and the western approach*. The Hague: Martinus Nijhoff.

Alston, P. (1979). Human rights and basic needs: A critical assessment. *Human Rights Journal, 12*, 19-67.

Alston, P. (1980). UNESCO's procedure for dealing with human rights violations. *Santa Clara Law Review, 20*, 665-696.

Alston, P. (1983a). The alleged demise of political human rights at the UN: A reply to Donnelly. International Organization, *37*, 537-546.

Alston, P. (1983b). The Universal Declaration at 35: Western and passé or alive and universal? *International Commission of Jurists Review, 31*, 60-70.

Alston, P. (1984). Conjuring up new human rights: A proposal for quality control. *American Journal of International Law, 78*, 607-721.

Alston, P. (1987). Out of the abyss: The challenges confronting the new U.N. Committee on Economic, Social and Cultural Rights. *Human Rights Quarterly, 9*, 332-381.

Alston, P. & Tomasevski, K. (Eds.). (1984). *The right to food.* Boston: Martinus Nijhoff.

Alt, A. (1934). Zur Talionsformel. *Zeitschrift für die Alttestamentliche Wissenschaft, 52*, 303-305.

Anand, R. P. (1962). Role of the "new" Asian-African countries in the present international legal order. *American Journal of International Law, 56*, 383-406.

Anonymous. (1947). Statement on human rights [by the American Anthropological Association]. *American Anthropologist, 49*, 539-543.

Anonymous. (1947-48). *Yearbook of the United Nations.* Lake Success, NY: Department of Public Information, United Nations, pp. 572-586.

Anonymous. (1948-49). *Yearbook of the United Nations.* New York: Columbia University Press and the United Nations, pp. 524-553.

Anonymous. (1970a). The rights of man. In K. R. Rahner (Ed.), *Sacramentum mundi* (pp. 365-368). New York: Herder and Herder.

Anonymous. (1970b). Vendetta. In *Encyclopedia Britannica* (Vol. 22, pp. 944-945). Chicago: William Benton.

Anonymous. (Ed.). (1981). *Human Rights in socialist society.* Moscow: Novosti Press Agency.

Anonymous. (1983a). *Professional ethics: Statement and procedures of the American Anthropological Association.* Washington, DC: American Anthropological Association.

Anonymous. (1983b). *Human rights documents.* Committee on Foreign Affairs. Washington, DC: United States Government Printing Office.

Anonymous. (1984a, January 18). The unkindest cut. *Nursing Times, 80*, 8-10.

Anonymous. (1984b). *Children in especially difficult circumstances.* London: Anti-Slavery Society. (Study prepared for UNICEF)

Anonymous. (1986a). Banjul charter comes into force. *Human Rights Internet Reporter, 11*(3), 46.

Anonymous. (1986b). *The concern for human rights: Real and false.* Moscow: Novosti Press Agency.

Anonymous. (1987a). *Is universality in jeopardy?* New York: United Nations. Department of Public Information.

Anonymous. (1987b). Shocking facts and figures about child labour in India. *Socio-Legal Concern Newsletter, 3*(4), 2-3.

Anonymous. (1988). Universal declaration of human rights. *Department of State Bulletin, 88* (2141), 1-9.

Anonymous. (1988-89). Introduction. Special Issue, Africa: Human Rights Directory and Bibliography. *Human Rights Internet Reporter, 12*(4), 5-8.

Arat, Z. F. (1986). Human rights and political instability in the Third World. *Policy Studies Review, 6*, 158-172.

Aron, R. (1959). Relativism in history. In H. Meyerhoff (Ed.), *The philosophy of history in our time* (pp. 152-161). Garden City, NY: Doubleday Anchor.

Aron, R. (1970).Sociology and the philosophy of human rights. In H. E. Kiefer &. M. X. Munitz (Eds.). *Ethics and social justice* (pp. 282-299). Albany: State University of New York Press.

Asante, S. K. B. (1968/1969). Nation building and human rights in emerging African nations. *Cornell International Law Journal, 1/2*, 72-107.

Asch, S. (1952). *Social Psychology*. New York: Prentice-Hall, Inc.

Attfield, R. (1979). How not to be a moral relativist. *The Monist, 62*, 510-521.

Ayers, E. L. (1984). *Vengeance and justice: Crime and punishment in the 19th-century south*. New York and Oxford: Oxford University Press.

Baehr, P. R. (1988, August-September). *Human rights in East and West: How common is the common standard of achievement?* Paper presented at the XIVth World Congress of the International Political Science Association, Washington, DC.

Bagish, H. (1983). Confessions of a former cultural relativist. In E. Angeloni (Ed.). *Anthropology 83/84* (pp. 22-29). Guilford, CT: Dushkin.

Bandman, B. (1978). Are there human rights? *Journal of Value Inquiry, 12*, 215-224.

Banks, D. L. (1986). The analysis of human rights data over time. *Human Rights Quarterly, 8*, 654-680.

Barnes, B., &. Bloor, D. (1982). Relativism, rationalism and the sociology of knowledge. In M. Hollis &. S. Lukes (Eds.), *Rationality and relativism* (pp. 21-47). Cambridge: MIT Press.

Barnett, H. G. (1948). On science and human rights. *American Anthropologist, 50*, 352-355.

Barnsley, J. H. (1972). *The social reality of ethics: The comparative analysis of moral codes*. London: Routledge and Kegan Paul.

Barth, F. (1953). *Principles of social organization in southern Kurdistan*. Universitetets Etnografiske Museum, Bulletin No. 7. Oslo: Brødrene Jorgensen A/S Boktrykkeri.

Barth, F. (1974). On responsibility and humanity: Calling a colleague to account. *Current Anthropology, 15*, 99-103.

Banon, J. (1979a). Reflections on cultural relativism—I. *Theology, 82*, 103-109.

Barton, J. (1979b). Reflections on cultural relativism—II. *Theology, 82*, 191-199.

Bassiouni, M. C (Ed.). (1982). *The Islamic criminal justice system*. London: Oceana Publications.

Baum, G. (1979). Catholic foundation of human rights. *Ecumenist, 18*, 6-12.

Baxi, U. (1972). Some remarks on Eurocentrism and the law of nations. In R.P. Anand (Ed.), *Asian states and the development of universal international law* (pp. 3-9). Delphi: Vikas.

Baxi, U. (1978). Human rights, accountability and development. *Indian Journal of International Law, 18*, 279-283.

Bay, C. (1979). A human rights approach to transnational politics. *Universal Human Rights, 1*, 19-43.

Bay, C. (1980a). Peace and critical political knowledge as human rights. *Political Theory, 8*, 293-318.

Bay, C. (1980b). On needs and rights beyond liberalism-A rejoinder to Flathman. *Political Theory, 8*, 331-334.

Beattie, J. M. H. (1984). Objectivity and social anthropology. In S. C. Brown (Ed.), *Objectivity and cultural divergence* (pp. 1-20). Cambridge: Cambridge University Press.

Becker, H. (1956). *Man in reciprocity.* New York: Praeger.

Bedau, H. A. (1968). Rights as claims, reasons and needs. *International Congress of Philosophy*, Proceedings, *3,* 132-136.

Bedau, H. A. (1978). Retribution and the theory of punishment. *Journal of Philosophy, 75*, 601-620.

Bedau, H. A.(1982). International human rights. In T. Regan &. D. V. DeVeer (Eds.), *And justice for* all (pp. 287-308). Totowa, NJ: Rowman &. Littlefield.

Beddard, R. (1980). *Human rights and Europe: A study of the machinery of human rights protection of the council of Europe* (2nd ed.). London: Sweet and Maxwell.

Beer, L. W. (1984). *Freedom of expression in Japan: A study in comparative law, politics and society.* Tokyo, New York and San Francisco: Kodansha International.

Beg, M. H. (1980). Human rights and Asia. *Santa Clara Law Review, 20*, 319-350.

Beitz, C. (1979). *Political theory and international relations.* Princeton, NJ: Princeton University Press.

Bell, L. (1975). Does ethical relativism destroy morality? *Man and World, 8*, 415-423.

Bell, R. (1960). *The Qur'an.* Translated with a critical re-arrangement of the Surahs (Vols. 1-2). Edinburgh: T. &. T. Clark. (Original work published 1937.)

Bello, E. (1981). Shared legal concepts between African customary norms and international conventions on humanitarian law. *Indian Journal of International Law, 21*, 79-95.

Bendix, R. (1963). Concepts and generalizations in comparative sociological studies. *American Sociological Review, 28*, 532-538.

Benedict, R. (1934). *Patterns of culture.* Boston: Houghton Mifflin.

Benedict, R. (1978). Anthropology and the abnormal. In R. Beehler & A. R. Drengson (Eds.), *The philosophy of society* (pp. 279-288). London: Methuen.

Benn, S. I. (1967). Rights. In P. Edwards (Ed.), *Encyclopedia of philosophy* (Vol. 7, pp.

191-195). New York and London: Macmillan and Free Press.

Benn, S. I. (1978). Human rights—For whom and for what? In E. Kamenka & A. E. S. Tay (Eds.), *Human rights* (pp. 59-73). London: Edward Arnold.

Bennett, J. (1949). Science and human rights: Reason and action. *American Anthropologist, 51,* 329-336.

Bentham, J. (1843). *The works of Jeremy Bentham* (J. Bowring, Ed.). London: Simpkin, Marshall.

Berger, P. (1977). Are human rights universal? *Commentary, 64,* 60-63.

Berman, H. (1984). Are human rights universal? *Interculture, 17*(2), 53-60.

Berman, H. J. (1965). Human rights in the Soviet Union. *Howard Law Journal, 11,* 333-341.

Berman, H. J. (1979). American and Soviet perspectives on human rights. *Worldview, 22*(11), 15-21.

Berreman, G. D. (1979). *Himachal: Science, People and "Progress."* Copenhagen: IWGIA.

Berreman, G. D. (1980, March). Are human rights merely a politicized luxury in the world today? *Anthropology and Humanism Quarterly,* pp. 2-13.

Berscheid, E., Boye, D., & Walster, E. (1968). Retaliation as a means of restoring equity. *Journal of Personality and Social Psychology, 10,* 370-376.

Biderman, S., & Kasher, A. (1984). Religious concepts of punishment and reward. *Philosophical and Phenomenological Research, 44,* 433-451.

Bidney, D. (1944). On the concept of culture and some cultural fallacies. *American Anthropologist, 46,* 30-44.

Bidney, D. (1953a). *Theoretical Anthropology.* New York: Columbia University Press.

Bidney, D. (1953b). The concept of value in modern anthropology. In A. L. Kroeber (Ed.), *Anthropology today* (pp. 682-699). Chicago: University of Chicago Press.

Bidney, D. (1959). The philosophical presuppositions of cultural relativism and cultural absolutism. In L.Ward (Ed.), *Ethics and the social sciences* (pp.51-76). Notre Dame, IN: University of Notre Dame Press.

Bidney, D. (1968). Cultural relativism. In D. Sills (Ed.), *International encyclopedia of the social sciences* (Vol. 3, pp. 543-547). New York: Free Press.

Bilder, R. B. (1969). Rethinking international human rights: Some basic questions. *Human Rights Journal, 2,* 557-608.

Bilder, R. B. (1984). An overview of international human rights. In H. Hannum (Ed.), *Guide to international human rights practice* (pp. 3-19). Philadelphia: University of Pennsylvania Press.

Black, M. (1962). Linguistic relativity: The views of Benjamin Lee Whorf. In M. Black (Ed.), *Models and metaphors.* Ithaca, NY: Cornell University Press.

Black-Michaud, J. (1975). *Cohesive force: Feud in the Mediterranean and the Middle East.* New York: St. Martin's.

Blackstone, W. T. (1968). Equality and human rights. *The Monist, 52,* 616-639.

Blackstone, W. T. (1971). The justification of human rights. In E. H. Pollack (Ed.), *Human rights* (pp. 90-105). Buffalo, NY: Jay Stewart for Amintaphil.

Blanchard, F. (1983). Report of the Director-General, Part 1, Child Labour. *International Labour Conference, 69th session.* Geneva: International Labour Office.

Blaser, A. W. (1984). The rhetoric, promise, and performance of human rights: Soviet and American perspectives. *Journal of Applied Behavioral Science, 20,* 471-489.

Blau, J. (1916). *Lex talionis.* New York: Central Conference of American Rabbis.

Blishtshenko, I. P. (1973). *Human rights practice in the USSR and its international impact.* Berlin: BDR Committee for Human Rights.

Bloch, M. (1961). *Feudal society.* Chicago: University of Chicago Press.

Blumentritt, F. (1891). The Quianganes of Luzon. *Popular Science Monthly, 39,* 388-393.

Boas, F. (1884-85). The central Eskimo. *Sixth Annual Report of the Bureau of Ethnology* (pp. 578-582). (Section entitled Social Order and Laws).

Boas, F. (1901). The mind of primitive man. *Journal of American Folklore, 14,* 1-11.

Boas, F. (1940). Liberty among primitive people. In R. N. Anshen (Ed.), *Freedom: Its meaning* (pp. 375-380). New York: Harcourt, Brace.

Boccassino, D. R. (1962). La vendetta del sangue praticata dagli Acioli dell'Uganda; riti e cannibalismo guerreschi. *Anthropos, 57,* 357-373.

Boehm, C. (1984). *Blood revenge: The anthropology of feuding in Montenegro and other tribal societies.* Lawrence: University Press of Kansas.

Bohannan, P. (1963). *Social anthropology.* New York: Holt, Rinehart & Winston.

Bohannan, P. (1972). Ethnography and comparison in legal anthropology. In L. Nader (Ed.), *Law in culture and* society (pp. 401-418). Chicago: Aldine.

Bohannan, P. (1973). Rethinking culture: A project for current anthropologists. *Current Antropology, 14,* 357-372.

Bollen, K. (1986). Political rights and political liberties in nations: An evaluation of human rights measures, 1950-1984. *Human Rights Quarterly, 8,* 567-591.

Boudhiba, A. (1982). *Exploitation of child labour.* New York: United Nations.

Boulware-Miller, K. (1985). Female circumcision: Challenges to the practice as a human rights violation. *Harvard Women's Law Journal, 8,* 155-177.

Boutros-Ghali, B. (1982). The league of Arab states. In K. Vasal &. P. Alston (Eds.). *The international dimensions of human rights* (Vol. 2, pp. 575-581). Westport, CT: Greenwood Press.

Boyle, K. (1984). Practice and procedure on individual applications under the European convention on human rights. In H. Hannum (Ed.), *Guide to international human rights practice* (pp. 133-152). Philadelphia: University of Pennsylvania Press.

Bozeman, A. B. (1971). *The future of law in a multicultural world.* Princeton. NJ: Princeton University Press.

Bozeman, A. B. (1980). The roots of the American commitment to the rights of man. In *Rights and responsibilities: international, social and individual dimensions* (pp. 51-102). Los Angeles: University of Southern California Press, Annenberg School of Communications.

Bozeman, A. B. (1982). Human rights and national security. *Yale Journal of World Public Order, 9,* 40-77.

Braham, R. L. (Ed.). (1980). *Human rights.* New York: Irvington.

Brandt, R. (1954). *Hopi ethics.* Chicago: University of Chicago Press.

Brandt, R. (1959). *Ethical theory.* Englewood Cliffs. NJ: Prentice-Hall.

Brandt, R. (1967). Ethical relativism. In P. Edward (Ed.), *The encyclopedia of philosophy* (Vol. 3, pp. 75-78). New York and London: Macmillan and Free Press.

Brandt, R. (1984). Relativism refuted? *The Monist, 67,* 297-307.

Braybrooke, D. (1972). The firm but untidy correlativity of rights and obligations. *Canadian Journal of Philosophy, 1,* 351-363.

Brown, D. (1986). *Toward a universal ethnography.* Unpublished manuscript.

Brown, P. G., & MacLean, D.(Eds.). (1979). *Human rights and U.S. foreign policy.* Lexington, MA: Lexington Books.

Brown, S. C. (Ed.). (1984). *Objectivity and cultural divergence.* Cambridge: Cambridge University Press.

Brown, S. M. (1955). Inalienable rights. *Philosophical Review, 64,* 192-211.

Bruce, M. K. (1971). Work of the UN relating to the status of women. *Revue des droils de l'homme/Human Rights Journal,* 365-412.

Buchanan, A. E. (1981). The Marxian critique of justice and rights. *Canadian Journal of Philosophy, 7,* 269-306.

Buergenthal, T. (1977). International and regional human rights law and institutions: Some examples of their interaction. *Texas International Law Journal, 12,* 321-330.

Buergenthal, T. (1984). The Inter-American system for the protection of human rights. In T. Meron (Ed.), *Human rights in international law* (pp.439-493). Oxford: Clarendon Press.

Bull, H., & Watson, A. (Eds.). (1984). *The expansion of international society.* Oxford: Clarendon Press.

Bureau, J. (1979). Une société sans vengeance? Les Gamo d'Ethiopie. *L'Ethnographie, 79,* 93-104.

Burke, T. E. (1979). The limits of relativism. *Philosophical Quarterly, 29,* 193-207.

Burks. A. W. (1986). Japan: The bellwether of East Asian human rights? In J. C. Hsiung (Ed.). *Human rights in East Asia* (pp. 31-53). New York: Paragon.

Burton, R. F. (1961). *The lake regions of central Africa: A picture of exploration.* New York: Horizon. (First published 1860).

Busquet, J. (1920). *Le Droit de la vendetta et les paci Corses.* Paris: Pedone.

Buultjens, R. (1980). Human rights in Indian political culture. In K. Thompson (Ed.), *The moral imperatives of human rights* (pp. 109-122). Washington, DC: University Press of America.

Bystricky. R. (1968).The universality of human rights in a world of conflicting ideologies. In A. Eide & A. Schou (Eds.), *International protection of human rights* (pp. 83-93). New York: Interscience.

Cahill, L. S. (1980). Toward a Christian theory of human rights. *Journal of Religious Ethics, 8,* 277-301.

Campbell, D. (1964). Distinguishing differences of perception from failures of communication in cross-cultural studies. In F. S. C. Northrop & H. H. Livingston (Eds.). *Cross-cultural understanding: Epistemology in anthropology* (pp. 308-336). New York: Harper & Row.

Campbell, D. (1972). Herskovits, cultural relativism and metascience. In M. Herskovits (Ed.), *Cultural relativism: Perspectives in cultural pluralism* (pp. v-xxiv). New York: Random House.

Campbell, D., & LeVine, R. (1961). A proposal for cooperative cross-cultural research on ethnocentrism. *Journal of Conflict Resolution, 5,* 82-108.

Cantril, H. (1955). Ethical relativity from the transactional point of view. *Journal of Philosophy, 52,* 677-687.

Capotorti, F. (1983). Human rights: The hard road towards universality. In R. St. J. MacDonald & D. M. Johnston (Eds.), *The structure and process of international law: Essays in legal philosophy, doctrine and theory* (pp. 977-1000). The Hague: Martinus Nijhoff.

Cassese, A. (1986). *International law in a divided world.* Oxford: Clarendon Press.

Cassin, R. S. (1951). *La déclaration universelle et la mise en oeuvre des droits de l'homme.* Paris: Librairie du Rccueil Sirey.

Castberg, R. (1968). Natural law and human rights: An idea-historical survey. In A. Eide & A. Schou (Eds.), *International protection of human rights* (pp. 13-34). New York: Interscience.

Cavoski, K. (1982). The attainment of human rights in socialism. *Praxis International, 1,* 365-375

Chafee, Z. (1963). *Documents on fundamental human rights,* 2 vols. New York: Atheneum.

Chalidze, V. (1974). *To defend these rights: Human rights and the Soviet Union.* New York: Random House.

Chan, P. (1980). The forgotten little people—A study of urban child labour in a developing economy. *Asian Economies, 35,* 67-79.

Chang, C. C. (1946). Political structure in the Chinese draft constitution. *American*

Academy of Political and Social Science, Annals, 243, 67-76.

Chelhod, J.(1980). Equilibre et parite dans la vengeance du sang chez les Bedouins de Jordanie. In R. Verdier (Ed.), *La vengeance* (Vol. I, pp. 125-143). Paris: Editions Cujas.

Cheng, C. (1979). Human rights in Chinese history and Chinese philosophy. *Comparative Civilizations Review, 1*, 1-19.

Chernenko, K. U. (1981). *Human rights in Soviet society*. New York: International Publishers.

Chiang, P. (1981). *Non-governmental organizations at the United Nations: Identity, role and function*. New York: Praeger.

Chiba, M. (1984). Cultural universality and particularity of jurisprudence. In M. L. Marasinghe & W. E. Conklin (Eds.), *Essays on Third World perspectives on jurisprudence* (pp. 303-326). Singapore: Malayan Law Journal (PTE).

Chiba, M. (1987). The identity postulate of a legal culture. *ARSP, Rechts und Sozialphilosophie*, Beiheft (IVR), *30*, 7-13.

Cingranelli, D. L. (Ed.). (1988). *Human rights: Theory and measurement*. London: MacMillan.

Christol C. Q. (1977). Human rights. *Encyclopaedia Americana Supplement*. New York: Americana Corporation.

Claude, I. L. (1951).The nature and status of the Sub-commission on Prevention of Discrimination and Protection of Minorities. *International Organization, 5*, 300-312.

Claude, R. (Ed.). (1976). *Comparative human rights*. Baltimore and London: Johns Hopkins University Press.

Clifford, J., & Marcus, G. E. (Eds.). (1986). *Writing culture: The poetics and politics of ethnography*. Berkeley: University of California Press.

Coakley, S. (1979). Theology and cultural relativism: What is the problem? *Neue Zeitschrift fur Systematische Theologie und Religionsphilosophie, 21*, 223-243.

Cobbah, J., & Hamalengwa, M. (1986). The human rights literature on Africa: A bibliography. *Human Rights Quarterly, 8*, 115-125.

Coburn, R. (1976). Relativism and the basis of morality. *Philosophical Review*, 87-93.

Cohn, H. (1971). Talion. *Encyclopedia Judaica* (Vol. 15, p. 741).

Cohn, H. (1972). A human rights theory of law: Prolegomena to a methodology of instruction. In René S. Cassin, *René Cassin Amicorum Discipulorumque Liber* (Vol. 4, pp. 31-60). Paris: Editions A. Pedone.

Colson, E. (1963). Social control and vengeance in Plateau Tonga society. *Africa, 23*, 199-212.

Contini, P. (1971). The evolution of blood-money for homicide in Somalia. *Journal of African Law, 15*, 77-84.

Cook, J. (1978). Cultural relativism as an ethnocentric notion. In R. Beehler & A. R.

Drengson (Eds.), *The Philosophy of Society* (pp. 289-315). London: Methuen.

Cooke, V. (1979). Justice in a world of conceptual relativism. In C. A. Kelbley (Ed.), *The value of justice: Essays on the theory and practice of social virtues* (pp. 29-38). New York: Fordham University Press.

Cooper, D. (1978). Moral relativism. *Midwest Studies in Philosophy, 3*, 97-108.

Copper, J. F., Michael, F., &. Wu, Y. (1985). *Human rights in post-Mao China.* Boulder and London: Westview Press.

Coulson, N. J. (1957). The state and the individual in Islamic law. *International and Comparative Law Quarterly, 6*, 49-60.

Cranston, M. (1967). Human rights: real and supposed. In D. D. Raphael (Ed.). *Political theory and the rights of man* (pp. 43-53). Bloomington: Indiana University Press.

Cranston, M. (1973). *What are human rights?* (2nd ed.). London: Bodley Head.

Cranston, M. (1983). Are there any human rights? *Daedalus, 112*, 1-17.

Crawford, J. (Ed.) (1988). *The rights of peoples.* Oxford: Clarendon Press.

Dalby, M. (1981). Revenge and the law in traditional China. *American Journal of Legal History, 25*, 267-307.

Daly, M. (1978). *Gynecology: The metaethics of radical feminism.* Boston: Beacon Press.

Daly, M. &. Wilson, M. (1988). *Homicide.* Hawthorne, NY: Aldine de Gruyter.

Danelski, D. J. (1966). A behavioral conception of human rights. *Law in Transition Quarterly, 3*, 63-73.

D'Angelo, E. (1973). A comparative concept of freedom. Fifteenth International Congress of Philosophy, Varna, Bulgaria. *Proceedings of the XVth World Congress of Philosophy* (Vol. 4, pp. 47-50).

Das, K. (1982). United Nations institutions and procedures founded on conventions on human rights and fundamental freedoms. In K. Vasak & P. Alston (Eds.), *The international dimensions of human rights* (Vol. I, pp. 303-362). Westport, CT: Greenwood Press.

Daube, D. (1969). *Studies in Biblical Law.* New York: Ktav Publishing House, Inc.

Dautrerner, J. (1885). The vendetta or legal revenge in Japan. *Transactions of the Asiatic Society of Japan, 13*, 82-89.

Davis, M. (1986). Harm and retribution. *Philosophy and Public Affairs, 15*, 236-266.

Dean, R. N. (1980). Beyond Helsinki: The Soviet view of human rights in international law. *Virginia Journal of International Law, 21*, 55-95.

Deats, R. L. (1978). Human rights: An historical and theological perspective. *Engage/Social Action, 6*, 10-14.

De Laguna, G. (1942). Cultural relativism and science. *The Philosophical Review, 51*, 141-166.

De Marneffe, J. (1974). Cultural relativism. *Indian Philosophical Quarterly, 1*, 313-323.

Dembitz, L. (1895). Retaliation. In I. Singer (Ed.) *Jewish encyclopedia* (Vol. 10, pp. 385-386). New York: Ktav Publishing.

de Neufville, J. I. (1986). Human rights reporting as a policy tool: An examination of the State Department country reports. *Human Rights Quarterly, 8*, 681-699.

Derian, P. (1978). Human rights: A world perspective. *Department of State Current Policy, 42*, 1-4.

de Waal, F. (1982). *Chimpanzee politics.* New York: Harper & Row.

Dewey, J. (1927). Anthropology and ethics. In W. F. Ogburn & A. Goldenweiser (Eds.). *The Social sciences and their interrelations* (pp. 24-36). Boston: Houghton Mifflin.

Diamond, A. S. (1957). An eye for an eye. *Iraq, 19*, 151-155.

Di Bella, M. P. (1980). Le code de la vengeance en Barbagia (Sardaigne) selon A. Pigliaru. *Production Pastorale et Société, 7*, 37-42.

Dinstein, Y. (1976). Collective human rights of peoples and minorities. *International and Comparative Law Quarterly, 25*, 102-120.

Dirio, J. A. (1976). Cognitive universalism and cultural relativity in moral education. *Educational Philosophy and Theory, 8*, 33-52.

Dobriansky, P. (1988). *U.S. human rights policy: An overview.* Current Policy No. 1091. Washington, DC: U.S. Department of State, Bureau of Public Affairs.

Dogramaci, I. (1985). Child labour: An overview. In P. M. Shah (Ed.), *Child labour: A threat to health and development* (pp. 7-12). Geneva: Defense for Children International.

Dominguez, J. I., Rodley, N. S., Wood, B., & Falk, R. (1979). *Enhancing global human rights.* New York: McGraw Hill.

Dominicé, C. (1982). The implementation of humanitarian law. In K. Vasak & P. Alston (Eds.), *The international dimensions of human rights* (Vol. 2, pp. 427-447). Westport, CT: Greenwood Press.

Donnelly, J. (1981). Recent trends in UN human rights activity: Description and polemic. *International Organization, 35*, 633-655.

Donnelly, J. (1982a). Human rights as natural rights. *Human Rights Quarterly, 4*, 391-405.

Donnelly, J. (1982b). Human rights and human dignity: An analytic critique of non-western conceptions of human rights. *American Political Science Review, 76*, 303-316.

Donnelly, J. (1982c). How are rights and duties correlative? *Journal of Value Inquiry, 16*, 287-294.

Donnelly, J. (1984). Cultural relativism and universal human rights. *Human Rights Quarterly, 6*, 400-419.

Donnelly, J. (1985). *The concept of human rights.* New York: St. Martin's.

Donnelly, J. (1986). International human rights: A regime analysis. *International*

Organization, 40, 599-642.

Donnelly, J., & Howard, R. E. (Eds.). (1987). *International Handbook of Human Rights*. Westport, CT: Greenwood Press.

Donnelly, J., & Howard, R. E. (1988). Assessing national human rights performance: A theorical framework. *Human Rights Quarterly, 10*, 214-248.

Doron, P. (1969). A new look at an old lex. *Journal of the Ancient Near Eastern Society of Columbia University, 1*, 21-27.

Downing, T. E., & Kushner, G. (Eds.). (1988). *Human rights and anthropology*. Cambridge, MA: Cultural Survival.

Driscoll, D. J. (1979). The development of human rights in international law. In W. Laqueur & B. Rubin (Eds.), *The human rights reader* (pp. 41-56). New York: New American Library.

Driver, G. R., & Miles, J. C. (1952). *The Babylonian laws: Vol. 1. Legal commentary*. Oxford: Clarendon Press.

Driver, G. R., & Miles, J. C. (1956). *The Babylonian laws: Vol 2. Transliterared text, translations, philological notes, glossary*. Oxford: Clarendon Press.

Drost, P. (1951). *Human rights as legal rights*. Leiden: A. W. S. Uitgeversmi.

D'Sa, R. M. (1981-83). The African Charter on Human and Peoples' Rights: Problems and prospects for regional action. *Australian Yearbook of International Law, 10*, 101-130.

Duchacek, I. D. (1973). *Rights and liberties in the world today: Constitutional promise and reality*. Santa Barbara, California and Oxford: ABC-Clio.

DuCros, P. (1926). De Ia vendetta a la loi du talion. *Revue d' Historie et de Philosophie Religieuses, 6*, 350-365.

Dudley, J. (1982). Human rights practices in the Arab states: The modern impact of shari'a values. *Georgia Journal of International and Comparative Law, 12*, 55-93.

Dugan, J. (1978). *Human rights and the South African legal order*. Princeton, NJ: Princeton University Press.

Dumont, L. (1980). *Homo hierarchicus: The caste system and its implications*. Chicago and London: University of Chicago Press.

Duncker, K. (1939). Ethical relativity. *Mind, 48*, 39-53.

Dundes, A. (1968). *Every man his way: Readings in cultural anthropology*. Englewood Cliffs, NJ: Prentice-Hall.

Dupree, L. (1980). Militant Islam and traditional warfare in Islamic south Asia. *American Universities Field Staff Reports, 1980/21 Asia*, 1-12.

Durkheim, E. (1966). *The division of labor in society*. New York: Free Press.

Dworkin, R. (1978). *Taking rights seriously*. Cambridge, MA: Harvard University Press.

Ebel, H. (1986). The strange history of cultural relativism. *Journal of Psychoanalytic Anthropology, 9*, 177-183.

Edel, A. (1962). Anthropology and ethics in common focus. *Journal of the Royal Anthropological Institute, 92,* 55-72.

Edel, A. (1970). On a certain value-dimension in analyses of moral relativism. *Journal of Philosophy, 67,* 584-588.

Edel, A. (1971). Some reflections on the concept of human rights. In E. H. Pollack (Ed.), *Human Rights* (pp. 1-23). Buffalo, NY: Jay Stewart for Amintaphil.

Edel, A. (1977). *Ethical judgment.* Glencoe, IL: Free Press.

Edel, A. (1982). Westermarck's formulation of ethical relativity in twentieth century perspective. In T. Stroup (Ed.), *Edward Westermarck: Essays on his life and work. Acta Philosophica Fennica, 34,* 71-98.

Edel, A., & Edel, M. (1963). The confrontation of anthropology and ethics. *The Monist, 47,* 489-505.

Edel, A., & Edel, M. (1968). *Anthropology and ethics: The quest for moral understanding.* Cleveland: The Press of Case Western Reserve University.

Edwards, R. R. (1986). Civil and social rights: Theory and practice in Chinese law today. In R. R. Edwards, L. Henkin, & A. J. Nathan (Eds.), *Human Rights in Contemporary China* (pp. 41-75). New York: Columbia University Press.

Edwards, R. R., Henkin, L., & Nathan, A. J. (1986). *Human rights in contemporary China.* New York: Columbia University Press.

Egorov, A. G. (1979). Socialism and the individual-Rights and freedoms. *Soviet Studies in Philosophy, 18,* 3-5I.

Eide, A. (1977). *Human rights in the world society.* Oslo-Bergen-Tromsø Universitetsforlaget.

Eide, A. (1979). The world of human rights as seen from a small, industrialized country. *International Studies Quarterly 23,* 246-272.

Eide, A., Eide, W. B., Goonatilake, S., Gussow, J., & Omawale (Eds.). (1984). *Food as a human right.* Tokyo: The United Nations University.

Eide, A., & Schou, A. (Eds.). (1968). *International protection of human rights.* New York: Interscience.

Eisler, R. (1987). Human rights: Toward an integrated theory for action. *Human Rights Quarterly 9,* 287-308.

Ekman, P. (1973). Cross-cultural studies of facial expressions. In P. Ekman (Ed.), *Darwin and facial expression* (pp. 169-222). New York and London: Academic Press.

El Dareer, A. (1983a). *Woman why do you weep? Circumcision and its consequences.* London: Zed Press.

El Dareer, A. (1983b). Attitudes of Sudanese people to the practice of female circumcision. *International Journal of Epidemiology, 12,* 138-144.

Elezi, I. (1966). Sur la vendetta en Albanie. *Studia Albanica, 3,* 305-318.

Elias, R. (1986). *The politics of victimization.* New York and Oxford: Oxford University Press.

Elias, T. O. (1979). The contribution of Asia and Africa to contemporary international law. In T. O. Elias, (Ed.), *New horizons in international law* (pp. 21-33). Alphen aan den Rijin: Sijthoff & Noordhoff.

El-Kayal, M. (1975). *The role of the United Nations in the protection of human rights.* J.S.D. thesis, University of Illinois at Champaign-Urbana.

Elkin, A. P. (1948).The rights of man in primitive society. In UNESCO (Ed.), *Human rights* (pp. 226-241). New York and London: Allan Wingate.

Ellenberger, H. F. (1981). La vendetta. *Revue Internationale de Criminologie et de Police Technique, 34,* 125-142.

El Naiem, A. A. (1984). A modern approach to human rights in Islam: Foundations and implications for Africa. In C. E. Welch, Jr. & R. I. Meltzer (Eds.). *Human rights and developmentment in Africa* (pp. 75-89). Albany: State University of New York Press.

El Naiem, A. A. (1987). Religious minorities under Islamic law and the limits of cultural relativism. *Human Rights Quarterly, 9,* 1-18.

Emerson, R. (1974-75). The fate of human rights in the Third World. *World Politics, 27,* 201-226.

Emmett, D. (1968). Ethical systems and social structure. In D. Sills (Ed.), *International Encyclopedia of the Social Sciences* (Vol. 5, pp. 157-160). New York: Macmillan and Free Press.

Evans-Pritchard, E. E. (1963). *The Nuer.* Oxford: Clarendon Press.

Ezejiofor, G. (1984). *Protection of human rights under the law.* London: Butterworths.

Falconer, A. D. (Ed.). (1980). *Understanding human rights: Interdisciplinary and interfaith study.* Dublin: Irish School of Ecumenics.

Falk, R. (1981). *Human rights and state sovereignty.* New York: Holmes & Meier.

Farabee, W. C. (1967). *The central Arawaks: Anthropological publications.* New York: Humanities Press.

Fareed, N.J. (1977). *The United Nations Commission on Human Rights and its work for human rights and fundamental freedoms.* Ph.D. dissertation, Washington State University.

Farer, T. J. (1979). On a collision course: The American campaign for human rights and the antiradical bias in the Third World. In D. P. Kommers & G. D. Loescher (Eds.), *Human rights and American foreign policy* (pp. 263-277). Notre Dame, IN: University of Notre Dame Press.

Farer, T. J. (1987). The United Nations and human rights: More than a whimper, less than a roar. *Human Rights Quarterly, 9,* 550-586.

Fawcett, J. E. S. (1969). *The application of the European convention on human rights.* Oxford: Clarendon Press.

Feinberg, J. (1966). Duties, rights and claims. *American Philosophical Quarterly, 3,* 137-144.

Feinberg, J. (1970). The nature and value of rights. *Journal of Value Inquiry, 4*, 243-257.

Feinberg, J. (1973). *Social philosophy*. Englewood Cliffs, NJ: Prentice-Hall.

Feinberg, J. (1980). *Rights, justice, and the bounds of liberty*. Princeton, NJ: Princeton University Press.

Ferguson, C. C. (1979). Global human rights: Challenges and prospects. *Denver Journal of International Law and Policy, 8*, 367-377.

Ferguson, J. A. (1986). The Third World. In R.J. Vincent (Ed.), *Foreign policy and human rights: Issues and responses* (pp. 203-226). Cambridge: Cambridge University Press.

Feyerabend, P. (1977). Rationalism, relativism and scientific method. *Philosophy in Context, 6*, 7-19.

Finkelstein, J. J. (1936). An eye for an eye. *The Menorah Journal, 24*, 207-218.

Finkelstein, J. J. (1961). Ammisaduqa's Edict and the Babylonian "law codes." *Journal of Cuneiform Studies, 15*, 91-104.

Firth, R. (1973). The study of values by social anthropologists. *Man, 53*, 230-260.

Fischer, D. D. (1982). Reporting under the Covenant on Civil and Political Rights: The first five years of the human rights committee. *American Journal of International Law, 76*, 142-153.

Fisher, E. F. (1982). Explorations and responses: *Lex talionis* in the Bible and rabbinic tradition. *Journal of Ecumenical Studies, 19*, 582-587.

Fitzmaurice, G. G. (1956). The foundations of the authority of international law and the problem of enforcement. *Modern Law Review, 19*, 1-13.

Flathman, R. E. (1976). *The practice of rights*. Cambridge: Cambridge University Press.

Flathman, R. E. (1980). Rights, needs, and liberalism. *Political Theory, 8*, 319-330.

Flew, A. (1979). What is a right? *Georgia Law Review, 13*, 1127-1141.

Foot, P. (1979). Morality and art. In T. Honderich & M. Burnyeat (Eds.). *Philosophy as it is* (pp. 7-29). New York: Penguin.

Foot, P. (1982). Moral relativism. The Lindley lecture: University of Kansas. In M. Krausz & J. W. Meilands (Eds.), *Relativism: Cognitive and moral* (pp. 152-166). Notre Dame, IN: University of Notre Dame Press.

Forsythe, D. P. (1982). Socioeconomic human rights: The United Nations, the United States, and beyond. *Human Rights Quarterly 4*, 433-449.

Forsythe, D. P. (1983). *Human rights and world politics*. Lincoln: University of Nebraska Press.

Forsythe, D. P. (1985). The United Nations and human rights, 1945-85. *Political Science Quarterly, 100*, 249-269.

Forsythe, D. P., & Wiseberg, L. S. (1979). Human rights protection: A research agenda. *Universal Human Rights, 1*, 1-24.

Fortin, E. L. (1982). The new rights theory and natural law. *The Review of Politics,* *44,* 590-612.

Frank. P. (1943). The relativity of truth and the objectivity of values. In L. Bryson & L. Finkelstein (Eds.), *Science, philosophy and religion* (pp. 12-32), 3rd Symposium. New York: Conference on Science, Philosophy and Religion and Their Relation to the Democratic Way of Life, Inc.

Frankena, W. K. (1939). The naturalistic fallacy. *Mind, 48,* 464-477.

Frankena, W. K. (1952). *Symposium: The concept of human rights. Science, language, and human rights.* Philadelphia: University of Pennsylvania Press.

Frankena, W. K. (1955). Natural and inalienable rights. *Philosophical Review, 64,* 212-232.

Frankena, W. K. (1973). *Ethics.* Englewood Cliffs, NJ: Prentice-Hall.

Fraser, D. M., & Salzberg, J. P. (1979). International political parties as a vehicle for human rights. *Annals, American Academy of Political and Social Science, 442,* 63-68.

Fraser, J. G. (1935). *The golden bough: A study in magic and religion,* Part 5, Vol. 2 (3rd ed.). New York: Macmillan.

Freeman, D. (1967). A matter of values. *Man, 2,* 132-133.

Freeman, E. (Ed.). (1963). Ethics and anthropology. *The Monist, 47,* 489-641.

Friedman, L. M. (1986). The law and society movement. *Stanford Law Review, 38,* 763-780.

Friedman, L. M. (1971). The idea of right as a social and legal concept. *Journal of Social Issues, 27,* 189-198.

Fryer, E. D. (1980). Contemplating Sinha's anthropocentric theory of international law as a basis for human rights. *Case Western Reserve Journal of International Law, 12,* 575-590.

Frymer-Kensky, T. (1980). Tit for tat: The principle of equal retribution in Near Eastern and Biblical law. *Biblical Archeologist, 43,* 230-234.

Fuchs, A. E. (1981). Taking absolute rights seriously. *Tenth World Congress on Philosophy of Law and Social Philosophy,* Vol. 2. Mexico.

Furer-Haimendorf, C. von. (1967). Morals and merit: *A study of values and social controls in South Asian societies.* London: Weidenfeld and Nicolson.

Galey, M. E. (1979). Promoting nondiscrimination against women: The UN Commission on the status of women. *International Studies Quarterly, 23,* 273-302.

Galtung, J., & Wirak, A. H. (1977). Human needs and human rights: A theoretical approach. *Bulletin of Peace Proposals, 8,* 251-258.

Ganji, M. (1962). *International protection of human rights.* Geneva: Librairie E. Droz.

Gardeniers, T., Hannum, H., & Kruger, J. (1982). The UN Sub-commission on Prevention of Discrimination and Protection of Minorities: Recent developments. *Human Rights Quarterly, 4,* 353-370.

Garet, R. (1983). Communality and existence: The rights of groups. *Southern California Law Review, 56*, 1001-1075.

Garine, I. D. (1980). Les etrangers, la vengeance et les parents chez les Massa et les Moussey (Tchad et Cameroun). In R. Verdier (Ed.), *La vengeance* (Vol. I, pp. 91-124). Paris: Editions Cujas.

Gazzali, M. (1962). *Human rights in the teaching of Islam.* Cairo: Al makhtabat al-Tjariyah.

Geertz, C. (1983). *Local knowledge: Further essays in interpretive anthropology.* New York: Basic Books.

Geertz, C. (1984). Anti anti-relativism. *American Anthropologist, 86*, 263-278.

Gerber, D. (1973). Cultural relativity and ethical relativism. *Proceedings International Congress of Philosophy* (Bulgaria) (Vol. I, pp. 159-163).

Gewirth, A. (1982). *Human rights: Essays on justifications and applications.* Chicago and London: University of Chicago Press.

Gewirth, A. (1983). The epistemology of human rights. *Social Philosophy and Policy, 1*, 1-24.

Gewirth, A. (1985). Why there are human rights. *Social Theory and Practice, 11*, 235-255.

Gilligan, C. (1982). *In a different voice.* Cambridge, MA: Harvard University Press.

Ginsburg, M. (1956). *On the diversity of morals.* New York: Macmillan.

Ginsburg, M. (1973). On the diversity of morals. *Journal of the Royal Anthropological Institute, 83*, 117-135.

Ginther, K., & Benedek, W. (Eds.). (1983). *New perspectives and conceptions of international law.* New York: Springer-Verlag.

Girard, R. (1977). *Violence and the sacred* (P. Gregory, Trans.). Baltimore and London: Johns Hopkins University Press.

Gittleman, R. (1982). The African Charter on Human and Peoples' Rights: A legal analysis. *Virginia Journal of International Law, 22*, 667-714.

Gittleman, R. (1984). The African Commission on Human and Peoples' Rights: Prospects and procedures. In H. Hannum (Ed.), *Guide to international human rights practice* (pp. 153-162). Philadelphia: University of Pennsylvania Press.

Gjoliku, L. (1984). The Socialist order is the most democratic. *Albania Today, 3*(76), 46-51.

Glaser, K., & Possony, S. T. (1979). *Victims of politics: The state of human rights.* New York: Columbia University Press.

Glasse, R. M. (1959). Revenge and redress among the Huli: A preliminary account. *Mankind, 5*, 273-289.

Gluckman, M. (1965). *Politics, law and ritual in tribal society.* New York and Toronto: New American Library.

Gluckman, M. (1966). The peace in feud. In M. Gluckman (Ed.), *Custom and*

Conflict in Africa (pp. 1-26). Oxford: Blackwell.

Gluckman, M. (1969). Concepts in the comparative study of tribal law. In L. Nader (Ed.), *Law in culture and society* (pp. 349-373). Chicago: Aldine.

Golding, M. P. (1968). Towards a theory of human rights. *The Monist, 52*, 521-549.

Golding, M. P. (1978). The concepts of rights: A historical sketch. In E. Bandman, & B. Bandman (Eds.), *Bioethics and human rights* (pp. 44-50). Boston: Little, Brown.

Goldman, M. (1983). Human rights in the People's Republic of China. *Daedalus, 112*, 111-138.

Goldschmidt, W. (1951). Ethics and the structure of society: An ethnological contribution to the sociology of knowledge. *American Anthropologist, 53*, 506-524.

Goldstein, R. J. (1986). The limitations of using quantitative data in studying human rights abuses. *Human Rights Quarterly, 8*, 607-653.

Gordenker, L. (1983). Development of the UN system. In T. Trister (Ed.), *The United States, the United Nations, and the management of global change* (pp. 11-21). New York: New York University Press.

Gouldner, A. W. (1960). The norm of reciprocity: A preliminary statement. *American Sociological Review, 25*, 161-178.

Grande, F. (1983). Tolerancia versus Ley Del Talion. *Cuadernos Hispanoamericanos. 395*, 203-211.

Green, J. F. (1958). *The UN and human rights*. Washington, DC: Brookings Institutions. (reprint).

Green, J. F. (1977). Changing approaches to human rights: the United Nations, 1954 and 1974. *Texas International Law Journal, 12*, 223-238.

Green, R. G. (1981). Basic human rights/needs: Some problems of categorical translation and unification. *Review of the International Commission of Jurists, 27*, 53-58.

Greidanus, S. (1984). Human rights in biblical perspective. *Calvin Theological Journal, 19*, 5-31.

Gros Espiell, H. (1979). The evolving concept of human rights: Western, socialist and Third World approaches. In B. G. Ramcharan (Ed.), *Human rights: Thirty years after the Universal Declaration* (pp. 41-65). The Hague, Boston, London: Martinus Nijhoff.

Gros Espiell, H. (1982). The organization of American states. In K. Vasak & P. Alston (Eds.), *The international dimensions of human rights* (Vol. 2, pp. 543-574). Westport, CT: Greenwood Press.

Gross, L. (1965). The United Nations and the role of law. *International Organization, 19*, 537-561.

Groult, B. (1975). *Ainsi soit-elle*. Paris: Grasset.

Guggenheim, M. H. (1977). The implementation of human rights by the UN

Commission on the Status of Women. *Texas International Law Journal, 12,* 239-249.

Haas, E. B. (1978). *Global evangelism rides again: How to protect human rights without really trying.* Berkeley, CA: Institute for International Studies.

Haider, S. M. (1978). *Islamic concept of human rights.* Lahore: Book House.

Haile, M. (1984). Human rights, stability, and development in Africa: Some observations on concept and reality. *Virginia Journal of International Law, 24,* 575-615.

Hakim, K. A. (1955). *Fundamental human rights.* Lahore: Institute of Islamic Culture Publications.

Haldane, J. B. S. (1940). A comparative study of freedom. In R. N. Anshen (Ed.), *Freedom: Its meaning* (pp. 447-472). New York: Harcourt, Brace.

Halderman, J. (1979). Advancing human rights through the United Nations. *Law and Contemporary Problems, 43,* 275-288.

Hall, J. (1983). Biblical atonement and modern criminal law. *Journal of Law and Religion, 1,* 279-295.

Hallpike, C. R. (1975). Two types of reciprocity. *Comparative Studies in Society and History, 17,* 113-119.

Hallpike, C. R. (1977). *Bloodshed and vengeance in the Papuan mountains.* Oxford: Clarendon Press.

Hamalengwa, M., Flinterman. C., & Dankwa, E. V. O. (1988). *The international law of human rights in Africa.* Dordrecht: Martinus Nijhoff.

Hannum, H. (1984). *Guide to international human rights practice.* Philadelphia: University of Pennsylvania Press.

Harakas, S. S. (1982). Human rights: An Eastern Orthodox perspective. In A. Swidler (Ed.), *Human rights in religious traditions* (pp. 13-24). New York: Pilgrim Press.

Hardy, M. J. L. (1963). *Blood feuds and the payment of blood money in the Middle East.* Beirut.

Harman, G. (1975). Moral relativism defended. *Philosophical Review, 84,* 3-22.

Harman, G. (1978a). Relativistic ethics: Morality as politics. *Midwest Studies in Philosophy, 3,* 109-121.

Harman, G. (1978b). What is moral relativism? In A. Goldman &. J. Kim (Eds.), *Values and morals: Essays in honor of William Frankena, Charles Stevenson, and Richard Brandt.* Dordrecht: Reidel.

Harris, J. S. (1924?) *Lex talionis and the Jewish law of mercy.* London: Pelican Press.

Harrison, G. (1976). Relativism and tolerance. *Ethics, 8,* 122-135.

Hart, H. L. A. (1948-49). The ascription of responsibility and rights. *Proceedings of the Aristotelian Society, 49,* 171-194.

Hart, H. L. A. (1961). *The concept of law.* Oxford: Clarendon Press.

Hart, H. L. A. (1973). Bentham on legal rights. In A. W. B. Simpson (Ed.), *Oxford Essays on Jurisprudence*, 2nd series (pp. 171-201). Oxford: Clarendon Press.

Hart, H. L. A. (1979). Are there any natural rights? In D. Lyons (Ed.), *Rights* (pp. 1-25). Belmont, CA: Wadsworth.

Hartung, F. (1954). Cultural relativity and moral judgments. *Philosophy of Science 21*, 118-126.

Hasluck, M. (1967). The Albanian blood feud. In P. Bohannan (Ed.), *Law and warfare* (pp. 381-408). Garden City, NY: Natural History Press.

Hassan, P. (1969). The word "arbitrary" as used in the Universal Declaration of Human Rights, illegal or unjust? *Harvard International Law Journal, 10,* 225-262.

Hassan, R. (1982). On human rights and the Qur'anic perspective. In A. Swidler (Ed.). *Human rights in religious traditions* (pp. 51-65). New York: Pilgrim Press.

Hatch, E. (1983). *Culture and morality: The relativity of values in anthropology.* New York: Columbia University Press.

Hauser, R. E. (1979). A First World view. In D. P. Kommers &. G. D. Loescher (Eds.). *Human rights and American foreign policy* (pp.85-89). Notre Dame, IN: University of Notre Dame Press.

Haver, P. (1982). The UN Sub-commission on Prevention of Discrimination and Protection of Minorities. *Columbia Journal of Transnational Law, 21,* 103-134.

Heelas, P. (1971). The odd philosopher. *Journal of the Anthropological Society of Oxford, 2,* 146-152.

Held, V. (1984). *Rights and Goods: Justifying Social Action.* New York and London: The Free Press and Macmillan.

Henderson, G. P. (1968). Moral nihilism. *Studies in Moral Philosophy*, 42-52.

Henkin, A. (Ed.). (1979). *Human dignity: The internationalization of human rights.* New York: Aspen Institute for Humanistic Studies.

Henkin, L. (1965). The United Nations and human rights. *International Organization, 19,* 504-517.

Henkin, L. (1976). Judaism and human rights. *Judaism: A Quarterly Journal of Jewish Life and Thought, 25,* 436-446.

Henkin, L. (1979a). Human rights: Reappraisal and readjustment. In D. Sidorsky (Ed.), *Essays on human rights* (pp. 68-87). Philadelphia: Jewish Publication Society of America.

Henkin, L. (1979b). Rights: American and human. *Columbia Law Review, 79,* 406-425.

Henkin, L. (1981). Economic-social rights as "rights": A United States perspective. *Human Rights Law Journal, 2,* 223-236.

Henkin, L. (1986). The human rights idea in contemporary China: A comparative perspective. In R. R. Edwards, L. Henkin, & A. J. Nathan (Eds.), *Human rights in contemporary China* (pp. 7-39). New York: Columbia University Press.

Henle, R. J. (1980). A Catholic view of human rights: A Thomistic reflection. In A. Rosenbaum (Ed.), *The philosophy of human rights* (pp. 87-93). Westport, CT: Greenwood Press.

Herczegh, G. (1984). *Development of international humanitarian law*. Budapest: Akadé Kiadó.

Herodotus. (1947). *The Persian wars*. New York: Modern Library.

Hersch, J. (1970). Is the declaration of human rights a Western concept? In H. E. Kiefer & M. K. Munitz (Eds.), *Ethics and social justice* (pp. 323-332). Albany: State University of New York Press.

Hersch, J. (1986). Human rights in Western thought: Conflicting dimensions. In *UNESCO* (pp. 131-148). Paris: UNESCO.

Herskovits, M. (1950). *Man and his works*. New York: Alfred A. Knopf. (First published 1947).

Herskovits, M. (1951). Tender- and tough-minded anthropology and the study of values in culture. *Southwestern Journal of Anthropology, 7*, 22-31.

Herskovits, M. (1958). Some further comments on cultural relativism. *American Anthropologist, 60*, 266-273.

Herskovits, M. (1964). *Cultural anthropology*. New York: Alfred Knopf.

Herskovits, M. (1972). *Cultural relativism: Perspectives in cultural pluralism*. New York: Random House.

Heuman, S. E. (1979). A Socialist conception of human rights: A model from prerevolutionary Russia. In A. Pollis & P. Schwab (Eds.), *Human rights* (pp. 44-59). New York: Praeger.

Hevener, H. K. (Ed.). (1981). *The dynamics of human rights in U.S. foreign policy*. New Brunswick and London: Transaction Books.

Hevener, N. K., & Mosher, S. A. (1978). General principles of law and the UN covenant on civil and political rights. *International and Comparative Law Quarterly, 27*, 596-614.

Higgins, R. (1979). *Human rights—Prospects and problems*. Thirty-fourth Montague Burton Lecture on International Relations. Leeds: Leeds University Press.

Higgins, R. (1989). Human rights: Some questions of integrity. *Modern Law Review, 52*, 1-21.

Hingorani, R. C. (1984). *Modern international law* (2nd ed.). New York: Oceana Publications.

Hirst, P. (1985). Is it rational to reject relativism? In J. Overing (Ed.). *Reason and morality* (pp. 5-103). London and New York: Tavistock.

Hirszowicz, M. (1966). The Marxist approach. *International Social Science Journal, 18*, 11-21.

Hoare, S. (1967). The UN Commission on human rights. In E. Luard (Ed.), *The international protection of human rights* (pp. 59-98). London: Thames & Hudson.

Hobhouse, L. T. (1915). *Morals in evolution: A study of comparative ethics*. London: Chapman & Hall.

Hoebel, E. A. (1949). [Review of *Man and his works* by M. Herskovits]. *American Anthropologist, 51,* 471-474.

Hoebel, E. A. (1954). *The law of primitive man*. Cambridge. MA: Harvard University Press.

Hoebel, E. A. (1970). Blood feud. *Encyclopedia Britannica* (Vol. 3, pp 803-804).

Hoebel, E. A. (1976). Feud: Concept, reality and method in the study of primitive law. In A. R. Desai (Ed.), *Essays on modernization of underdeveloped societies* (Vol. I., pp. 500-513). Atlantic Highlands, NJ: Humanities Press.

Hoffman, S. (1981). *Duties beyond borders*. Syracuse: Syracuse University Press.

Hohfeld, W. N. (1964). *Fundamental legal conceptions*. New Haven, CT: Yale University Press.

Holborow, L. (1985). Benn, Mackie and basic rights. *Australasian Journal of Philosophy, 63,* 11-25.

Holleman, W. L. (1987). *The human rights movement: Western values and theological perspectives*. New York: Praeger.

Hollenbach, D. (1979). Claims in conflict: *Retrieving and renewing the Catholic human rights tradition*. New York: Paulist.

Hollenbach, D. (1982a). Human rights and religious faith in the Middle East: Reflections of a Christian theologian. *Human Rights Quarterly, 4,* 94-109.

Hollenbach, D. (1982b). Human rights and interreligious dialogue: The challenge to mission in a pluralistic world. *International Bulletin of Missionary Research, 6,* 98-104.

Hollis, M., & Lukes, S. (Eds.). (1982). *Rationality and relativism*. Cambridge: MIT Press.

Holmes, H. B. (1983). A feminist analysis of the Universal Declaration of Human Rights. In C. C. Gould (Ed.), *Beyond domination: New perspectives on women and philosophy* (pp. 250-264). Totowa, NJ: Rowman & Allanheld.

Holy Bible (1952). [King James version.] New York: Oxford University Press.

Hook, S. (1970). Reflections on human rights. In H. E. Kiefer & M. K. Munitz (Eds.), *Ethics and social justice* (pp. 252-281). Albany: State University of New York Press.

Hose, C., & McDougall, W. (1901). The relations between men and animals in Sarawak. *Journal of the Anthropological Institute of Great Britain and Ireland, 31,* 173-213.

Hosken, F. P. (1976). *Women's International Network News, 2*(1), 30-44.

Hospers, J. (Ed.). (1984). Is relativism defensible? *The Monist, 67,* 293-482.

Hountondji, P. J. (1986). The master's voice—Remarks on the problem of human rights in Africa. In *UNESCO* (pp. 319-332). Paris: UNESCO.

Howard, R. (1983). The full belly thesis: Should economic rights take priority over civil and political rights? Evidence from sub-Saharan Africa. *Human Rights Quarterly, 4,* 467-490.

Howard, R. (1984a). Evaluating human rights in Africa: Some problems of implicit comparisons. *Human Rights Quarterly, 6,* 160-179.

Howard, R. (1984b). Women's rights in English-speaking sub-Saharan Africa. In C. E. Welch, Jr., & R. I. Meltzer (Eds.). *Human rights and development in Africa* (pp. 46-74). Albany: State University of New York Press.

Howard, R. (1986a). *Human rights in commonwealth Africa.* Totowa, NJ: Rowman & Littlefield.

Howard, R. (1986b). Is there an African concept of human rights? In R. J. Vincent (Ed.), *Foreign policy and human rights* (pp. 11-32). Cambridge: Cambridge University Press.

Howard, R., & Donnelly, J. (1986). Human dignity, human rights and political regimes. *American Political Science Review, 80,* 801-817.

Howard, V. A. (1968). Do anthropologists become moral relativists by mistake? *Inquiry, 11,* 175-189.

Hsiung, J. C. (Ed.). (1986). *Human rights in East Asia: A cultural perspective.* New York: Paragon House.

Hsu, F. (1964). Rethinking the concept "primitive." *Current Anthropology, 5,* 169-178.

Huang, M. (1979). Human rights in a revolutionary society: The case of the People's Republic of China. In A. Pollis & P. Schwab (Eds.), *Human rights: Cultural and ideological perspectives* (pp. 60-85). New York: Praeger.

Hudson, S. D. (1979). A note on Feinberg's analysis of legal rights in terms of the activity of claiming. *Journal of Value Inquiry, 13,* 155-156.

Hudson, S. D., &. Husak, D. N. (1980). Legal rights: How useful is Hohfeldian analysis? *Philosophical Studies, 37,* 45-53.

Hudson, W. D. (Ed.). (1969). *The is/ought question.* New York: St. Martin's.

Huelsman, B. R. (1976). An anthropological view of clitoral and other female genital mutilations. In T. P. Lowry &. T. S. Lowry (Eds.), *The clitoris* (pp. 111-161). St. Louis, MO: Warren H. Green.

Humphrey, J. P. (1967). The UN Charter and the Universal Declaration of Human Rights. In E. Luard (Ed.), *The international protection of human rights* (pp. 39-58). New York: Praeger.

Humphrey, J. P. (1968). The UN Sub-Commission on the Prevention of Discrimination and Protection of Minorities. *American Journal of International Law, 62,* 869-888.

Humphrey, J. P. (1969). The UN Commission on Human Rights and its parent body. In René S. Cassin, *René Cassin Amicorum Discipulorumque Liber* (Vol. I, pp. 108-113). Paris: Editions A. Pedone.

Humphrey, J. P. (1973). The international law of human rights in the middle twentieth century. In M. Bos (Ed.), *The present state of international law and other essays* (pp.75-105). Deventer: Kluwer.

Humphrey, J. P. (1975). The Sub-Commission on the Prevention of Discrimination and the Protection of Minorities. *American Journal of International Law, 66,* 869-888.

Humphrey, J. P. (1979). The Universal Declaration of Human Rights: Its history, impact and juridical character. In B. G. Ramcharan (Ed.), *Human rights: Thirty years after the universal declaration* (pp. 21-31). The Hague: Martinus Nijhoff.

Humphrey, J. P. (1984). *Human rights and the United Nations: A great adventure.* Dobbs Ferry, NY: Transnational Publishers.

Husak, D. N. (1984). Why there are no human rights. *Social Theory and Practice, 10,* 125-141.

Husak, D. N. (1985). The motivation for human rights. *Social Theory and Practice, 11,* 249-255.

Husson, L. (1982). Contenu et signification des notions de morale naturelle et de droit naturel. *Archives de Philosophie, 45,* 529-548.

Inada, K. K. (1982). The Buddhist perspective on human rights. In A. Swidler (Ed.), *Human rights in religious traditions* (pp. 66-76). New York: Pilgrim Press.

Inagaki, R. (1986). Some aspects of human rights in Japan. In *UNESCO* (pp. 179-192). Paris: UNESCO.

Ingarden, R. (1975). Remark concerning the relativity of values. *Journal of the British Society for Phenomenology, 6,* 102-108.

Ingram, P. (1981). Natural rights: A reappraisal. *Journal of Value Inquiry, 15,* 3-18.

International Commission of Jurists. (1976 [1978]). *Human rights in a one-party state.* London: Search Press.

Ishaque, K. M. (1974). Human rights in Islamic law. *Review of the International Commission of Jurists, 123,* 30-39.

Iwe, N. S. S. (1986). The history and contents of human rights. New York: Peter Lang.

Jackson, B. S. (1973). The problem of Exod. XXI 22-5 (IUS Talionis). *Vestus Testamentum, 23,* 273-304.

Jacobs, F. O. (1975). *The European convention on human rights.* Oxford: Clarendon Press.

Jacoby, S. (1983). *Wild justice: The evolution of revenge.* New York: Harper & Row.

Jaeger, F., & Selznick, P. (1964). A normative theory of culture. *American Sociological Review, 29,* 653-669.

Jaffa, H. V. (1984). Human rights and the crisis of the West. In H. V. Jaffa (Ed.), *American conservatism and the American Founding* (pp. 216-236). Durham, NC: Carolina Academic Press.

Janis, J. W. (1986). The utility and relativity of international law theory. *Proceedings, American Society of International Law*, 8th Annual Meeting, Washington, DC (pp. 152-157).

Jarvie, I. C. (1964a). *The revolution in anthropology*. London: Routledge & Kegan Paul.

Jarvie, I. C. (1964b). [Review of *Relativism and the study of man*]. *British Journal for the Philosophy of Science, 15*, 141-158.

Jarvie, I. C. (1975a). Cultural relativism again. *Philosophy of the Social Sciences, 5*, 343-355.

Jarvie, I. C. (1975b). Epistle to the anthropologists. *American Anthropologist, 77*, 253-255.

Jarvie, I. C. (1983). Rationality and relativism. *British Journal of Sociology, 34*, 44-60.

Jayatilleke, K. N. (1967). The principles of international law in Buddhist doctrine. *Recueil des Cours, 120*, 445-464.

Jenkins, I. (1980). The concept of rights. In I. Jenkins (Ed.), *Social order and the limits of the law* (pp. 241-267). Princeton. NJ: Princeton University Press.

Jenks, C. W. (1970). *Social justice in the law of nations: The ILO impact after fifty years*. London: Oxford University Press.

Jhabvala, F. (1984). The practice of the Covenant's Human Rights Committee, 1976-1982: Review of state party reports. *Human Rights Quarterly, 6*, 81-106.

Johnson, M. G. (1987). The contributions of Eleanor and Franklin Roosevelt to the development of international protection for human rights. *Human Rights Quarterly, 9*, 19-48.

Johnson, W. G. (1986). Human rights practices in divergent ideological settings: How do political ideas influence policy choices? *Policy Studies Review, 6*, 58-70.

Jones, J. W. (1926). Acquired and guaranteed rights. In *Cambridge Legal Essays* (pp. 223-242). Cambridge, UK: W. Heffer & Sons, Ltd.

Kabir, H. (1948). Human rights: The Islamic tradition and the problems of the world today. In UNESCO (Ed.), *Human Rights* (pp. 191-194). London and New York: Allan Wingate.

Kadarkay, A. (1982). *Human rights in American and Russian political thought*. Washington, DC: University Press of America.

Kamenka, E., & A. Tay (Eds.). (1978). *Human Rights*. London: Edward Arnold.

Kamenka, E., & A. Tay. (1986). Human rights: Perspectives from Australia. In *UNESCO* (pp. 151-177). Paris: UNESCO.

Kamminga, M., & Rodley, N. S. (1984). Direct intervention at the UN: NGO participation in the Commission on Human Rights and its Sub-commission. In H. Hannum (Ed.), *Guide to international human rights* (pp. 186-199). Philadelphia: University of Pennsylvania Press.

Kanger, H. (1984). *Human rights in the U.N. Declaration*. Uppsala: Academia

Upsaliensis.

Kannyo, E. (1980). *Human rights in Africa: Problems and prospects.* International League for Human Rights.

Kannyo, E. (1984). The Banjul Charter on Human and People's Rights: Genesis and political background. In C. Welch & R. Meltzer (Eds.), *Human rights in Africa.* Albany: State University of New York Press.

Kant, I. (1981). *Foundations of the metaphysics of morals.* Indianapolis: Bobbs-Merrill.

Kaplan, A. (1980). Human relations and human rights in Judaism. In A. Rosenbaum (Ed.), *The philosophy of human rights* (pp. 53-85). Westport, CT: Greenwood Press.

Karsten, R. (1923). *Blood revenge, war, and victory feasts among the Jibaro Indians of Eastern Ecuador* (U.S. Bureau of American Ethnology, Bulletin 79). Washington, DC: Government Printing Office.

Kartashkin, V. (1982a). The Socialist concept of human rights. In K. Vasak & P. Alston (Eds.), *The international dimensions of human rights* (Vol. 2, pp. 631-643). Westport, CT: Greenwood Press.

Kartashkin, V. (1982b). Economic, social and cultural rights. In K. Vasak & P. Alston (Eds.), *The international dimensions of human rights* (Vol. 1, pp. 111-134). Westport, CT: Greenwood Press.

Kartashkin, V. A. (1977). Covenants on human rights and Soviet legislation. *Revue des Droits de l'Homme, 10,* 97-115.

Kataio, N. L. (1981). The rights and duties of young people. In *Human rights in socialist society* (pp. 90-101). Moscow: Novosti Press.

Kaufman, N. G., & Whiteman, D. (1988). Opposition to human rights treaties in the United State Senate: The legacy of the Bricker Amendment. *Human Rights Quarterly, 10,* 309-337.

Kay, P., & Kempton, W. (1984). What is the Sapir-Whorf hypothesis? *American Anthropologist, 86,* 65-79.

Kearns, T. R. (1975). Rights, benefits and normative systems. *Archiv für Rechts- und Sozialphilosophie, 61,* 465-483.

Keith, K. J. (1967). Asian attitudes to international law. *Australian Yearbook of International Law, 1967,* 1-35.

Kelley, R. (1984). Comparing the incomparable: Politics and ideas in the United States and the Soviet Union. *Comparative Studies in Society and history, 26,* 672-708.

Kelman, H. C. (1977). Conditions, criteria, and dialectics of human dignity. *International Studies Quarterly, 21,* 529-552.

Kelsen, H. (1941). Causality and retribution. *Philosophy of Science, 8,* 533-556.

Kelsen, H. (1946). *Society and nature: A sociological inquiry.* London: Kegan Paul, Trench, Trubner.

Kennan, E. L. (1980). Human rights in Soviet political culture. In K. Thompson

(Ed.), *The moral imperatives of human rights* (pp. 69-79). Washington, DC: University Press of America.

Kenyatta, J. (1965). *Facing Mount Kenya: The tribal life of the Gikuyu.* New York: Vintage.

Khadduri, J. (1946). Human rights in Islam. *Annals, American Academy of Political and Social Science, 243*, 77-81.

Khadduri, M. (1984). *The Islamic conception of justice.* Baltimore and London: Johns Hopkins University Press.

Khanna, H. R. (1978). Future of human rights in contemporary world. *Indian Journal of International Law, 18*, 133-138.

Khatchadourian, H. (1985). Toward a foundation for human rights. *Man and World, 13*, 219-240.

Khushalani, Y. (1983). Human rights in Asia and Africa. *Human Rights Law Journal, 4*, 403-442.

Kidd, D. (1969). *Kafir socialism and the dawn of individualism: An introduction to the study of the native problem.* New York: Negro Universities Press.

Kim, I. (1986). Human rights in South Korea and U.S. relations. In J. C. Hsiung (Ed.), *Human rights in East Asia* (pp. 55-75). New York: Paragon.

Kirk, G., & Chamberlain, L. (1945). The organization of the San Francisco conference. *Political Science Quarterly, 60*, 321-342.

Kleinig, J. (1973). *Punishment and desert.* The Hague: Martinus Nijhoff.

Kleinig, J. (1978). Human rights, legal rights and social change. In E. Kamenka & A. Tay (Eds.), *Human rights* (pp. 36-47). London: Edward Arnold.

Kleinig, J. (1981). Cultural relativism and human rights. In A. Tay (Ed.), *Teaching human rights* (pp. 111-118). Canberra: Australian Government Publishing Service.

Klenner, H. (1984). Freedom and human rights. *GDR Committee for Human Rights Bulletin, 10*, 13-22.

Kluckhohn, C. (1949). The philosophy of the Navaho Indians. In S. C. Northrop (Ed.), *Ideological differences and world order* (pp. 356-384). New Haven, CT: Yale University Press.

Kluckhohn, C. (1951). Values and value-orientations in the theory of action. In T. Parsons & E. A. Shils (Eds.), *Toward a general theory of action* (pp. 388-433). Cambridge, MA: Harvard University Press.

Kluckhohn, C. (1952). Universal values and anthropological relativism. *Modern Education and Human Values*, Pitcairn-Crabbe Foundation Lecture Series, *4*, 87-112.

Kluckhohn, C. (1953). Universal categories in culture. In A. L. Kroeber (Ed.), *Anthropology Today* (pp. 524-553). Chicago: University of Chicago Press.

Kluckhohn, C. (1955). Ethical relativity: Sic et non. *Journal of Philosophy, 52*, 663-

677.

Kluckhohn, C. (1956a). New uses for "barbarians." In L. D. White, Jr. (Ed.), *Frontiers of knowledge in the study of man* (pp. 33-47). New York: Harper.

Kluckhohn, C. (1956b). Toward a comparison of value-emphases in different cultures. In L. D. White (Ed.), *The state of the social sciences* (pp. 116-132). Chicago: University of Chicago Press.

Kluckhohn, F. R. & Strodtbeck, F. T. (1961). *Variations in value orientations*. Evanston, IL: Row, Peterson.

Knight, S. (1984). Three varieties of cultural relativism. *Educational Philosophy and Theory, 16,* 23-36.

Kohlberg, L., & Elfenbein, D. (1975). The development of moral judgments concerning capital punishment. *American Journal of Orthopsychiatry, 45,* 614-640.

Kolakowski, L. (1983). Marxism and human rights. *Daedalus, 112,* 81-92.

Koldayev, V. (1976). *Soviet citizens: Their rights and duties.* Moscow: Novosti Press Agency.

Kommers, D. P., & Loescher, G. D. (Eds.). (1979). *Human rights and American foreign policy.* Notre Dame, IN: University of Notre Dame Press.

Koso-Thomas, O. (1987). *The circumcision of women: A strategy for eradication.* London: Zed Books.

Kramer, D. C. (1982). *Comparative civil rights and liberties.* Washington, DC: University Press of America.

Krappe, A. H. (1944). Observations on the origin and development of the idea of justice. *University of Chicago Law Review, 12,* 179-197.

Krausz, M., & Meiland, J. W. (Eds.). (1982). *Relativism: Cognitive and moral.* Notre Dame, IN: University of Notre Dame Press.

Kronenberg, A. (1984). Where are the barbarians? Ethnocentrism versus the illusion of cultural universalism: The answer of an anthropologist to a philosopher. *Ultimate Reality and Meaning, 7,* 233-236.

Kudryavtsev, V. N. (1986). Human rights and the Soviet constitution. In *UNESCO* (pp. 83-94). Paris: UNESCO.

Kugelmass, H. J. (1981). *Lex talionis in the Old Testament.* Unpublished doctoral thesis, University of Montreal.

Kumar, S. (1981). Human rights and economic development: The Indian tradition. *Human Rights Quarterly, 3,* 47-55.

Kunig, P. (1982). The protection of human rights by international law in Africa. *German Yearbook of International Law, 25,* 138-168.

Kunz, J. L. (1949).The UN declaration of human rights. *American Journal of International Law, 43,* 316-323.

LaBurthe-Tolra, P. (1980). Note sur la vengeance chez les Beti. In R. Verdier (Ed.), *La vengeance* (Vol. I, pp. 157-166). Paris: Editions Cujas.

Lackland, T. H. (1974-75). Toward creating a philosophy of fundamental human rights. *Columbia Human Rights Law Review, 6*, 473-503.

Ladd, J. (1957). *The structure of a moral code.* Cambridge, MA: Harvard University Press.

Ladd, J. (1963). The issue of relativism. *The Monist, 47*, 585-609.

Ladd, J. (Ed.). (1973). *Ethical relativism.* Belmont, CA: Wadsworth.

Ladd, J. (1982). The poverty of absolutism. In T. Stroup (Ed.), *Edward Westermarck: Essays on his life and works* (Vol. 34, pp. 158-180). Helsinki: Acta Philosophica Fennica.

LaGrange, F. M. J. (1916). L'homicide d'apres le Code de Hammourabi et d'apres la Bible. *Revenue Biblique, 13*, 440-471.

Lamont, W. D. (1950). Rights. *Aristotelian Society*, Suppl. Vol. 24, pp. 83-94.

Landy, E. A. (1980). The implementation procedures of the international labor organization. *Santa Clara Law Review, 20*, 633-663.

Langan, J. (1982). Human rights in Roman Catholicism. In A. Swidler (Ed.), *Human rights in religious traditions* (pp. 25-39). New York: Pilgrim Press.

LaPenna, I. (1977). Human rights: Soviet theory and practice. *Conflict studies, 83*, 1-15. Laqueur, W., & Rubin, B. (Eds.). (1979). *The human rights reader.* New York: New American Library.

Laubier, P. de. (1985). Sociology of human rights: Religious forces and human rights policy. *Labour and Society, 10*, 97-104.

Laubier, P. de. (1985). Sociology of human rights: The state as an actor in human rights policy. *Labour and Society, 10*, 259-266.

Lauterpacht, E. (1965). Some concepts of human rights. *Howard Law Journal, 11*, 264-274.

Lauterpacht, H. (1950). *International law and human rights.* New York: Praeger.

Lazari-Pawlowska, I. (1970). On cultural relativism. *Journal of Philosophy, 67*, 577-583.

Lean, M. E. (1970). Aren't moral judgments "factual"? *The Personalist, 51*, 259-285.

Lear, J. (1984). Moral objectivity. In S. C. Brown (Ed.), *Objectivity and cultural divergence* (pp. 135-170). Cambridge: Cambridge University Press.

LeBlanc, L. J. (1973). *The OAS and the promotion of human rights.* Ph.D. dissertation, University of Iowa.

Lee, H. W. (1977). *Human rights in Korea: The crisis of relevance.* Seoul: The Academy of Korean Studies.

Lee, M. (1986). North Korea and the Western notion of human rights. In J. C. Hsiung (Ed.). *Human Rights in East Asia* (pp. 129-151). New York: Paragon.

Lee, S. H. (1985). The status of the debate on rights in the USSR. *Studies in Soviet Thought, 30*, 149-164.

Leenhardt, M. (1930). Notes d'Ethnologie Neo-Caledonienne. Universite de Paris, *Travaux et Memoires de l'Institut d'Ethnologie, 8.*

Legesse, A. (1980). Human rights in African political culture. In K. Thompson (Ed.), *The Moral Imperatives of Human Rights* (pp. 123-138). Washington, DC: University Press of America.

Leng, S. (1980). Human rights in Chinese political culture. In K. Thompson (Ed.), *The Moral Imperatives of Human Rights* (pp. 81-107). Washington, DC: University Press of America.

Leonidov, E. (1982). Democracy—True and false. *International Affairs* (Moscow), *11,* 3-10.

Levi, W. (Ed.). (1976). *Law and politics in the international society.* Beverly Hills, CA: Sage.

LeVine, R. A. (1984). *Child labor and ethical relativism.* Paper presented at the Symposium on Ethical Relativism, American Anthropological Association, Washington, DC.

LeVine, R. A., & Campbell. D. T. (1972). *Ethnocentrism: Theories of conflict, ethnic attitudes, and group behavior.* New York: John Wiley.

LeVine, R. A., & White, M. I. (1986). *Human conditions: the cultural basis of educational development.* New York and London: Routledge & Kegan Paul.

Lewis, W. H. (1961). Feuding and social change in Morocco. *Journal of Conflict Resolution, 5,* 43-54.

Lieberam, E. (1979). Criticism of bourgeois attacks on basic rights under socialism. *GDR Committee for Human Rights Bulletin, 3,* 12-23.

Lihau, E. (1986). Comments on the Banjul Charter. *Human Rights Internet Reporter, 11*(4), 12-15.

Lillich, R., & Newman, F.C. (1979). *International human rights: Problems of law and policy.* Boston and Toronto: Little, Brown.

Linton, R. (1952). Universal ethical principles: An anthropological view. In R. N. Anshen (Ed.), *Moral principles of action: Man's ethical imperative* (pp. 645-660). New York and London: Harper.

Linton, R. (1954). The problem of universal values. In R. F. Spencer (Ed.), *Method and perspective in anthropology* (pp.145-168). Minnesota: University of Minnesota Press.

Lister, G. (1988). *Good news: Our human rights policy.* Current Policy No. 1125. Washington. DC: U.S. Department of State, Bureau of Public Affairs.

Little, D. (1988). *Human rights and the conflict of cultures: Western and Islamic perspectives on religious liberty.* Columbia: University of South Carolina Press.

Livezey, L. W. (1988). *Nongovernmental organizations and the ideas of human rights.* Princeton, NJ: The Center for International Studies, Princeton University.

Lo, C. (1948). Human rights in the Chinese tradition. In UNESCO (Ed.), *Human rights* (pp. 186-190). London and New York: Allan Wingate.

Lockman, J. (1743). *Travels of the Jesuits into Various Parts of the World: Compiled from Their Letters*, Vol. 2. London.

Loflin, M. D., & Winogrond, I. R. (1976). A culture as a set of beliefs. *Current Anthropology, 17*, 723-725.

Lomansky, L. (1983). Personal projects as the foundation for basic rights. *Social Philosophy and Policy, 1*, 35-55.

Lombardi, L. G. (1986). The nature of rights. *Philosophy Research Archives, 11*, 431-439.

Lopatka, A. (1979). On the notion of human rights. *GDR Committee for Human Rights Bulletin, 4*, 5-11.

Lucy, J., & Shweder. R. (1979). Whorf and his critics: Linguistic and non-linguistic influences on color memory. *American Anthropologist, 81*, 581-615.

Lukes, S. (1974). Relativism: Cognitive and moral. *Aristotelian Society, Suppl.* Vol. 48, pp. 165-189.

Lukes, S. (1982). Can a Marxist believe in human rights? *Praxis International, 1*, 334-345.

Lum, L. (Ed.). (1988). *Cross Cultural aspects of human rights: Asia.* Symposium Proceedings, No. 1. Washington, DC: U.S. Department of State, Foreign Service Institute.

Lyons, D. (1969). Rights, claimants and beneficiaries. *American Philosophical Quarterly, 6*, 173-185.

Lyons, D. (1970). The correlativity of rights and duties. *Nous, 4*, 45-57.

Lyons, D. (1976a). Ethical relativism and the problem of incoherence. *Ethics, 86*, 107-121.

Lyons, D. (1976b). Rights against humanity. *Philosophical Review, 85*, 208-215.

Lyons, D. (1977). Human rights and the general welfare. *Philosophy and Public Affairs, 6*, 113-129.

Lyons, D. (Ed.). (1979). *Rights.* Belmont, CA: Wadsworth.

Lyons, H. (1981). Anthropologists, moralities and relativities: The problem of genital mutilalions. *Canadian Review of Sociology and Anthropology, 18*, 499-518.

Mabbott, J. D. (1946). Is anthropology relevant to ethics? *Aristotelian Society, Suppl.* Vol. 22, pp. 85-93.

MacBeath, A. M. (1946). Is anthropology relevant to ethics? *Aristotelian Society, Suppl.* Vol. 22, pp. 94-121.

MacBeath, A. M. (1952). *Experiments in living: A study of the nature and foundations of ethics or morals in the light of recent work in social anthropology* (Gifford lectures). London: Macmillan.

MacClintock, S. S. (1901). Kentucky mountaineers and their feuds. *American Journal of Sociology, 7*, 171-187.

MacCormack, G. (1973). Revenge and compensation in early law. *American Journal of*

Comparative Law, 21, 69-85.

MacDonald, M. (1946-47). Natural rights. *Proceedings of the Aristotelian Society, 47*, 225-250.

Macdonald, R. St. J. (1978). The United Nations and the promotion of human rights. In R. St. J. Macdonald, Johnston, D. M., & Morris, G. L. (Eds.), *The international law and policy of human welfare* (pp. 203-237). Alphen aan den Rijn: Sijthoff & Noordhoff.

Macfarlane, L. J. (1982). Marxist theory and human rights. *Government and Opposition, 17*, 414-428.

Macfarlane, L. J. (1988, August-September). *Human rights as global rights.* Paper presented at the XIVth World Congress of the International Political Science Association, Washington, DC.

MacGibbon, I. C. (1957). Customary international law and acquiescence. *British Yearbook of International Law, 33*, 115-145.

Machan, T. R. (1975). *Human rights and human liberties.* Chicago: Nelson Hall.

Machan, T. R. (1980). Some recent work in human rights theory. *American Philosophical Quarterly, 17*, 103-115.

MacIntyre, A. (1973). The essential contestability of some social concepts. *Ethics, 84*, 1-9.

MacIntyre, A. (1981). *After virtue.* Notre Dame, IN: University of Notre Dame Press.

Mackie, J. L. (1977). *Ethics: Inventing right and wrong.* Harmondsworth: Penguin.

Mackie, J. L. (1978). Can there be a rights-based moral theory? *Midwest Studies in Philosophy, 3*, 350-359.

Macrae, J. (1801). Account of the Kookies or Lunctas. *Asiatic Researches, 7*, 183-198.

Maki, L. J. (1980). General principles of human rights law recognized by all nations: Freedom from arbitrary arrest and detention. *California Western International Law Journal, 10*, 272-313.

Malik, J. I. (1981). The concept of human rights in Islamic jurisprudence. *Human Rights Quarterly, 3*, 56-67.

Malinowski, B. (1944). *A scientific theory of culture and other essays.* Chapel Hill: University of North Carolina Press.

Malinowski, B. (1949). *Crime and custom in savage society.* London: Routledge & Kegan Paul.

Mandelbaum, M. (1979). Subjective, objective, and conceptual relativisms. *The Monist, 62*, 403-428.

Manglapus, R. S. (1978). Human rights are not a western discovery. *Worldview, 21*(10), 4-6.

Maquet, J. (1958). Le relativisme culturel. *Présence Africaine, 22*, 65-73.

Maquet, J. (1958-59). Le relativisme culturel. *Présence Africaine, 23*, 59-68.

Maquet, J. (1964). Objectivity in anthropology. *Current Anthropology, 5*, 47-65.

Marasinghe, L. (1984). Traditional conceptions of human rights in Africa. In C. E. Welch, Jr., & R. I. Meltzer (Eds.), *Human rights and development in Africa* (pp. 32-45). Albany: State University of New York Ptess.

Marasinghe, M. L., & Conklin, W. E. (Eds.). (1984). *Essays on Third World perspectives in jurisprudence.* Singapore: Malayan Law Journal PTE.

Marcus, G. E., & Fischer, M. M. J. (1986). *Anthropology as cultural critique.* Chicago and London: University of Chicago Press.

Marett, R. R. (1906). [Review of *The origin and development of the moral ideas* by E. Westermarck]. *Mind, 15*, 403-407.

Margolin, A. (1933-34).The element of vengeance in punishment. *Journal of Criminal Law, Criminology, and Police Science, 24*, 755-767.

Margolis, J. (1976). Robust relativism. *Journal of Aesthetics and Art Criticism, 35*, 37-46.

Maritain, J. (1943). *The rights of man and natural law.* New York: Scribners.

Markovic, M. (1982). Philosophical foundations of human rights. *Praxis International, 1*, 386-400.

Markovic, M. (1986). Differing conceptions of human rights in Europe: Towards a resolution. In UNESCO, *Philosophical foundations of human rights* (pp. 113-130). Paris: UNESCO.

Marks, S. (1984). The complaint procedure of the United Nations Educational, Scientific and Cultural Organization. In H. Hannum (Ed.), *Guide to international human rights practice* (pp. 94-107). Philadelphia: University of Pennsylvania Press.

Marshall, T. (1968). Human rights: An American view. In K. J. Keith (Ed.), *Essays on Human Rights* (pp. 45-48). Wellington: Sweet and Maxwell.

Martin, R. (1979). The nature of human rights. *Archiv für Rechts- und Sozialphilosophie*—Supplementa, Vol. 1, Contemporary Conceptions of Law, 9th World Congress (Basel, 1979) (pp. 379-393).

Martin, R. (1980). Human rights and civil rights. *Philosophical Studies, 37*, 391-403.

Martin, R. (1985). *Rawls and rights.* Lawrence: University of Kansas Press.

Martin, R. & Nickel, J. W. (1978). A bibliography on the nature and foundations of rights, 1947-1977. *Political Theory, 6*, 395-413.

Martin, R., & Nickel, J. W. (1980). Recent work on the concept of rights. *American Philosophical Quarterly, 17*, 165-180.

Masahiko, K. (1985). Asian perspective—Human rights—A Western standard? *Japan Christian Quarterly, 51*(2), 110-112.

Masson-Oursel, P. (1923). *La philosophie comparée.* Paris: Librairie Felix Alcan.

Masson-Oursel, P. (1951). True philosophy is comparative philosophy. *Philosophy East and West, 1*, 6-9.

Mauss, M. (1954). *The gift*. London: Cohen & West.

Mawdudi, A. A. (1976). *Human rights in Islam*. London: Islam Foundation.

Mayo, B. (1965). Human rights. *Aristotelian Society, Suppl.* Vol. 39, pp. 219-236.

M'Baye, K. (1982). Human rights in Africa. In K. Vasak & P. Alston (Eds.), *The international dimensions of human rights* (Vol. 2, pp. 583-600). Westport, CT: Greenwood Press.

McCamant, J. F. (1981). Social science and human rights. *International Organization, 35*, 531-552.

McClintock, T. (1963). The argument for ethical relativism from the diversity of morals. *The Monist, 47*, 528-544.

McClintock, T. (1969). The definition of ethical relativism. *The Personalist, 50*, 435-447.

McClintock, T. (1971a). The basic varieties of ethical skepticism. *Metaphilosophy, 2*, 29-43.

McClintock, T. (1971b). Relativism and affective reaction theories. *Journal of Value Inquiry, 5*, 90-104.

McClintock, T. (1971c). Skepticism about basic moral principles. *Metaphilosophy, 2*, 150-157.

McClintock, T. (1973). How to establish or refute ethical relativism. *The Personalist, 54*, 318-324.

McCloskey, H. J. (1965). Rights. *Philosophical Quarterly, 15*, 115-127.

McCloskey, H. J. (1975). The right to life. *Mine, 84*, 403-425.

McCloskey, H. J. (1976a). Rights—Some conceptual issues. *Australasian Journal of Philosophy, 54*, 99-115.

McCloskey, H. J. (1976b). Human needs, rights and political values. *American Philosophical Quarterly, 13*, 1-11.

McClosky, H., & Brill, A. (1983). *Dimensions of tolerance: What Americans believe about civil liberties*. New York: Russell Sage.

McCoy, T. W. (1976). *The McCoys: Their story as told to the author by eye witnesses and descendants*. Pikeville, Kentucky; Preservation Council Press of the Preservation Council of Pike County.

McLean, S., & Graham, S. E. (1983). *Female circumcision, excision, and infibulation: The facts and proposals for change*. Report No. 47. London: Minority Rights Group.

McNair, L. (1957). The general principles of law recognized by civilized nations. *British Yearbook of International Law, 33*, 1-9.

McRae, D. M. (1971). Sovereignty and the international legal order. *Western Ontario Law Review, 10*, 56-86.

McWhinney, E. (1962). "Peaceful co-existence" and Soviet-Western international law. *American Journal of International Law, 56*, 951-970.

McWhinney, E. (1984a).The time dimension in international law, historical relativism and intertemporal law. In J. Makarczyk (Ed.), *Essays in international law in honour of Judge Manfred Lachs* (pp. 179-199). The Hague: Martinus Nijhoff.

McWhinney, E. (1984b). *United Nation lawmaking: Cultural and ideological relativism and international law making for an era of transition.* New York and London: Holmes & Meier.

Meachling, C. (1983). Human rights dehumanized. *Foreign Policy, 52,* 118-135.

Mead, M. (1942). The comparative study of culture and the purposive cultivation of democratic values. In L. Bryson & L. Finkelstein (Eds.), *Science, Philosophy and Religion* (pp. 56-97), 2nd Symposium. New York: Conference on Science, Philosophy and Religion and Their Relation to the Democratic Way of Life, Inc.

Mead, M. (1961). Some anthropological considerations concerning natural law. *Natural Law Forum, 6,* 51-84.

Mead, M. (1967). The rights of primitive peoples. *Foreign Affairs, 45,* 304-318.

Medvedev, F., & Kulikov, G. (1981). *Human rights and freedoms in the USSR.* Moscow: Progress Publishers.

Meijer, M. J. (1980). An aspect of retribution in traditional Chinese law. *T'oung Pao, 66,* 199-216.

Meiland, J. (1980a). Relativism, criteria, and truth. *Philosophical Quarterly, 30,* 229-231.

Meiland, J. (1980b). On the paradox of cognitive relativism. *Metaphilosophy, 11,* 115-126.

Melden, A. I. (1952). Symposium: The concept of universal human rights. *Science, Language, and Human Rights* (pp. 167-188). Philadelphia: University of Pennsylvania Press.

Melden, A. I. (1977). *Rights and persons.* Oxford: Basil Blackwell.

Mendelievich, E. (Ed.). (1979). *Children at work.* Geneva: International Labour Office.

Merelman, R. M. (1986). Revitalizing political socialization. In M. G. Hermann (Ed.), *Political psychology* (pp. 279-319). San Francisco: Jossey-Bass.

Meron, T. (1982). Norm making and supervision in international human rights: Reflections on institutional order. *American Journal of International Law, 76,* 754-778.

Meron, T. (1984). *Human rights in international law: Legal and policy issues* (2 vols.) Oxford: Clarendon Press.

Meron, T. (1986). *Human rights law-making in the United Nations: A critique of instruments and process.* Oxford: Clarendon Press.

Meyers, D. T. (1981). Human rights in pre-affluent societies. *Philosophical Quarterly, 31,* 139-144.

Meyers, D. T. (1985). *Inalienable rights: A defense.* New York: Columbia University

Press.

Miller, D., &. Orr, J. (1980). Beyond the relativism myth. *Change, 12*, 11-15.

Mills, D. E. (1976). Kataki-uchi: The practice of blood-revenge in pre-modern Japan. *Modern Asian Studies, 10*, 525-542.

Milne, A. J. M. (1986). *Human rights and human diversity: An essay in the philosophy of human rights.* Albany: State University of New York Press.

Mitias, M. H. (1983). Is retributivism inconsistent without *lex talionis*? *Rivista Internazionale di Filosofia del Diritto, 56*, 43.

Mitra, K. (1982). Human rights in Hinduism. In A. Swidler (Ed.), *Human rights in religious traditions* (pp. 77-84). New York: Pilgrim Press.

Mojekwu, C. C. (1980). International human rights: The African perspective. In J. L. Nelson & V. M. Green (Eds.). *International human rights* (pp. 85-95), New York: Human Rights Publishing.

Monro, D. H. (1955). Anthropology and ethics. *Australasian Journal of Philosophy, 33*, 160-176.

Montague, P. (1980). Two concepts of rights. *Philosophy and Public Affairs, 9*, 372-384.

Montague, P. (1986). Is there a right to freedom? *Philosophical Studies, 49*, 71-81.

Montgomery, J. W. (1986). *Human rights and human dignity.* Dallas, TX: Zondervan.

Moore, M. (1982). Moral reality. *Wisconsin Law Review, 1982*, 1061-1156.

Moore, S. F. (1969). Comparative studies. In L. Nader (Ed.), *Law in culture and society* (pp. 337-348). Chicago: Aldine.

Moore, S. F. (1972). Legal liability and evolutionary interpretation: Some aspects of strict liability, self-help and collective responsibility. In M. Gluckman (Ed.), *The allocation of responsibility* (pp. 51-107). Manchester: Manchester University Press.

Moore, S. F. (1983). *Law as process.* London: Routledge & Kegan Paul.

Morris, H. (1981). The status of rights. *Ethics, 92*, 40-56.

Moser, S. (1968). *Absolutism and relativism in ethics.* Springfield, IL: Charles C. Thomas.

Mower, A. G., Jr. (1976). Human rights in Africa: A double standard? *Revue des droits de l'homme, 9*(1), 39-70.

Mulgan, R. G. (1968). The theory of human rights. In K. J. Keith (Ed.), *Essays on Human Rights* (pp. 13-29). Wellington: Sweet and Maxwell.

Murdock, G. P. (1945). The common denominator of cultures. In R. Linton (Ed.), *The science of man in the world crisis* (pp. 123-142). New York: Columbia University Press.

Murphy, A. (1943). *The uses of reasons.* New York: Macmillan.

Murphy, C. (1971-1972). Ideological interpretations of human rights. *Paul Law Review, 21*, 287-306.

Murphy, C. (1981). Objections to western conceptions of human rights. *Hofstra Law Review, 9*, 433-447.

Murphy, J. G. (1979). *Retribution, justice, and therapy.* Dordrecht: D. Reidel.

Murphy, P. L. (1972). *The constitution in crisis times.* New York: Harper & Row.

Murphy, P. L. (1979). *WWI and the origin of civil liberties.* New York: W. W. Norton.

Murumba, S. K. (1986). *The cultural and conceptual basis of human rights norms in international law.* Ph.D. dissertation, Monash University, Melbourne, Australia.

Mutzenberg, C. G. (1917). *Kentucky's famous feuds and tragedies.* New York: R. F. Fenno.

Myres, J. L. (1916).The influence of anthropology on the course of political science. *University of California Publications in History, 4,* 1-81.

Nadel, S. F. (1947). *The Nuba.* London: Oxford University Press.

Nader, L. (Ed.). (1969). *Law in culture and society.* Chicago: Aldine.

Nader, L. (1975). Forums for justice: A cross-cultural perspective. *Journal of Social Issues, 31,* 151-170.

Nader, L., & Starr, J. (1973). Is equity universal? In R. A. Newman (Ed.). *Equity in the World's Legal Systems: A Comparative Studies Dedicated to René Cassin* Brussels: E. Bruylant.

Nader, L., & Sursock, A. (1987). Anthropology and justice. In R. L. Cohen (Ed.), *Justice: Views from the social sciences.* New York: Plenum.

Nanda, V. P. (1976). From Gandhi to Gandhi—International legal responses to the destructtion of human rights and fundamental freedoms in India. *Denver Journal of International Law and Policy, 6,* 1942.

Narain, B. J. (1985). Absolutism vs. relativism in social and legal philosophy: Human rights. *Rechtstheorie, 8,* 351-356.

Nasr, S. H. (1980). The concept and reality of freedom in Islam and Islamic civilization. In A. Rosenbaum (Ed.), *The philosophy of human rights* (pp. 95-101). Westport, CT: Greenwood Press.

Nathan, A. J. (1986a). Political rights in Chinese constitutions. In R. R. Edwards, L. Henkin, & A. J. Nathan, *Human rights in contemporary China* (pp. 77-124). New York: Columbia University Press.

Nathan, A. J. (1986b). Sources of Chinese rights thinking. In R. R. Edwards, L. Henkin, & A. J. Nathan (Eds.), *Human rights in contemporary China* (pp. 125-164). New York: Columbia University Press.

Nawaz, M. K. (1965). The concept of human rights in Islamic law. *Howard Law Journal, 11,* 325-332.

Ndiaye, B. (1982). The place of human rights in the Charter of the Organization of African Unity. In K. Vasak & P. Alston (Eds.), *The international dimensions of human rights* (Vol. 2, pp. 601-616). Westport, CT: Greenwood.

Neff, S. C. (1984). Human rights in Africa. *International and Comparative Law*

Quarterly, 33, 331-347.

Nelson, J. L., & Green, V. M. (1980). *International human rights: Contemporary issues.* New York: Human Rights Publishing.

Nelson, W. N. (1974). Special rights, general rights, and social justice. *Philosophy and Public Affairs*, 3, 410-430.

Newman, J. (1972). Ethical relativism. *Laval Theologique et Philosophique, 28*, 63-74.

Newman, J. (1974). Metaphysical relativism. *Southwestern Journal of Philosophy, 12*, 435-448.

Newman, J. (1977). Popular pragmatism and religious belief. *International Journal of the Philosophy of Religion, 8*, 94-110.

Newman, J. (1978). The idea of religious tolerance. *American Philosophical Quarterly, 15*, 187-195.

Newsom, D. D. (Ed.). (1986). *The diplomacy of human rights.* Lanham: University Press of America.

Nickel, J. W. (1977). Dworkin on the nature and consequences of rights. *Georgia Law Review, 11*, 1115-1142.

Nickel, J. W. (1980a). Cultural diversity and human rights. In J. L. Nelson & V. M. Green (Eds.) *International human rights: Contemporary issues* (pp. 43-56). New York: Human Rights Publishing.

Nickel, J. W. (1980b). Is there a human right to employment? *Philosophical Forum, 11*, 149-170.

Nickel, J. W. (1982). Are human rights utopian? *Philosophy and Public Affairs, 11*, 246-264.

Nickel, J. W. (1987). *Making sense of human rights: Philosophical reflections on the universal declaration of human rights.* Berkeley: University of California Press.

Nielsen, K. (1968). Scepticism and human rights. *The Monist, 52*, 573-594.

Nielsen, K. (1970). Varieties of ethical subjectivism. *Danish Yearbook of Philosophy, 7*, 73-87.

Nielsen, K. (1971). Anthropology and ethics. *Journal of Value Inquiry, 5*, 253-266.

Nielsen, K. (1972). On locating the challenge of relativism. *Second Order, 1*(2), 14-25.

Nielsen, K. (1974a). On the diversity of moral beliefs. *Cultural Hermeneutics, 2*, 281-303.

Nielsen, K. (1974b). Principles of rationality. *Philosophical Papers, 3*, 55-89.

Nielsen, K. (1974c). Rationality and relativism. *Philosophy of the Social Sciences, 4*, 313-331.

Nielsen, K. (1977). The embeddedness of conceptual relativism. *Dialogos, 11*, 85-111.

Nielsen, K. (1982a). Grounding rights and a method of reflective equilibrium. *Inquiry, 25*, 277-306.

Nielsen, K. (1982b). Capitalism, socialism and justice. In T. Regan & D. Van

DeVeer (Eds.), *And Justice for All* (pp. 264-286). Totowa, NJ: Rowman & Littlefield.

Nielsen, N. C., Jr. (1964). Freedom as a transcultural value. *Proceedings of the Thirteenth International Congress of Philosophy* (Mexico) (Vol. 7, pp. 359-367).

Niset, J. (1977). La doctrine du Bouddha et les droits de l'hommes. *Revue des droits de l'homme, 10*, 5-13.

Nissim-Sabat, C. (1987). On Clifford Geertz and his anti anti-relativism. *American Anthropologist, 89*, 935-939.

Nolde, O. F. (1946). Possible functions of the Commission on Human Rights. *Annals, American Academy of Political and Social Science, 243*, 144-149.

Nonet, P., & Selznick, P. (1978). *Law and society in transition: Toward responsive law.* New York: Harper & Row.

Noorani, A. G. (1978). The judiciary and the bar in India during the emergency. *Verfassung und Recht in Ubersee, 11*, 403-411.

Nordenbo, S. E. (1978). Pluralism, relativism, and the neutral teacher. *Journal of the Philosophy of Education, 12*, 129-139.

Nordenstreng, K. (1984). *The mass media declaration of UNESCO.* Norwood. NJ: Ablex.

Norris, R. E. (1980). Bringing human rights petitions before the Inter-American Commission. *Santa Clara Law Review, 20*, 733-772.

Norris, R. E. (1984). The individual petition procedure of the inter-American system for the protection of human rights. In H. Hannum (Ed.), *Guide to international human rights practice* (pp. 108-132). Philadelphia: University of Pennsylvania Press.

Northrop, F. S. C. (Ed.). (1949). Ideological differences and world order*: Studies in the philosophy and science of the world's cultures.* New Haven, CT: Yale University Press.

Northrop, F. S. C. (1953). Cultural values. In A. L. Kroeber (Ed.), *Anthropology today* (pp. 668-681). Chicago: University of Chicago Press.

Northrop, F. S. C. (1955). Ethical relativism in the light of recent developments in social science. *Journal of Philosophy, 52*, 649-662.

Northrop, F. S. C., & Livingston, H. H. (Eds.). (1964). *Cross-cultural understanding: Epistemology in anthropology.* New York: Harper & Row.

Novak, M. (1986). *Human rights and the new realism.* New York: Freedom House.

Novak, M., & Papaioannau, Y. (1985). Annotated bibliography of human rights. *Labour and Society, 10*, 105-114.

Nowak, L. (1975). Relative truth, the correspondence principle, and absolute truth. *Philosophy of Science, 42*, 187-202.

Nowell-Smith, P. H. (1971). Cultural relativism. *Philosophy of the Social Sciences, 1*, 1-18.

Obeyesekere, G. (1966). Methodological and philosophical relativism. *Man, 1,* 368-374.

O'Boyle, M. (1980). Practice and procedure under the European convention on human rights. *Santa Clara Law Review, 20,* 697-732.

Oesterreicher, J. M. (1980, December 21). Christianity, Judaism and the law of retaliation (Letter to the editor). *New York Times,* p. 16.

Okafor, F. U. (1985). Human right and justice: The African perspective. *Philosophy and Social Action, 11*(3), 25-33.

Olcere, B. O. (1984). The protection of human rights in Africa and the African charter on human and peoples'rights: A comparative analysis with the European and American systems. *Human Rights Quarterly, 6,* 141-159.

Okoli, E. (1982).Toward a human rights framework in Nigeria. In P. Schwab & A. Pollis (Eds.). *Toward a human rights framework* (pp. 203-222). New York: Praeger.

Ortique, R. O. (1984). Philosophical and moral underpinnings of human rights beyond constitutional rights: Why domestic courts should be concerned. *Southern University Law Review, 11,* 104-125.

Orwin, C., & Pangle, T. (1984). The philosophical foundations of human rights. In M. F. Plattner (Ed.), *Human rights in our time: Essays in memory of Victor Baras* (pp. 1-22). Boulder and London: Westview Press.

Otterbein, K. F. (1970). *The evolution of war: A cultural study.* New Haven, CT: HRAF Press.

Otterbein, K. F. (1986). *The ultimate coercive sanction: A cross-cultural study of capital punishment.* New Haven, CT: HRAF Press.

Otterbein, K. F., & Otterbein, C. W. (1965). An eye for an eye, a tooth for a tooth: A cross-cultural study of feuding. *American Anthropologist, 67,* 1470-1482.

Overing, J. (Ed.). (1985). *Reason and morality.* London and New York: Tavistock.

Pagels, E. (1979a). Human rights: Legitimizing a recent concept. *Annals, American Academy of Political and Social Science, 442,* 57-62.

Pagels, E. (1979b). The roots and origins of human rights. In A. Henkin (Ed.), Human dignity: *The internationalization of human rights* (pp. 1-8). New York: Aspen Institute for Humanistic Studies.

Pahr, W. P. (1985, December). Human rights in a pluralistic world. *Revue des droits de l'homme / Human Rights Journal* (pp. 101-105).

Pandeya, R. C. (1986) Human rights: An Indian perspective. In *UNESCO* (pp. 267-277). Paris: UNESCO.

Panichas, G. E. (1985). The structure of basic human rights. *Law and Philosophy, 4,* 343-375.

Parulekar, R. (1979). *Myth, faith and hermeneutics.* New York: Paulist Press.

Panikkar, R. (1982). Is the notion of human rights a Western concept? *Diogenes, 120,* 75-102.

Pappu, S. S. R. R. (1969). The idea of human rights. *International Review of History and Political Sciences, 6,* 44-54.

Pappu, S. S. R. R. (1982). Human rights and human obligations: An East-West perspective. *Philosophy and Social Action, 8,* 15-28.

Parle, H. S. (1987). Correlates of human rights: Global tendencies. *Human Rights Quarterly, 9,* 405-413.

Parsons, T. (1964). Evolutionary universals in society. *American Sociological Review, 29,* 339-357. Also reprinted in A. R. Desai (Ed.), *Essays on modernization of underdeveloped societies,* Vol. 1. Atlantic Heights, NJ: Humanities Press (1976).

Patterson, O. (1973-74). On guilt, relativism, and black-white relations. *American Scholar, 43,* 122-132.

Patyulin, V. (1981). The socialist conception of human rights. *In Human Rights in Socialist Society* (pp. 7-23). Moscow: Novosti Press Agency Publishing House.

Paul, E. F., Paul, J., & Miller, F. D., Jr. (Eds.). (1984). *Human rights.* Oxford: Basil Blackwell.

Peffer, R. (1978). A defense of rights to well-being. *Philosophy and Public Affairs, 8,* 65-87.

Pennock, J. R., & Chapman, J. W. (Eds.). (1981). *Human rights.* New York and London: New York University Press.

Percy, J. D. (1943). Revenge and retribution. *London Quarterly and Holborn Review, 168,* 69-71.

Perelman, C. (1982). The safeguarding and foundation of human rights. *Law and Philosophy, 1,* 119-129.

Perkins, R. L. (1984). Conceptual relativism and Europocentrism: The reply of a philosopher to an anthropologist. *Ultimate Reality and Meaning, 7,* 237-240.

Perry, T. D. (1977). A paradigm of philosophy: Hohfeld on legal rights. *American Philosophical Quarterly, 14,* 41-50.

Peters, E. L. (1967). Some structural aspects of the feud among the camel-herding Bedouin of Cyrenaica. *Africa, 37,* 261-282.

Peterson, S. (1985). Remarks on three formulations of ethical relativism. *Ethics, 95,* 887-908.

Petro, N. N. (1983). *The Predicament of Human. Rights: The Carter and Reagan Policies.* Lanham, MD: University Press of America.

Phillips, A. (1977). Another look at murder. *Journal of Jewish Studies, 28,* 105-126.

Pictet, J. (1985). *Development and principles of international humanitarian law.* Dordrecht: Maninus Nijhoff; Geneva: Henry Dunant Institute.

Pilling, A. R. (1957). Law and feud in an aboriginal society of North Australia. Doctoral dissertation, University of California, Berkeley.

Piscatori, J. (1980). Human rights in Islamic political culture. In K. Thompson (Ed.), *The moral imperatives of human rights* (pp. 139-167). Washington, DC: University Press of America.

Plato. (1968). *The republic.* New York: Basic Books.

Plattner, M. F. (Ed.). (1984). *Human rights in our time: Essays in memory of Victor Baras.* Boulder and London: Westview Press.

Pocklington, T. C. (1982). Against inflating human rights. *Windsor Yearbook of Access to Justice, 2,* 77-86.

Pogge, T. W. (1986). Liberalism and global justice: Hoffmann and Nardin on morality in international affairs. *Philosophy and Public Affairs, 15,* 67-81.

Polish, D. F. (1982). Judaism and human rights. In A. Swidler (Ed.), *Human rights in religious traditions* (pp. 40-50). New York: Pilgrim Press.

Pollis, A. (1982). Liberal, socialist, and Third World perspectives of human rights. In A. Pollis & P. Schwab (Eds.), *Toward a human rights framework* (pp. 1-26). New York: Praeger.

Pollis, A. (1987). The state, the law, and human rights in modern Greece. *Human Rights Quarterly, 9,* 587-614.

Pollis, A., & Schwab, P. (Eds.). (1979a). *Human rights: Cultural and ideological perspectives.* New York: Praeger.

Pollis, A., & Schwab, P. (1979b). Human rights: A Western construct with limited applicability. In A. Pollis & P. Schwab (Eds.), *Human rights: Cultural and ideological perspectives* (pp. 1-18). New York: Praeger.

Popper, K. (1966). Facts, standards, and truth: A further criticism of relativism. In K. Popper, *The open society and its enemies* (5th rev. ed.) (pp. 369-398). New York: Harper.

Posner, R. A. (1980a). Retribution and related concepts of punishment. *Journal of Legal Studies, 10,* 71-92.

Posner, R. A. (1980b). A theory of primitive society, with special reference to primitive law. *Journal of Law and Economics, 23,* 1-53.

Pospisil, L. (1968). Feud. *International Encyclopedia of the social sciences* (Vol. 5, 389-393). New York: Macmillan and Free Press.

Postow, B. C. (1978). Ethical relativism and the ideal observer. *Philosophy and Phenomenological Research, 39,* 120-121.

Postow, B. C. (1979). Moral relativism avoided. *The Personalist, 60,* 95-100.

Pound, R. (1949). Toward a new jus gentium. In F. S. C. Northrop (Ed.), *Ideological differences and world order* (pp. 1-17). New Haven, CT: Yale University Press.

Poupko, C. K. (1975). The religious basis of the retributive approach to punishment. *The Thomist, 39,* 528-541.

Primorac, I. (1979). On some arguments against the retributive theory of punishment. *Rivista Internazionale di Filosofia del Diritto, 56,* 43-60.

Primorac, I. (1981). Is retributivism analytic? *Philosophy, 56,* 203-211.

Primorac, I. (1984). On retributivism and the *lex talionis. Rivista Internazionale di*

Filosofia del Diritto, 61, 83-94.

Pritchard, K. (1986). An integrative approach to explaining human rights conditions. *Policy Studies Review, 6*, 110-122.

Przetacznik, F. (1977). The socialist concept of human rights: Its philosophical background and political justification. *Revue Belge de Droit International, 13*, 238-278.

Pospisil, L. (1956). The nature of law. *New York Academy of Sciences Transactions, 18*, 746-755.

Puntambekar, S. V. (1948). The Hindu concept of human rights. In UNESCO (Ed.), *Human Rights* (pp. 195-198). London and New York: Allan Wingate.

Quesada, F. M. (1986). Human rights in Latin America. In *UNESCO* (pp. 301-317). Paris: UNESCO.

Rabbath, E. (1959). La theorie des droits de l'homme dans le droit musulman. *Revue Internationale de Droit Comparé, 11*, 672-693.

Radcliffe-Brown, A. R. (1940). Preface. In M. Fortes & E. E. Evans-Pritchard (Eds.), *African political systems* (pp. xi-xxiii). Oxford: Oxford University Press.

Radcliffe-Brown, A. R. (1951). The comparative method in social anthropology. *Journal of the Royal Anthropological Institute, 81*, 15-22.

Radcliffe-Brown, A. R. (1952). *Structure and function in primitive society.* New York: Free Press.

Rahman, S. A. (1978). The Qur'an and fundamental human rights. *Hamdard Islamicus, 1*, 71-85.

Rai, L. D. (1981). Human rights development: In ancient Nepal. *Human Rights Quarterly, 3*, 37-46.

Ramcharan, B. G. (Ed.). (1979). *Human rights: Thirty years after the Universal Declaration.* The Hague, Boston, and London: Martinus Nijhoff.

Ramcharan, B. G. (1983). The concept of human rights in contemporary international law. *Canadian Human Rights Yearbook, 1983* (pp. 267-281).

Ramcharan, B. G. (Ed.). (1985). *The right to life in international law.* Dordrecht: Martinus Nijhoff.

Ranck, S. H. (1901). Punishment to fit the crime. *American Journal of Sociology, 6*, 695-706.

Raphael, D. D. (1966). The liberal Western tradition of human rights. *International Social Science Journal, 18*, 22-30.

Raphael, D. D. (1967). Human rights, old and new. In D. D. Raphael (Ed.), *Political Theory and the Rights of Man* (pp. 101-118). Bloomington: Indiana University Press.

Rawls, J. (1955). Two concepts of rules. *Philosophical Review, 64*, 3-32.

Rawls, J. (1971). *A theory of justice.* Cambridge, MA: Harvard University Press.

Reddaway, P. B. (1979). Theory and practice of human rights in the Soviet Union. In

D. P. Kommers & G. D. Loescher (Eds.), *Human rights and American foreign policy* (pp. 115-144). Notre Dame. IN: University of Notre Dame Press.

Redfield, R. (1957). The universally human and the culturally variable. *Journal of General Education, 10*, 150-160.

Redfield, R. (1962). *The primitive world and its transformations.* Ithaca, NY: Cornell University Press.

Regan, T. (1983). *The case for animal rights.* Berkeley: University of California Press.

Reid, C. (1970). Popular subjectivism and relativism. *Journal of Critical Analysis, 2*, 36-42.

Renteln, A. D. (1985). The unanswered challenge of relativism and the consequences for human rights. *Human Rights Quarterly, 7*, 514-540.

Reynolds, T. H. (1978). Highest aspirations on barbarous acts…The explosion in human rights documentation: A bibliographic survey. *Law Library Journal, 71*, 1-48.

Richards, B. A. (1969). Inalienable rights: Recent criticism and old doctrine. *Philosophy and Phenomenological Research, 29*, 391-404.

Ridley, W. (1975). *Kamilaroi and other Australian languages* (2nd ed.). Sydney: T. Richards, Government Printer.

Rieder, J. (1984). The social organization of vengeance. In D. Black (Ed.), *Toward a general theory of social control* (Vol. 1, pp. 131-162). Orlando, FL: Academic Press.

Rimlinger, G. V. (1983). Capitalism and human rights. *Daedalus, 112*, 51-79.

Rioux, M. (1957). Relativisme culturel et jugements de valeur. *Anthropologica, 4*, 61-77.

Ritchie-Calder, L. (1967). *On human rights.* London: H. G. Wells Society.

Roberts, A., & Kingsbury, B. (Eds.) (1988). *United Nations, divided world: The UN's roles in international relations.* Oxford: Clarendon Press.

Roberts, R. (1971). *The social laws of the Qoran, considered and compared with those of the Hebrew and other ancient code*s. London and Dublin: Curzon Press.

Robertson, A. H. (1977). *Human rights in Europe* (2nd ed.). Manchester: Manchester University Press.

Robinson, N. (1958). *The universal declaration of human rights: Its origin, significance, application, and interpretation.* New York: Institute of Jewish Affairs.

Rodgers, G., & Standing, G. (Eds.). (1981). *Child work, poverty, and underdevelopment.* Geneva: International Labour Office.

Rodinson, M. (1955). Ethnographie et relativisme. *Nouvelle Critique, 69*, 46-63.

Rosan, L. J. (1971). Human dignity and human rights in the philosophy of absolute idealism. *The Philosophy Forum, 9*, 99-105.

Rosch, E. (1974). Linguistic relativity. In A. Silverstein (Ed.), *Human communication: Theoretical explorations* (pp. 95-121). New York: John Wiley.

Rose, A. M., & Prell, A. E. (1955). Does the punishment fit the crime? A study in social valuation. *American Journal of Sociology, 61,* 247-259.

Rosenbaum, A. S. (Ed.). (1980). *The philosophy of human rights: International perspectives.* Westport, CT: Greenwood Press.

Rosenbaum, A. S. (1985). On the philosophical foundations of the conception of human rights. *Philosophy Research Archives, 10,* 543-565.

Rosenne, S. (1965). The court and the judicial process. *International Organizaion, 19,* 518-536.

Roshwald, M. (1958-59). The concept of human rights. *Philosophy and Phenomenological Research, 19,* 354-379.

Ross, M. H. (1985). Internal and external conflict and violence: Cross-cultural evidence and a new analysis. *Journal of Conflict Resolution, 29,* 547-579.

Rossi, P. H., Waite, E., Bose, C. E., & Berk, R. E. (1974). The seriousness of crimes: Normative structure and individual differences. *American Sociological Review, 39,* 224-237.

Rotenstreich, N. (1977). On ethical relativism. *Journal of Value Inquiry, 11,* 81-103.

Runciman, W. G. (1974). Relativism: Cognitive and moral. *Aristotelian Society, Suppl.* Vol. 48, pp. 191-208.

Rusis, A. (1968).The International protection of human rights. *The Quarterly Journal of the Library of Congress, 25,* 244-271.

Russell, L. J. (1946). Is anthropology relevant to ethics? *Aristotelian Society, Suppl.,* Vol. 22, pp. 61-84.

Saba, H. (1982). UNESCO and human rights. In K. Vasak & P. Alston (Eds.), *The international dimensions of human rights* (Vol. 1, pp. 401-426). Westport, CT: Greenwood Press.

Said, A. A. (Ed.). (1978). *Human rights and world order.* New Brunswick, NJ: Transaction Books.

Said, A. A. (1979a). Precept and practice of human rights in Islam. *Universal Human Rights, 1,* 63-79.

Said, A. A. (1979b). Human rights in Islamic perspectives. In A. Pollis & P. Schwab (Eds.), *Human rights: cultural and ideological perspectives* (pp. 86-100). New York: Praeger.

Said, A. A., & Nassar, J. (1980). The use and abuse of democracy in Islam. In J. L. Nelson & V. M. Green (Eds.), *International Human Rights* (pp. 61-83). New York: Human Rights Publishing.

Salzberg, J. P. (1973). *The United Nations Sub-commission on Prevention of Discrimination and Protection of Minorities.* Ph.D. dissertation, New York University.

Sanders, A. J. G. M. (1978). On African socialism and natural law thinking. *Comparative and International Law Journal of South Africa, 11,* 68-75.

Sanderson, L. P. (1986). *Female genital mutilation, excision, and infibulation: A bibliography*. London: Anti-Slavery Society for the Protection of Human Rights.

Sapontzis, S. F. (1978). The value of human rights. *Journal of Value Inquiry, 12*, 210-214.

Sartorius, R. (1985). Utilitarianism, rights and duties to self. *American Philosophical Quarterly, 22*, 241-249.

Sastry, K. R. R. (1966). Hinduism and international law. *Recueil des Cours, 117*, 507-614.

Schall, J. V. (1981). Human Rights: The "so-called" Judaeo-Christian tradition. *Communio, 8*, 51-61.

Scheingold, S. A. (1974). *The politics of rights: Lawyers, public policy, and political change*. New Haven, CT: Yale University Press.

Schifter, R. (1988a). *Human rights: A western cultural bias?* Current Policy No. 1105. Washington, DC: U.S. Department of State, Bureau of Public Affairs.

Schifter, R. (1988b). *Witnessing the changes in human rights*. Current Policy No. 1142. Washington, DC: U.S. Department of State, Bureau of Public Affairs.

Schildkraut, E. (1980). Children's work reconsidered. *International Social Science Journal, 32*, 479-489.

Schiller, M. (1969). Are there any inalienable rights? *Ethics, 79*, 309-315.

Schirmer, J. (1988). The dilemma of cultural diversity and equivalency in universal human rights standards. In T. E. Downing & G. Kushner (Eds.), *Human rights and anthropology* (pp. 91-106). Cambridge, MA: Cultural Survival.

Schirmer, J., Renteln, A. D., & Wiseberg, L. (1988a). Anthropology and human rights: A selective annotated bibliography. *Human Rights Teaching Bulletin, 6*, 74-114.

Schirmer, J., Renteln, A. D., & Wiseberg, L. (1988b). Anthropology and human rights: A selected bibliography. In T. E. Downing and G. Kushner (Eds.), *Human rights and anthropology* (pp. 125-196). Cambridge, MA: Cultural Survival.

Schmidt, P. (1955). Some criticisms of cultural relativism. *Journal of Philosophy, 70*, 780-791. Schoeck, H., & Wiggins, J. (Eds.). (1961). *Relativism and the study of man*. Princeton, NJ: Van Nostrand.

Schoenfeld, C. G. (1966). In defense of retribution in the law. *Psychoanalytic Quarterly, 35*, 108-121.

Scholte, B. (1984). Reason and culture: The universal and particular revisited. *American Anthropologist, 86*, 960-965.

Schott, R. (1980). Vengeance and violence among the Bulsa of northern Ghana. In R. Verdier (Ed.), *La vengeance* (Vol. 1, pp. 167-199). Paris: Editions Cujas.

Schoultz, L. (1981). *Human rights and United States policy toward Latin America*. Princeton, NJ: Princeton University Press.

Schreiber, A. (1970). *The Inter-American Commission on human rights*. Leiden: Sijthoff.

Schwab, P., & Pollis, A. (Eds.). (1982). *Toward a human rights framework*. New York: Praeger.

Schwelb, E. (1959).The influence of the Universal Declaration of Human Rights on international and national law. *Proceedings of the American Society of International Law, 1959,* 217-229.

Schwelb, E. (1964). *Human rights and the international community: the roots and growth of the Universal Declaration of Human Rights 1948-1963.* Chicago: Quadrangle.

Schwelb, E. (1970). The international protection of human rights: A survey of recent literature. *International Organization, 24,* 75-92.

Schwelb, E. (1977). The international measures of implementation of the international covenant on civil and political rights and of the optional protocol. *Texas International Law Journal, 12,* 141-186.

Schwelb, E., & Alston, P. (1982). The principal institutions and other bodies founded under the Charter. In K. Vasak & P. Alston (Eds.), *The International Dimensions of Human Rights* (Vol. 1, pp. 231-301). Westport, CT: Greenwood Press.

Scoble, H. M., & Wiseberg, L. (Eds.). (1982). *Access to justice*. London: Zed Books.

Segal, R. A. (1987). Relativism and rationality in the social sciences. *The Journal of Religion, 67,* 353-362.

Seligman, C. G. (1910). *The Melanesians of British New Guinea*. Cambridge: Cambridge University Press.

Sellers, J. (1979). Human rights and the American tradition of justice. *Soundings, 62,* 226-255.

Selznick, P. (1961). Sociology and natural law. *Natural Law Forum, 6,* 84-108.

Shah, P. M. (Ed.). (1985). *Child labour: A threat to health and development*. Geneva: Defence for Children International.

Shapiro, M. (1981). *Courts: A comparative and political analysis*. Chicago: University of Chicago Press.

Shelton, D. L. (1984). Individual complaint machinery under the United Nations 1503 procedure and the Optional Protocol to the International Covenant on Civil and Political Rights. In H. Hannum (Ed.), *Guide to international human rights practice* (pp. 59-73). Philadelphia: University of Pennsylvania Press.

Shepherd, G. W., Jr., & Nanda, V. P. (Eds.). (1985). *Human rights and Third World development*. Westport, CT: Greenwood Press.

Shestack, J. J. (1982). The Commission on Human Rights. In S. M. Finger & R. J. Harbert (Eds.), *U.S. policy in international institutions: Defining reasonable options in an unreasonable world* (pp. 71-82). Boulder, CO: Westview Press.

Shestack, J. J. (1984). The jurisprudence of human rights. In T. Meron (Ed.), *Human rights in international law: Legal and policy issues* (Vol. 1, pp. 69-107). Oxford: Clarendon Press.

Shih, H. (1940). The modernization of China and Japan: A comparative study in cultural conflict and a consideration of freedom. In R. N. Anshen (Ed.), *Freedom: Its meaning* (pp. 14-122). New York: Harcourt, Brace.

Shimahara, N. (1970). Enculturation—A reconsideration. *Current Anthropology, 11*, 143-154.

Shue, H. (1979). Rights in light of duties. In P. G. Brown & D. MacClean (Eds.), *Human rights and U.S. foreign policy* (pp. 65-81). Lexington, MA: Lexington Books.

Shue, H. (1980). *Basic rights: Subsistence, affluence, and U.S. foreign policy.* Princeton, NJ: Princeton University Press.

Shweder, R. A., & Bourne, E. J. (1982). Does the concept of the person vary cross-culturally? In A. J. Marsella & G. M. White (Eds.), *Cultural Conceptions of Mental Health and Therapy* (pp. 97-137). Dordrecht: D. Reidel.

Shweder, R. A., & LeVine, R. A. (1984). *Culture theory: Essays on mind, self, and emotion.* Cambridge: Cambridge University Press.

Sidgwick, H. (1922). *The methods of ethics* (7th ed.). London: Macmillan.

Sidorsky, D. (1979a). Contemporary reinterpretations of the concept of human rights. In D. Sidorsky (Ed.), *Essays on human rights* (pp. 88-109). Philadelphia: Jewish Publication Society of America.

Sidorsky, D. (Ed.). (1979b). *Essays on human rights: Contemporary issues and Jewish perspectives.* Philadelphia: Jewish Publication Society of America.

Sieghart, P. (1985). *The lawful rights of mankind: An introduction to the international legal code of human rights.* Oxford and New York: Oxford University Press.

Simic, A. (1967). The blood feud in Montenegro. Essays in Balkan ethnology, *Kroeber Anthropological Society*, Special Publications, No. 1, pp. 83-94.

Simmel, G. (1950). *The Sociology of Georg Simmel* (K. H. Wolff, Trans. & Ed.). Glencoe, IL: The Free Press.

Sinaceur, M. A. (1986). Islamic tradition and human rights. In *UNESCO* (pp. 193-225). Paris: UNESCO.

Sinclair, I. (1987). *The international law commission.* Cambridge: Grotius Publications.

Singer, M. (1972). The basis of rights and duties. *Philosophical Studies, 23*, 48-57.

Singh, J. (1982). *Human rights and the future of mankind.* Atlantic Highlands, NJ: Humanities Press.

Sinha, S. P. (1978a). The anthropocentric theory of international law as a basis for human rights. *Case Western Reserve Journal of International Law, 10*, 469-502.

Sinha, S. P. (1978b). Human rights philosophically. *Indian Journal of International Law, 18*, 139-159.

Sinha, S. P. (1981). Human rights: A non-western viewpoint. *Archiv für Rechts- und Sozialphilosophie, 67*, 76-91.

Sinha, S. P. (1982). Why and how human rights. *International Journal of Legal*

Information, 10, 308-319.

Sirkin, A. M. (1979). Can a human rights policy be consistent? In P. G. Brown & D. MacLean (Eds.), *Human rights and U.S. foreign policy* (pp. 199-213). Lexington, MA: Lexington Books.

Smoger, G. (1979). Whither the Commission on human rights: A report after the 35th session. *Vanderbilt Journal of Transnational Law, 12,* 943-968.

Smolik, J. (1980). Theological comments on the question of human rights. *Communio Viatorium, 23,* 189-192.

Smolowe, J., et al. (1983, January 24). All work and no play—The world's youngest laborers sacrifice their childhood in days of endless toil. *Newsweek* (International edition), pp. 20-25.

Snyder, F. E., & Sathirathai, S. (Eds.). (1987). *Third World attitudes toward international law.* Dordrecht: Martinus Nijhoff.

Sohn, L. (1973). *International protection of human rights.* Indianapolis: Bobbs-Merrill.

Sohn, L. (1977). The human rights law of the Charter. *Texas International Law Journal, 12,* 129-140.

Somerville, J. (1948). Comparison of the Soviet and western democratic principles, with special reference to human rights. In UNESCO (Ed.), *Human rights* (pp. 152-155). London and New York: Allan Wingate.

Sonnichsen, C. L. (1951). *I'll die before I'll run: The story of the great feuds of Texas.* New York: Harper.

Sonnichsen, C. L. (1971). *Ten Texas feuds.* Albuquerque: University of New Mexico Press.

Sophocles. (1974). Antigone. *The Theban plays.* Harmondsworth: Penguin. (Originally written 442-441 B.C.)

Southall, A. W. (1956). *Alur society: A study in processes and types of domination.* Cambridge: W. Heffner.

Spasov, B. (1981). The political and civil rights of the individual under socialism. In *Human rights in socialist society* (pp. 72-89). Moscow: Novosti Press Agency.

Spencer, H. (1900). *The principles of sociology* (Vol. 2). New York: D. Appleton.

Spiro, M. E. (1978). Culture and human nature. In G. Spindler (Ed.), *The making of psychological anthropology* (pp. 330-360). Berkeley: University of California Press.

Spiro, M. E. (1984). Some reflections on cultural determinism and relativism with special reference to emotion and reason. In R. A. Shweder & R. A. LeVine (Eds.), *Culture Theory* (pp. 323-346). Cambridge: Cambridge University Press.

Spiro, M. E. (1986). Cultural relativism and the future of anthropology. *Cultural Anthropology, 1,* 259-286.

Stace, W. T. (1962). *The concept of morals.* New York: Macmillan.

Stackhouse, M. L. (1984). *Creeds, society, and human rights: A study in three cultures.* Grand Rapids, MI: William B. Eerdmans.

Stavropoulos, P. (1984/1985). Human rights and the sovereign state. *Melbourne Journal of Politics, 16*, 35-52.

Stein, H. (1986). Cultural relativism as the central organizing resistance in cultural anthropology. *Journal of Psychoanalytic Anthropology, 9*, 157-175.

Stevenson, C. (1958). Relativism and nonrelativism in the theory of values. In C. Stevenson (Ed.), *Facts and values* (pp. 71-93). New Haven, CT: Yale University Press.

Steward, J. H. (1948). Comments on the statement on human rights. *American Anthropologist, 50*, 351-352.

Stillschweig, K. (1947). International protection of human rights and fundamental freedoms. *Historica Judaica, 9*, 35-56.

Stirling, A. P. (1960). A death and a youth club: Feuding in a Turkish village. *Anthropological Quarterly, 33*, 51-75.

Stocking, G. W., Jr. (1968). *Race, culture, and evolution.* New York: Free Press; London: Collier-Macmillan.

Stocking, G. W., Jr. (1982). Afterword: A view from the center. *Ethnos, 47*, 172-186.

Stohl, M., Carleton, D., Lopez, G., & Samuels, S. (1986). State violation of human rights: Issues and problems of measurement. *Human Rights Quarterly, 8*, 592-606.

Strauss, I. (1953). *Natural right and history.* Chicago and London: University of Chicago Press.

Stroup, T. (1984). Edward Westermarck: A reappraisal. *Man, 19*, 575-592.

Summers, R. (Ed.). (1968). *Essays in legal philosophy.* Berkeley: University of California Press.

Sumner, W. G. (1911). *Folkways: A study of the sociological importance of usages, manners, customs, mores, and morals.* Boston: Ginn, Athanaeum.

Sumner, W. G. (1969). Rights. In A. G. Keller & M. R. Davie (Eds.), *Essays of William Graham Sumner* (pp. 358-368). Hamden, CT: Archon.

Sutter, R. B. (1978). *Human rights in China.* Congressional Research Service, Library of Congress.

Swartz, M. (1961). Negative ethnocentrism. *Journal of Conflict Resolution, 5*, 75-81.

Swepston, L. (1984). Human rights complaint procedures of the International Labor Organization. In H. Hannum (Ed.), *Guide to international human rights practice* (pp. 74-93). Philadelphia: University of Pennsylvania Press.

Swidler, A. (Ed.). (1982). *Human rights in religious traditions.* New York: Pilgrim Press.

Szabo, I. (1968).The theoretical foundations of human rights. In A. Eide & A. Schou (Eds.). *International protection of human rights* (pp. 35-45). New York: Interscience.

Szabo, I. (1982). Historical foundations of human rights and subsequent developments. In K.Vasak & P. Alston (Eds.), *The international dimensions of human rights* (Vol. 1, pp. 11-42). Westport, CT: Greenwood Press.

Szymanski, A. (1984). *Human rights in the soviet union.* London: Zed Books.

Tabandeh, S. H. (1970). *A Muslim Commentary on the Universal Declaration of Human Rights.* London: F. T. Goulding.

Tai, H. (1986). Human rights in Taiwan: Convergence of two political cultures? In J. C. Hsiung (Ed.), *Human Rights in East Asia* (pp. 79-108). New York: Paragon.

Takirambudde, P. N. (Ed.). (1982). *The individual under Africa Law.* Proceedings of the First All-Africa Law Conference, Oct. 11-16, 1981. University of Swaziland, Department of Law, Private Bay, Kwaluseni, Swaziland.

Talhami, G. (1985). The human right of women in Islam. *Journal of Social Philosophy, 16,* 1-7.

Taperell, K. (1985). Islam and human rights. *Australian Foreign Affairs Record, 56,* 1177-1184.

Tardu, M. E. (1980). United Nations response to gross violations of human rights: The 1503 Procedure. *Santa Clara Law Review, 20,* 559-601.

Tay, A. E. (1978). Marxism, socialism and human rights. In E. Kamenka & A. E. Tay (Eds.), *Human Rights* (pp. 105-112). London: Edward Arnold.

Tay, A. E. (1981a). Socialism and human rights. In A. E. Tay (Ed.), *Teaching human rights* (pp. 73-76). Canberra: Australian Government Publishing Service.

Tay, A. E. (Ed.) (1981b). *Teaching human rights.* Canberra: Australian Government Publishing.

Taylor, P. (1958). Social science and ethical relativism. *Journal of Philosophy, 55,* 32-44.

Taylor, P. (1974). Four types of ethical relativism. *Philosophical Review, 63,* 500-516.

Tchechko, B. (1948). The conception of the rights of man in the U.S.S.R. based on official documents. In UNESCO (Ed.), *Human rights* (pp. 158-176). London and New York: Allan Wingate.

Tennekes, J. (1971). *Anthropology, relativism, and method.* Assen: Van Gorcum.

Teson, F. R. (1984-85). International human rights and cultural relativism. *Virginia Journal of International Law, 25,* 869-898.

Thakur, R. (1982). Liberalism, democracy, and development: Philosophical dilemmas in Third World politics. *Political Studies, 30,* 333-349.

Thapar, R. (1966). The Hindu and Buddhist traditions. *International Social Science Journal, 18,* 31-40.

Thapar, R. (1978). The ramifications of human rights. *Indian Journal of International Law, 18,* 274-278.

Thompson, K. W. (1980a). Tensions between human rights and national sovereign rights. In N. T. Horn (Ed.), *Rights and responsibilities: International, social, and individual dimensions* (pp. 113-158). Los Angeles: University of Southern California Press.

Thompson, K. W. (Ed.). (1980b). *The moral imperatives of human rights: A world survey.* New York and London: University Press of America.

Thomson, A. S. (1970). *The story of New Zealand* (2 vols.). New York: Praeger. (First published 1859).

Thomson, J. J. (1986). *Rights, restitution, and risk.* Cambridge, MA: Harvard University Press.

Thurnwald, R. (1930). Blood vengeance feud. *Encyclopedia of the social sciences* (Vol. 2, pp. 598-599). New York: Macmillan.

Tieya, W. (1983). The Third World and international law. In R. St. J. MacDonald & D. M. Johnston (Eds.), *The structure and process of international law: Essays in legal philosophy, doctrine and theory* (pp. 955-976). The Hague: Martinus Nijhoff.

Todd, W. (1976). Relativism. *Methodology and Science, 9,* 174-194.

Tolley, H., Jr. (1983). Decision-making at the UN Commission on Human Rights, 1979-1982. *Human Rights Quarterly, 5,* 27-57.

Tolley, H., Jr. (1984). The concealed crack in the citadel: The UN Commission on Human Rights' response to confidential communications. *Human Rights Quarterly, 6,* 420-462.

Tolley, H., Jr. (1987). *The U.N. Commission on human rights.* Boulder and London: Westview Press.

Tomeh, A. (1968). Moral values in a cross-cultural perspective. *Journal of Social Psychology, 74,* 137-138.

Tomuschat, C. (1981). Is universality of human rights standards an outdated and utopian concept? In R. Bieber & D. Nickel (Eds.), *Das Europa der zweiten Generation: Gedächtnisschrift für Christoph Sasse* (Vol. 2, pp. 585-609) Strassburg: Engel Verlag, Kehl am Rhein.

Toulmin, S. (1972). Conceptual change and the problem of relativity. In M. Krausz (Ed.), *Critical essays on the philosophy of R. G. Collinwood* (pp. 201-221). Oxford: Clarendon Press.

Tower, M. (1984). Popular misconceptions: A note on the *lex talionis. Law and Justice, 80-81,* 21-27.

Tuck, R. (1981). *Natural rights theories: Their origin and development.* Cambridge: Cambridge University Press.

Turack, D. C. (1984). The African Charter on Human and Peoples' Rights: Some preliminary thoughts. *Akron Law Review, 17,* 365-381.

Turlington, E. (1945). The UN Commission on human rights. *American Journal of International Law, 39,* 757-758.

Turnbull, C. M. (1972). *The mountain people.* New York: Touchstone Book, Simon & Schuster.

Turnbull, C. M. (1975). Reply. *Current Anthropology, 16,* 354-358.

Tyagi, Y. K. (1981). Third World response to human rights. *Indian Journal of International Law, 21*, 119-140.

Tylor, E. B. (1873). Primitive society. *Contemporary Review, 21*, 701-718.

Umozurike, U. O. (1983). The African Charter on Human and Peoples' Rights. *American Journal of International Law, 77*, 902-912.

UNESCO. (Ed.). (1948). *Human rights: Comments and interpretations.* London and New York: Allan Wingate.

UNESCO. (1979). *Meeting of experts on the place of human rights in cultural and religious traditions.* (SS-79/CONF. 607/1-9). Paris: UNESCO.

UNESCO. (1986). *Philosophical foundations of human rights.* Paris: UNESCO.

Unwin, N. (1985). Relativism and moral complacency. *Philosophy, 60*, 205-214.

Valcarenghi, M. (1981). *Child labour in Italy.* London: Anti-Slavery Society.

Valticos, J. (1969). Universalité des droits de l'homme et diversité des conditions nationales. In René S. Cassin, *René Cassin Amicorum Discipulorumque Liber* (Vol. 1, pp. 383-403). Paris: Editions A. Pedone.

Valticos, N. (1982). The International Labour Organization. In K. Vasak & P. Alston (Eds.), *The international dimensions of human rights* (Vol. 1, pp. 363-399). Westport, CT: Greenwood Press.

van Boven, T. C. (1968). The UN Commission on human rights and violations of human rights and fundamental freedoms. *Netherlands International Law Review, 15*, 374-393.

van Boven, T. C. (1977). The UN and human rights: A critical reappraisal. *Bulletin of Peace Proposals, 11*, 198-208.

van Boven, T. C. (1982a). Distinguishing criteria of human rights. In K. Vasak & P. Alston (Eds.), *The international dimensions of human rights* (Vol. 1, pp. 43-60). Westport, CT: Greenwood Press.

van Boven, T. C. (1982b). *People matter: Views on international human rights policy.* The Netherlands: Muelenhoff Amsterdam.

van Boven, T. C. (1984). Protection of human rights through the United Nations system. In H. Hannum (Ed.), *Guide to international human rights practice* (pp. 46-56). Philadelphia: University of Pennsylvania Press.

Vance, C. R. (1986). The human rights imperative. *Foreign Policy, 63*, 3-19.

Van de Veer, D. (1979). Are human rights alienable? *Philosophical Studies, 37*, 165-176.

Van Dyke, V. (1980). The cultural rights of peoples. *Universal Human Rights, 2*, 1-21.

Vasak, K. (1982). The Council of Europe. In K. Vasak & P. Alston (Eds.), *The international dimensions of human rights* (Vol. 2, pp. 457-542). Westport, CT: Greenwood Press.

Vasak, K., & Alston, P. (Eds.). (1982). *The international dimensions of human rights, 2* vols. Westport, CT: Greenwood Press.

Verdier, R. (1980). *La vengeance*, Vol. 1. Paris: Editions Cujas.

Verdier, R. (1984a). *La vengeance*, Vol. 3. Paris: Editions Cujas.

Verdier, R. (1984b). *La vengeance*, Vol. 4. Paris: Editions Cujas.

Verdoodt, A. (1964). *Naissance et signification de la déclaration universelle des droits de l'homme.* Louvain: E. Warny.

Vincent, R. J. (1978). Western conceptions of a universal moral order. *Journal of International Studies, 4*, 43-60.

Vincent, R. J. (Ed.). (1986a). *Foreign policy and human rights.* Cambridge: Cambridge University Press.

Vincent, R. J. (1986b). The response of Europe and the Third World to United States human rights diplomacy. In D. D. Newsom (Ed.), *The diplomacy of human rights* (pp. 31-42). Lanham, MD: University Press of America.

Vincent, R. J. (1986c). *Human rights and international relations.* Cambridge, UK: Cambridge University Press.

Vlastos, G. (1970). Justice and equality. In A. I. Melden (Ed.), *Human rights* (pp. 76-95). Belmont, CA: Wadsworth.

von Hirsch, A. (1978). Proportionality and desert: A reply to Bedau. *Journal of Philosophy, 75*, 622-624

Wai, D. M. (1979). Human rights in sub-Saharan Africa. In A. Pollis & P. Schwab (Eds.), *Human rights* (pp. 115-144). New York: Praeger.

Wainwright, W. J. (1967). Natural rights. *American Philosophical Quarterly, 4*, 79-84.

Waldron, J. (Ed.). (1984). *Theories of rights.* Oxford: Oxford University Press.

Wall, G. B. (1967). Primitive cultures and ethical universals. *International Philosophical Quarterly, 7*, 470-482.

Washburn, W. E. (1987). Cultural relativism, human rights, and the AAA. *American Anthropologist, 89*, 939-943.

Wasserstrom, R. (1964). Rights, human rights and racial discrimination. *Journal of Philosophy, 61*, 628-641.

Wasserstrom, R. (1978). Retributivism and the concept of punishment. *Journal of Philosophy, 75*, 620-622.

Watson, J. S. (1979). Legal theory, efficacy and validity in the development of human rights norms in international law. *University of Illinois Law Forum, 5*, 609-641.

Webster, A. F. C. (1983). Human rights in the USSR: Two views of socialist reality. *Religious Humanism, 17*, 14-21.

Weeramantry, C. G. (1988). *Islamic Jurisprudence: An International perspective.* New York: St. Martin's.

Weichelt, W. (1979). Some observations on the notion of human rights. *GDR Committee for Human Rights Bulletin, 2*, 3-15.

Weil, P. (1983). Towards relative normativity in international law. *American Journal of International Law, 77,* 413-442.

Weingreen, J. (1976). The concepts of retaliation and compensation in Biblical law. *Royal Irish Academy, Proceedings, 76,* Section C, 510.1, pp. 1-11.

Weinstein, M. (1975). A problem of relativism: A reinterpretation. *Human Context, 7,* 422-425.

Weinstein, W. (1976). Africa's approach to human rights at the United Nations. *Issues, 6,* 14-21.

Weiss, P. (1942). Democracy and the rights of man. *Science, Philosophy and Religion,* 2nd Symposium, 273-296.

Welch, C. E., Jr., & Meltzer, R. I. (Eds.). (1984). *Human rights and development in Africa.* Albany: State University of New York Press.

Wellman, C. (1963). The ethical implications of cultural relativity. *Journal of Philosophy, 60,* 169-184.

Wellman, C. (1975). Ethical disagreement and objective truth. *American Philosophical Quarterly, 12,* 211-221.

Wellman, C. (1978). A new conception of human rights. In E. Kamenka & A. E. Tay (Eds.), *Human Rights* (pp. 48-58). London: Edward Arnold.

Wellman, C. (1985). *A theory of rights: Persons under laws, institutions, and morals.* Totowa, NJ: Rowman & Allanheld.

Werhane, P. H., Gini, A. R., & Ozar, D. R. (Eds.). (1986). *Philosophical issues in human rights: Theories and applications.* New York: Random House.

Westermarck, E. (1898). The essence of revenge. *Mind, 7,* 289-310.

Westermarck, E. (1924). *The origin and development of the moral ideas,* 2 vols. London: Macmillan.

Westermarck, E. (1932a). *Early beliefs and their social influence.* London: Macmillan.

Westermarck, E. (1932b). *Ethical relativity.* New York: Harcourt, Brace.

White, F. C. (1982a). Knowledge and relativism—I. *Educational Philosophy and Theory, 14*(1), 1-13.

White, F. C. (1982b). Knowledge and relativism—II. *Educational Philosophy and Theory, 14*(2), 1-13.

White, F. C. (1984). On total cultural relativism: A rejoinder. *Educational Philosophy and Theory, 16,* 43-44.

Whorf, B. (1956). *Language, thought and reality.* Cambridge: MIT Press.

Wiarda, H. J. (1978). Democracy and human rights in Latin America: Toward a new conceptualization. *Orbis, 22,* 137-160.

Wiarda, H. J. (1981). The ethnocentrism of the social science implications for research and policy. *The Review of Politics, 43,* 163-197.

Williams, B. (Ed.). (1972). *Morality: An introduction to ethics.* New York: Harper &

Row.

Williams, B. (1974-75). The truth in relativism. *Aristotelian Society, 75*, 215-228.

Williams, E. (1947). Anthropology for the common man. *American Anthropologist, 49*, 84-90.

Williams, F. E. (1941). Group sentiment and primitive justice. *American Anthropologist, 43*, 523-539.

Williams, G. (1956).The concept of a legal liberty. *Columbia Law Review, 56*, 1129-1150.

Williams, P. (Ed.). (1981). *The International Bill of Rights*. Glen Ellen, CA: Entwhistle Books.

Williams, P. C. (1978). Losing claims of rights. *Journal of Value Inquiry, 12*, 178-197.

Wilson, B. (Ed.). (1970). *Rationality*. Oxford: Basil Blackwell.

Wilson, P. J., McCall, G., Geddes, W. R., Mark, A. K., Pfeiffer, J. E., &. Boskey, J. B. (1975). More thoughts on the Ik and anthropology. *Current Anthropology, 16*, 343-354.

Wilson, R. W. (1986). Rights in the People's Republic of China. In J. C. Hsiung (Ed.), *Human rights in East Asia* (pp. 111-126). New York: Paragon.

Wilson, S. (1988). *Feuding, conflict and banditry in nineteenth century Corsica*. Cambridge: Cambridge University Press.

Winch, P. (1964). Understanding a primitive society. *American Philosophical Quarterly, 1*, 307-324.

Winfield, R. D. (1982). The injustice of human rights. *Philosophy and Social Criticism, 9*, 81-96.

Winston, M. E. (1988). The Universal Declaration of Human Rights: A brief history. *Human Rights Education: The Fourth R, 1*, 8-9.

Winthrop, H. (1977). Ethical relativism and its irrelevancy for the issues of a complex society. *Religious Humanism, 11*, 2-10.

Wisdom, C. (1940). *The Chorti Indians of Guatemala*. Chicago: University of Chicago Press.

Wiseberg, L. (1976). Human rights in Africa: Toward a definition of the problem of a double standard. *Issues, 6*, 3-13.

Wiseberg, L., &. Scoble, H. (1981). Problems of comparative research on human rights. In V. P. Nanda, J. R. Scarritt & G. W. Shepherd, Jr. (Eds.), *Global human rights: Public policies: comparative measures, NGO strategies* (pp. 147-171). Boulder, CO: Westview Press.

Wong, D. (1984). *Moral relativity*. Berkeley: University of California Press.

Woo, P. K. Y. (1980). A metaphysical approach to human rights from a Chinese point of view. In A. Rosenbaum (Ed.), *The philosophy of human rights* (pp. 113-124). Westport, CT: Greenwood Press.

Worsley, A. (1938). Infibulation and female circumcision: A Study of a little-known custom. *Journal of Obstetrics and Gynecology of the British Empire*, *45*, 686-691.

Wright, M. (1989). How problematical are the moral foundations of human rights? In D. M. Hill (Ed.), *Human Rights and Foreign Policy: Principles and Practice* (pp. 45-53). London: Macmillan.

Wu, Y., Michael, F., Copper, J. F., Lee, T., Chang, M. H. & Gregor, A. J. (1988). *Human Rights in the People's Republic of China*. Boulder and London: Westview Press.

Wyzanski, C. E., Jr. (1979). The philosophical background of the doctrines of human rights. In A. Henkin (Ed.), *Human dignity: The internationalization of human rights* (pp. 9-13). New York: Aspen Institute for Humanistic Studies.

Yamane, H. (1982). Asia and human rights. In K. Vasak &. P. Alston (Eds.). *The international dimensions of human rights* (Vol. 2, pp. 651-670). Westport, CT: Greenwood Press.

Zakaria, F. (1986). Human rights in the Arab world: The Islamic context. In *UNESCO* (pp. 227-241). Paris: UNESCO.

Znaniecki, I. F. (1915). Relativism and absolutism. *Philosophical Review*, *24*, 150-164.

Zuijdwijk, T. J. M. (1982). *Petitioning the United Nations: A study in human rights*. New York: St. Martin's.

Zvobgo, E. J. M. (1979). A Third World view. In D. P. Kommers & G. D. Loescher (Eds.), *Human rights and American foreign policy* (pp. 90-106). Notre Dame, IN: University of Notre Dame Press.

Index

[Page numbers below reference the pagination of the original 1990 edition and are found in this contemporary edition embedded into the text by the use of {brackets}.]

191

About the Author

ALISON DUNDES RENTELN is Professor of Political Science at the University of Southern California, where since 1987 she has taught Law and Public Policy with an emphasis on international law and human rights. She holds holds joint appointments in Anthropology, the Price School of Public Policy, and the Gould School of Law. A graduate of Harvard (History and Literature), she has a Ph.D. in Jurisprudence and Social Policy from the University of California, Berkeley, and a J.D. from the USC Gould School of Law. She served as Director of the Jesse Unruh Institute of Politics, and Vice-Chair and Chair of Political Science. In 2005 she received the USC campus-wide Associates Award for Excellence in Teaching.

She is the author of, among other works, *The Cultural Defense* (Oxford University Press, 2004), and coauthor with James Nafziger and Robert Paterson of *Cultural Law* (Cambridge University Press, 2010). Two of her essays appeared in a special issue of *Judicature* on cross-cultural jurisprudence (Mar.–Apr. 2009), and another in *The Judges' Journal* (Spring, 2010).

Professor Renteln has collaborated with the United Nations on the Convention on the Rights of Persons with Disabilities, most recently participating in a UN forum in Croatia. She lectured on comparative legal ethics in Bangkok and Manila at ABA-sponsored conferences. She has often taught seminars on the rights of ethnic minorities for judges, lawyers, court interpreters, jury consultants, and police officers. During the past few years she participated on panels on cross-cultural justice at the meetings of the American Bar Association, the National Association of Women Judges, the North American South Asian Bar Association, the American Society of Trial Consultants, and others. She served on several California civil rights commissions including the Attorney General's hate crimes task force and a California committee of Human Rights Watch. Currently she is a member of the California State Judicial Council "Cultural Competency" working group. She is married and has two sons.

Visit us at *www.quidprobooks.com*.

Made in the USA
Columbia, SC
10 March 2019